LIBRARY OF NEW TESTAMENT STUDIES

342

formerly the Journal for the Study of the New Testament Supplement series

Editor
Mark Goodacre

READING JAMES WITH NEW EYES

Methodological Reassessments of the Letter of James

EDITED BY
ROBERT L. WEBB
AND
JOHN S. KLOPPENBORG

t&t clark

Published by T&T Clark International
A Continuum imprint
The Tower Building, 11 York Road, London SE1 7NX
80 Maiden Lane, Suite 704, New York, NY 10038

www.tandtclark.com

British Library Cataloguing-in-Publication Data
A catalogue record for this book is available from the British Library

ISBN-10: 056703125X (hardback)
ISBN-13: 9780567031259 (hardback)

Typeset by Data Standards Ltd, Frome, Somerset, UK.

CONTENTS

CONTRIBUTORS

Alicia Batten, Pacific Lutheran University, Tacoma, Washington, USA.

K. Jason Coker, Drew University, Madison, New Jersey, USA.

John S. Kloppenborg, University of Toronto, Toronto, Ontario, Canada.

Darian Lockett, The King's College, East Rutherford, New Jersey, USA.

Margaret M. Mitchell, University of Chicago, Chicago, Illinois, USA.

Wesley H. Wachob, First United Methodist Church, Pensacola, Florida, USA.

Duane F. Watson, Malone College, Canton, Ohio, USA.

Robert L. Webb, McMaster University, Hamilton, Ontario, Canada.

ABBREVIATIONS

AB	Anchor Bible
ANRW	Hildegard Temporini and Wolfgang Haase (eds), *Aufstieg und Niedergang der römischen Welt: Geschichte und Kultur Roms im Spiegel der neueren Forschung* (Berlin: de Gruyter, 1972–)
BDAG	Bauer, W., F. W. Danker, W. F. Arndt and F. W. Gingrich, *Greek-English Lexicon of the New Testament and Other Early Christian Literature* (Chicago: University of Chicago Press, 3rd edn, 1999)
BETL	Bibliotheca ephemeridum theologicarum lovaniensium
BHT	Beiträge zur historischen Theologie
Bib	*Biblica*
BIS	Biblical Interpretation Series
BNTC	Black's New Testament Commentaries
BTB	*Biblical Theology Bulletin*
BWANT	Beiträge zur Wissenschaft vom Alten und Neuen Testament
BZAW	Beihefte zur *ZAW*
CBQ	*Catholic Biblical Quarterly*
CRBS	*Currents in Research: Biblical Studies*
ExpTim	*Expository Times*
FB	Forschung zur Bibel
FFNT	Foundations and Facets: New Testament
GBS	Guides to Biblical Scholarship
HNT	Handbuch zum Neuen Testament
HNTC	Harper's New Testament Commentaries
HTKNT	Herders theologischer Kommentar zum Neuen Testament
HUT	Hermeneutische Untersuchungen zur Theologie
HvTSt	*Hervormde teologiese studies*
ICC	International Critical Commentary
IG	*Inscriptiones graecae* (Editio minor; Berlin, 1924–)
Int	*Interpretation*
JBL	*Journal of Biblical Literature*
JSNTSup	Journal for the Study of the New Testament, Supplement Series
JSOTSup	Journal for the Study of the Old Testament, Supplement Series
JSP	*Journal for the Study of the Pseudepigrapha*
KNT	Kommentar till Nya Testamentet
LB	*Linguistica biblica*

LEC	Library of Early Christianity
LM	*Le Muséon*
NCBC	New Century Bible Commentary
Neot	*Neotestamentica*
NIBC	New International Biblical Commentary
NICNT	New International Commentary on the New Testament
NIGTC	The New International Greek Testament Commentary
NIV	New International Version
NovT	*Novum Testamentum*
NovTSup	Novum Testamentum, Supplements
NRSV	New Revised Standard Version
NTOA	Novum Testamentum et Orbis Antiquus
NTS	*New Testament Studies*
NTTS	New Testament Tools and Studies
PG	J.-P. Migne (ed.), *Patrologia cursus comletus: Series graeca* (166 vols; Paris: Petit-Montrouge, 1857–86)
PL	J.-P. Migne (ed.), *Patrologia cursus completus: Series latina* (217 vols; Paris: J.-P. Migne, 1844–64)
PNTC	Pillar New Testament Commentary
RB	*Revue biblique*
RevExp	*Review and Expositor*
RSV	Revised Standard Version
SBL	Society of Biblical Literature
SBLDS	SBL Dissertation Series
SBLSBS	SBL Sources for Biblical Study
SBLSP	SBL Seminar Papers
SBLSS	SBL Symposium Series
SBLTT	SBL Texts and Translations
SNTSMS	Society for New Testament Studies Monograph Series
SNTU	*Studien zum Neuen Testament und seiner Umwelt*
SNTW	Studies of the New Testament and Its World
SP	Sacra Pagina
ST	*Studia theologica*
SUNT	Studien zur Umwelt des Neuen Testaments
TDNT	Gerhard Kittel and Gerhard Friedrich (eds), *Theological Dictionary of the New Testament* (trans. Geoffrey W. Bromiley; 10 vols; Grand Rapids: Eerdmans, 1964–76)
THKNT	Theologischer Handkommentar zum Neuen Testament
WBC	Word Biblical Commentary
WUNT	Wissenschaftliche Untersuchungen zum Neuen Testament
ZNW	*Zeitschrift für die neutestamentliche Wissenschaft*
ZPE	*Zeitschrift für Papyrologie und Epigraphik*

Abbreviations of ancient sources are cited according to the lists provided in Patrick H. Alexander *et al.* (eds), *The SBL Handbook of Style for Ancient Near Eastern, Biblical, and Early Christian Studies* (Peabody, MA: Hendrickson, 1999).

Reading James with New Eyes: An Introduction

John S. Kloppenborg and Robert L. Webb

In the first half of the twentieth century the dominant paradigm used by those within the biblical-studies guild was the historical-critical method. In the second half of the century, there were voices that have called into question this hegemony. For some it was bankrupt and needed to be replaced, while for others it was limited and needed to be supplemented. And thus the past half-century has been a tumultuous period in biblical studies – a time in which other methods[1] have been proposed and used. Some of these methods arise from crossing disciplinary boundaries. For example, the study of the NT has been greatly enhanced by incorporating methodological approaches gleaned from the social sciences such as sociology, cultural anthropology, ethnography, etc. – often referred to within biblical studies as social-scientific criticism. Another example of crossing disciplinary boundaries, though in a very different direction, is literary criticism. Here, methods of reading gleaned from modern literary studies and even film studies are applied to the NT. Other methods arise from broadening ancient contexts. For example, a recognition of the significant role played by rhetoric in the Mediterranean world has led to its application to the NT in the form of rhetorical criticism. And a recognition of the different social experiences of early Christians has broadened this to what is known as socio-rhetorical criticism. Still other methods arise from the impact of a variety of philosophical implications of postmodernism. For example, recognizing the significant role played by the reader of a text in the production of meaning has given rise to reader-response criticism. Similarly the significance of social location, whether of an ancient author/reader or of the modern interpreter has led to a variety of methodological approaches including feminist criticism, ideological criticism, as well as the use of post-colonial theory.

---

1. Some methods might better be called paradigms, approaches or interpretive analytics. But for the sake of simplicity here, we simply use the term 'method' in its broadest possible sense to incorporate all of these.

This vast array of methodological diversity has led to exciting times in the study of the NT, and it has led to significant new insights concerning the NT. But these methods have been largely developed and applied with reference to the Gospels and the Pauline literature. Other NT texts have been relatively neglected, especially the so-called General Letters. This neglect may be observed at an educational level in the expression of outdated views concerning these letters being reproduced in supposedly up-to-date textbooks used in universities and theological schools. The neglect may also be observed at an academic level, for at the Annual Meeting of the Society of Biblical Literature there has not been a section devoted to the General Letters for almost a decade (apart from the Letters of John being considered as part of the Johannine literature).

Thus the current state of NT studies warrants a focused examination of at least some of these neglected NT letters particularly with reference to these new methodological developments. So in 2004 a committee of scholars who are working on one or more of these letters gathered to propose a new SBL Consultation: 'Methodological Reassessments of the Letters of James, Peter, and Jude'. This committee consists of Betsy Bauman-Martin, Peter H. Davids, John H. Elliott, John S. Kloppenborg, Duane F. Watson, and Robert L. Webb (chair). The consultation's focus is 'an examination of the impact of recent methodological developments to the Letters of James, Peter, and Jude, including, for example, rhetorical, social-scientific, socio-rhetorical, ideological and hermeneutical methods, as they contribute to understanding these letters and their social contexts'.

At the 2005 Annual Meeting of the Society of Biblical Literature two sessions were held, with the papers concerning themselves with the Letter of James. The quality of the papers was excellent and the audience interest was overwhelming – both times the meeting room was packed. It is the committee's intention to give attention to 1 Peter in 2006 and the Letters of Jude and 2 Peter in 2007.

The essays in this volume represent a majority of the papers on the Letter of James. Each has been revised in light of their discussion by the presenters and the audience. In particular, each essay includes a discussion of the particular methodology concerned as well as an exploration of its relevance to understanding James.

The essays in this volume can be grouped around three distinct and new approaches to James. In attempting to specify the orientation of James, three of these essays push well beyond traditional historical criticism by bringing to bear insights from the study of ideology, post-colonial studies and contemporary anthropology. In discussing the much-belaboured topic of James' view of poverty and riches, Alicia Batten asks key questions concerning the modes of economic production presupposed by the letter writer and his addressees and therefore the social configurations and ideological rationalizations sustained by these modes of production. Her essay shows how the Mediterranean values of honour and shame are related to modes of production and, consequently, points a direction for a more comprehensive understanding of the import of James' critique of wealth.

The topic that has perhaps been given even more attention than James and the poor is Jas 2.14-26. This pericope has provoked nearly endless debate as to whether James here engages Pauline thinking or not, whether James is prior to Galatians and Romans, whether the author of James understands Pauline distinctions or not, or whether Jas 2.14-26 has anything to do with Paul. Jason Coker's essay assumes that Jas 2.14-26 is anti-Pauline, but does so not from within the usual framework of assessing the conceptual context of James and Paul, but by looking at the debate through the optic of post-colonial theory. On his showing, James represents a 'nativist' answer to Paul's hybrid response to the dominant and dominating ideology of the Roman Empire. The great advantage of Coker's approach is that it sees *both* Paul and James as responses to dominating ideologies, and conceives their disagreement as one of social and ideological strategy. *En passant*, Coker offers some provocative suggestions as to why it was Paul's and not James' conceptualization of diasporic identity that was to succeed in the empire.

Darian Lockett complements Coker's approach by examining the construction of the 'world' in James. Developing an insight of John Elliott,[2] Lockett shows how the language of purity and contamination creates a symbolic map in which God, true piety and moral perfection are pitted against the world and its contaminating features. Such a construction of the world is dramatically at odds with the view of Paul, for example in 1 Corinthians, where on the topics of marriages between pagans and believers, and believers' participation at banquets – the two most basic of human activities, eating and sex – Paul counsels forms of accommodation with pagan society.

While the overwhelming majority of Jacobean scholars have imagined the relationship between James and Paul on a spectrum ranging from hostility and polemic to ignorance or indifference to each other's views, Margaret Mitchell's essay suggests a very different reading: that 'James knows some collection of Paul's letters, and writes from within Paulinism (rather than in opposition to Paul), creating a compromise document which has as one of its purposes reconciling "Paul with Paul" and "Paul with pillars" '. In support of this thesis Mitchell contends that James is born from the literary/epistolary culture generated by Paul, that James betrays knowledge of both Galatians and Romans and, hence, some early

2. John H. Elliott, 'The Epistle of James in Rhetorical and Social Scientific Perspective: Holiness-Wholeness and Patterns of Replication', *BTB* 23 (1993), pp. 71-81.

collection of Paul's letters, that James therefore may have been attempting to referee the well-known tensions between Galatians and Romans, and that James shares with other letters from the 'Pauline' orbit a harmonizing hermeneutic. The significance of Mitchell's conclusions is obvious, for if they are sustained, they call for a rewriting of a good deal of Jacobean and Pauline scholarship.

The final three essays all approach James from the standpoint of the study of rhetoric. Duane Watson, himself one of the pioneers in the application of rhetorical theory to James, offers a survey of the fruits of rhetorical analysis. But Watson's own proposal recognizes not only that James is one of the more rhetorically self-conscious compositions of the early Jesus movement, but also that James was itself at the forefront of the 'rhetorizing' of Jewish wisdom and the emergence of a form of rhetoric which, while displaying the influence of Greek and Roman rhetorical practices, also displayed its own peculiarities and characteristics.

Rhetorical analysis also figures in John Kloppenborg's essay on James' relationship to the Jesus tradition. One of the enduring puzzles is that while James shows many conceptual contacts with the Jesus tradition, in particular the sayings from the Sayings Gospel Q, there are very few verbal contacts. Traditional literary criticism, which insisted on a model of verbal copying if sources and influences were to be posited, has been at a loss to make sense of this puzzle. Yet, Kloppenborg argues, if one understands the rhetorical practice of *aemulatio* or 'recitation', where predecessor texts were taken up not as 'sources' but as 'resources', and transformed, reworded and redeployed, it is possible both to acknowledge James' debt to the Jesus tradition and to see his rhetorical skill in action.

Finally, Wesley Wachob continues the approach and insights of Vernon Robbins,[3] and his own socio-rhetorical analysis of James 2,[4] by elaborating the 'rhetorolects' or conceptual-linguistic domains that are operative in James. In this case, Wachob perceives two domains being engaged: the wisdom rhetorolect 'blends human experiences of the household and the created world...with the cultural space of God's cosmos' into a third 'space' that aims at engendering goodness as a reflection of God's ordering of the cosmos. The prophetic rhetorolect has in view not the cosmos but the kingdom and aims at creating 'a governed realm on earth where God's righteousness is enacted among all of God's people in the realm with the aid of God's specially transmitted word in the form of prophetic action and speech'. James partakes of both domains of discourse. James 1 is dominated especially by the wisdom rhetorolect

---

3. Vernon K. Robbins, *The Tapestry of Early Christian Discourse: Rhetoric, Society and Ideology* (London and New York: Routledge, 1996).

4. Wesley H. Wachob, *The Voice of Jesus in the Social Rhetoric of James* (SNTSMS, 106; Cambridge and New York: Cambridge University Press, 2000).

while the construction of Jas 2.1-13 suggests that an originally sapiential saying (Q 6.20b) has been taken up by James and moved into the domain of prophetic speech (Jas 2.5), focusing on God's kingdom and the law of the divine king (Jas 2.8). Wachob's suggestive analysis of James 1.2–2.13 could be extended to the entire letter in an effort to further specify the linguistic and conceptual world in which James moves.

The essays in this volume, taken together, illustrate programmatically both the rich insight that is to be had with the application of methods outside the purview of traditional historical criticism, and the distance that scholarship on Christian origins has come from Martin Dibelius' estimation of James as disjointed paraenesis, lacking conceptual coherence. James indeed displays various sorts of coherences, but these are only visible once one enters into the symbolic, ideological and rhetorical world in which James dwelt.

Ideological Strategies in the Letter of James

Alicia Batten

Although Martin Luther's attitude towards the Letter of James[1] has had an impact upon its history of interpretation, the text's blatant criticisms of riches and the activities of rich persons have surely played a role in its reception, at least in the post-Reformation era.[2] James does not receive nearly as much attention as Pauline literature or the gospel material, but when it does, its attack upon wealth is often toned down or massaged, such that it can be accommodated to the social and economic structures which the interpretive community inhabits. Even John Calvin, who admired the letter, observes that the beginning of James 2, in which the letter writer disparages the showing of partiality manifest in giving the best seat to the rich man and ordering the poor man to stand or sit at one's feet, does not mean that that James lacks respect for the rich, because, says Calvin, 'it is one of the duties of courtesy, not to be neglected, to honour those who are elevated in the world'. The reformer argues that it is wrong to show such partiality only when the poor are being despised, but, he says, the idea that 'a person sins who respects the rich' is 'absurd'.[3] Addressing the same passage, J. B. Mayor's magisterial 1892 commentary admits that 'if James were to visit English churches, he would not find much improvement'[4] with regard to who sits where. Mayor goes on to say, however, that:

> While there is perhaps no objection either to the appropriation of sittings, in so far as it assures to regular attendants the right to sit in

---

1. Indeed, Luther granted that there were good teachings in James in his *Preface to the New Testament*, but his assessment of it as a 'right strawy epistle' has affected the reception of the letter within the history of biblical interpretation.

2. Although representatives of the early church who often criticized wealth and usury such as the Cappadocians recognize James as Scripture, to my knowledge they do not refer to the letter's censure of affluence in their discussions of these issues.

3. John Calvin, *Commentaries on the Catholic Epistles* (trans. John Owen; Grand Rapids: Eerdmans, 1948), pp. 300–301.

4. J. B. Mayor, *The Epistle of St. James* (London: Macmillan, 1892), p. 197.

their accustomed place, or to the exactment of a fixed payment from the well-to-do members of the congregation for the use of their seats; it is surely most contrary to the spirit of God that all the best seats should be monopolized by the highest bidders... The free and open seats should at least be as good as the paying seats, and it should not be in the power of a seat-holder to prevent any unoccupied sitting from being used.[5]

Although Mayor advocates a more democratic seating system, he cannot accept the notion that paid-for pews should disappear from late-nineteenth-century British churches, nor should wealthy regular church-goers have to give up their accustomed spot.

There are other moments, however, when readers or listeners do not accommodate the letter to their context, and receive the letter quite differently, although not sympathetically, such as when James was read in a wealthy Chilean church during Pinochet's rule, and apparently half the congregation got up and left.[6] Another example is evident in Elsa Tamez's comment that some 'national security' governments would brand James as a Marxist–Leninist infiltration of the churches if it were sent to certain Latin American countries.[7]

The above examples illustrate an obvious point: a response to a text is determined in part by a person's or community's set of values and commitments – religious, political, economic and cultural – that uphold and promote specific interests. It is this fact that has contributed to the development of ideological criticism within literary studies, which in turn, has spread to biblical scholarship. Ideological criticism is now a mainstream approach within the guild, perhaps most strongly developed in Hebrew Bible study by scholars such as Norman Gottwald[8] and in the study of Christian origins through the work of John H. Elliott on 1 Peter,[9] and Vernon K. Robbins' attention to the ideological textures of texts.[10] The method examines ideology at multiple levels: author, text and

5. Mayor, *St. James*, p. 197.

6. José Míguez Bonino, comment on the dust jacket of Elsa Tamez's book, *The Scandalous Message of James* (trans. Mortimer Arias; New York: Crossroad, 1990).

7. Tamez, *Scandalous Message*, p. 1.

8. For example, see Norman K. Gottwald, *The Tribes of Yahweh: A Sociology of the Religion of Liberated Israel, 1250–1050 BCE* (Maryknoll, NY: Orbis, 1979).

9. See John H. Elliott, *A Home for the Homeless: A Sociological Analysis of 1 Peter, Its Situation and Strategy* (Philadelphia: Fortress, 1981).

10. See Vernon K. Robbins, *The Tapestry of Early Christian Discourse: Rhetoric, Society and Ideology* (London and New York: Routledge, 1996). A recent example of attention to ideology in James is Wesley H. Wachob, 'The Epistle of James and the Book of Psalms', in *Fabrics of Discourse* (Festschrift Vernon K. Robbins; ed. David B. Gowler, L. Gregory Bloomquist and Duane F. Watson; Harrisburg, London, New York: Trinity, 2003), pp. 64–88.

reader.[11] Although the word 'ideology' has a complicated history[12] and is often negatively understood as 'false consciousness', ideology can be understood in a variety of ways. As Raymond Geuss has explained, one can examine ideology in a purely descriptive sense insofar as one is identifying beliefs held, concepts used, rituals practised etc. by the members of a group. In this sense, every group of people has an ideology and the identification of it is non-evaluative and non-judgmental.[13] We can also understand ideology pejoratively, however, when we criticize 'a form of consciousness because it incorporates beliefs which are false, or because [ideology] functions in a reprehensible way, or because it has a tainted origin'.[14] Thirdly, ideology is also perceived positively in that it is not something to be found 'out there', but something to be constructed in order to serve the best interests of a particular group; 'it is a *verité à faire*'.[15] Contemporary ideological criticism tends to use the term neutrally and in as descriptive a sense as possible, but with attention to how ideologies have functioned negatively in texts and in history as well as how they have served constructive purposes. This means that historians attempt to locate and understand ideologies in and behind texts in order to locate the texts historically, in relation to other texts and with regard to subsequent interpretations up to and including those of the contemporary period.

A common definition of ideology used by many biblical scholars, therefore, is a set of values and beliefs held by a group, which represents the group's interests in conflicts over social, economic and political power.[16] To focus upon ideologies in texts is, as Gottwald has argued, 'to attempt to uncover the actual social relations masked by the limiting and self-serving group interests expressed in the ideas'.[17] These self-serving

11. For a brief summary of the approach, see Gale A. Yee, 'Ideological Criticism', in *Dictionary of Biblical Interpretation* (ed. John H. Hayes; Nashville: Abingdon, 1999), pp. 534–37.

12. For a detailed history of the term, see John B. Thompson, *Ideology and Modern Culture* (Stanford: Stanford University Press, 1990).

13. Raymond Geuss, *The Idea of Critical Theory: Habermas and the Frankfurt School* (Cambridge: Cambridge University Press, 1981), p. 5.

14. Geuss, *Critical Theory*, p. 21.

15. Geuss, *Critical Theory*, p. 23.

16. This definition is borrowed from John H. Elliott's book, *What is Social Scientific Criticism?* (GBS; Minneapolis: Fortress, 1993), p. 130, who builds on that of David Brion Davis, *The Problem of Slavery in the Age of Revolution, 1770–1823* (Ithaca: Cornell University Press, 1975), p. 14, as well as Terry Eagleton's work (*Ideology* [London: Verso, 1991]), although Eagleton does not settle on a single definition of ideology.

17. Norman K. Gottwald, 'Ideology and Ideologies in Israelite Prophecy', in *Prophet and Paradigms* (Festschrift Gene M. Tucker; ed. Stephen Breck Reid; JSOTSup, 229; Sheffield: Sheffield Academic Press, 1996), pp. 136–49 (138).

group interests could be positive or negative. The same could be said for the ideologies and interests of authors and readers.

This essay centres upon what ideologies are at work in the text of James especially as they pertain to questions of rich and poor. The approach begins with an examination of what the dominant ideology of James' context may have been before analysing to what extent James upholds or challenges that ideology. Given that ideologies are always rooted in the material world and modes of production, the method demands some attention to those issues. Then the study turns to an intrinsic analysis of the text in order to understand how the letter expresses and reinforces its ideology. How does James challenge the widespread ideology of his day, or expose that ideology as objectionable; and second, with what does he replace that ideology? In other words, how does he construct an ideology in a positive sense?[18] In particular, how does James take pre-existing materials and refashion them to suit his own ideological purposes?

While working through passages in James, I will incorporate the notion of ideological strategies using the work of literary critic Terry Eagleton.[19] Eagleton has identified ways in which ideologies seek to assert themselves, or how they are rhetorical, such that they do not remain purely theoretical, but are actually lived out, even if only partially. For example, ideologies seek to *unify* social groups, given that most groups contain people of different points of view. Thus ideologies want to foster a sense of social identity, especially in opposition to competing ideologies. Ideologies are *action oriented*, in that they seek to link the practical with the theoretical; they move people from a set of ideas to a set of practices. Ideologies also *rationalize* or give reasons for actions that may otherwise be subject to criticism, and they seek to *legitimate* a particular set of social relations, especially when a more powerful group attempts to gain compliance from others beneath it, and they present themselves as *natural*, as if they are self-evident and simply common sense. Finally, feminist scholars have also noted the strategy of *stereotyping*, in which a few features of a particular group are identified as characteristic of the group as a whole.[20] Such a strategy often takes the effects of specific material and sociological conditions and treats those effects as if they form the constitutive or essential identity of the group in question.[21]

Using ideological criticism is a heuristic tool in that it aids in uncovering aspects of texts that without the tool may not be as obvious.

18. See Geuss, *Critical Theory*, pp. 22–26.

19. See Eagleton, *Ideology*, pp. 33–61.

20. See Michèle Barrett, 'Ideology and the Cultural Construction of Gender', in *Women's Oppression Today: The Marxist/Feminist Encounter* (London: Verso, rev. edn, 1988), pp. 84–113 (108).

21. For example, Gale A. Yee (*Poor Banished Children of Eve: Woman as Evil in the Hebrew Bible* [Minneapolis: Fortress, 2003], p. 16) points out that the stereotype of

As the following examination attempts to show, an ideological examination of the Letter of James, at least with regard to those sections that deal
with rich and poor, reveals that although there might be some rich people
who potentially pose a threat to James' audience, the denigration of the
rich in James serves primarily to unify and build communal identity, and
exhort the audience to action. By casting the rich as 'the other' in this
letter, James constructs a positive identity and ideology for his audience as
the honourable poor who must care for the poor among them. Such an
ideology would contain countercultural or subcultural seeds or strains
that challenge the dominant ideology of the Roman empire, in which the
honourable and good were associated with those of power and status.
James roots this vilification of the rich and honouring of the poor in the
Jewish tradition and, to some extent, in selective teachings of Jesus.
Through such a construction, James reflects an ideology that draws upon
pre-existing ideas and images that would be familiar and presumably
authoritative for his audience.

1. *General Mode of Production*

Describing the mode of production that forms the background of this
letter is difficult for several reasons. First, there is no consensus as to the
provenance or audience of James; second, the details of socio-economic
life within the first-century Roman Empire were variable depending upon
the peculiarities of each region. Thus a discussion of this background will
need to rest upon some degree of generalization, although James does
offer a few clues that enable a little more specificity.

But first, we can say that the letter reflects an agrarian economy
dominated by the power of Rome. Society was highly stratified, with the
elites generally occupying the cities and large estates while peasants lived
on the outskirts or in rural towns and villages. Approximately 10 per cent
of the population consisted of elites (imperial elites making up roughly 1
per cent, and civic elites the remaining 9), and the majority of the
population consisted of a variety of urban and rural dwellers;[22] non-elites,
whose social status could be quite diverse, included dealers, shippers,
soldiers, and a large population of landless peasants, artisans and traders.
Social mobility was possible, but highly limited, and the flow of goods

---

submissive housewives is due in part to housewives' economic dependence upon their
husbands, as well as legal and religious ideologies. Thus the transformation of the stereotype
of housewives as submissive requires a 'change in the material grounds that sustain it'.

    22. See Philip A. Harland, 'Connections with Elites in the World of the Early Christians',
in *Handbook of Early Christianity* (ed. Anthony J. Blasi, Jean Duhaime, Paul-André
Turcotte; Walnut Creek, Lanham, New York and Oxford: Altamira, 2002), pp. 385–408 (esp.
386–88).

primarily vertical[23]whereby peasants produced goods for consumption by the city dwellers. Elite control over the peasantry was further entrenched by taxation, and requirements to pay rent and repay debts. The patron-client model formed the backdrop for most exchanges of goods and services between people of unequal social status, with the stronger party generally controlling the nature of the exchange. This exchange could, and in many cases did, become overtly exploitative, leading some to suggest that 'we should see the ideology of patronage as subverting village solidarity in some areas of the ancient world'.[24] There was no 'middle class' and the majority of people struggled to survive through subsistence living, but could easily fall into destitution. Thus we can imagine that a small elite and powerful class depended largely on the manual labour of the majority to provide for their needs through a complex web of patron-client relations that usually served the interests of the strongest parties involved. To be sure, there were ways of cushioning the effects of this sort of system, such as trade guilds, benefaction, almsgiving and general village mutuality, but by and large a system that worked in favour of the privileged was the norm.

Given the brutal and probably miserable lives of most people in the ancient world, one might ask why people did not rise up and revolt. Revolution was simply not an option. As T. F. Carney indicates, the preconditions for revolution did not exist in antiquity. There was no notion that all persons were politically equal, or that an individual had inalienable rights as a human being. Moreover, the notion of a brighter future for the majority of people was not expected. Carney writes:

> History was seen as a cyclical process in antiquity, or as a process of regression from a golden age or movement towards a day of doom and judgement by the Most High. Consequently movements for social change in antiquity tended to be of two varieties. One was millenarian: it involved a transcendental, otherworldly process. The other involved movements to restore some ideal order of bygone days.[25]

Therefore, although life was harsh for most people in the ancient world, we cannot assume that they anticipated or hoped for social progress.

There is no consensus upon where James was written from, although Syria or Palestine are likely candidates when one considers some of the

---

23. K. C. Hanson and Douglas E. Oakman, *Palestine in the Time of Jesus: Social Structures and Social Conflicts* (Minneapolis: Fortress, 1998), p. 128.

24. Peter Garnsey and Greg Woolf, 'Patronage of the Rural Poor in the Roman World', in *Patronage in Ancient Society* (ed. Andrew Wallace-Hadrill; London: Routledge, 1989), pp. 153–70 (157).

25. T. F. Carney, *The Shape of the Past: Models and Antiquity* (Lawrence, KS: Coronado Press, 1975), p. 120.

imagery of the letter such as the early and late rain in Jas 5.7.[26] The recipients of the letter, addressed as the 'twelve tribes in the diaspora', could be in a variety of places, but they are most likely urban areas given the references to things such as the 'crown' (στέφανος) of life (1.12), and to a man with gold rings and fancy clothes (2.2). Even if the man described in 2.2 is imaginary, the author assumes that the audience has heard of or seen such a figure. The author contrasts the treatment of this man, presumably an example of a rich (πλούσιος) person who oppresses the audience and drags people into court (2.6), with the treatment of the poor man (πτωχός). A πτωχός was an absolutely poor person who had no guarantee of the minimum required for existence such as 'itinerant and local beggars (especially people with disabilities and the chronically ill), many day laborers in the city and in the country, runaway slaves, many poor peasants and tenants'.[27] Given that James exhorts his audience regarding their comportment towards the rich and the poor, it is likely that the majority of the audience was neither, but were either relatively poor or relatively prosperous (given that there were certainly gradations in the ancient world), meaning that they could provide for themselves and for their families to varying degrees.[28] It is also possible that there were retainers within the audience – people of influence who depended on the goodwill of the elites for whom they worked. Ekkehard and Wolfgang Stegemann classify such people within the upper stratum of the ancient world, but they are still quite distinct from the elite.[29]

2. *Literary Mode of Production*

In such an economic and social context, texts were not mass produced. Most literature was created to supply administrative and religious needs which represented the elite perspective. Scribes, however, were not universally of the same social status nor were they all mechanistic bureaucrats. Many scribes worked as retainers for the powerful, but others, as John Kloppenborg points out, were 'not too high on the professional ladder', or functioned as 'free lance professionals' and did not necessarily serve the interests of the elites.[30] Kim Haines-Eitzen has

26.   See Peter H. Davids, 'Palestinian Traditions in the Epistle of James', in *James the Just and Christian Origins* (ed. B. Chilton and C. A. Evans; NovTSup, 98; Leiden: E. J. Brill, 1999), pp. 33–57 (esp. 47–48).

27.   Ekkehard W. Stegemann and Wolfgang Stegemann, *The Jesus Movement: A Social History of Its First Century* (trans. O. C. Dean; Minneapolis: Fortress, 1995), p. 84.

28.   Stegemann and Stegemann, *The Jesus Movement*, p. 71.

29.   Stegemann and Stegemann, *The Jesus Movement*, p. 71.

30.   John S. Kloppenborg, *Excavating Q: The History and Setting of the Sayings Gospel* (London: T&T Clark, 2000), pp. 200–201.

found that individual scribes could be 'multifunctional and multi-contextual',[31] and that sometimes texts could be produced and copied by people who were not professional scribes at all. Thus it is quite possible to conceive that a fairly sophisticated text such as James, which exhibits a good facility with Greek, rare vocabulary, familiarity with traditions from Jewish Scripture and tradition, as well as some form of Jesus' teachings, could emerge from a group that was distant from the very rich, or disaffected and alienated in some way, and not sympathetic to the interests of the wealthy and powerful.

3. Dominant Ideology

It would be inappropriate to argue for a uniform ideology throughout the Roman Empire, but we can speak of a *dominant ideology*, even though not all shared it. This was an ideology of honour configured in a specific way. Honour is usually defined as a person's feeling of self-worth and the public's acknowledgment of that worth. It stands for a person's place in society.[32] Males were expected to uphold it, defend it and gain more of it if possible. Honour was central to family and community identity, and always connected to one's social status whether that be in a rural village or the emperor's household.

I call the centrality of honour an ideology because it was so closely connected to material conditions, and reflected a whole set of values and beliefs that served the interests of a specific group of people, that is, primarily elite males. For example, honour was intimately tied to the structure of power relations within the family, and to the division of labour insofar as the more highly honoured people in society did not do manual work, while those lower on the social scale, possessing less honour, obviously did. Moreover, this division was largely gender-based, and thus it would be extremely dishonourable for males to be doing women's work etc. Concern for honour thus functioned as a type of social control, for it restricted the kinds of activities and behaviours in which people could engage.

Moving from family and village life to armies, cities and the empire as a whole, J. E. Lendon has shown how honour was central at all administrative levels. As he writes:

> Emperors, officials and officers used the lure of honour and the threat of disgrace to control those they ruled over or commanded. They took

---

31. Kim Haines-Eitzen, *Guardians of Letters: Literacy, Power and the Transmitters of Early Christian Literature* (New York and Oxford: Oxford University Press, 2000), p. 22.

32. Bruce J. Malina, *The New Testament World: Insights from Cultural Anthropology* (Atlanta: John Knox, 1981), p. 47.

advantage also of the fact that spirited parochial loyalty – civic loyalty in a civilian world, unit loyalty in an army – manifested itself as vigorous concern for the honour which the ancient mind invested in cities and legions. Thus cities and legions too could be honoured and dishonoured by their rulers, and since their citizens and soldiers felt an intense anxiety about their honour, about their place in relation to their hated rivals, a wise government could use their particularistic devotion as a basis for political power.[33]

Whether one was strong or weak, in the army or trying to run a household, concerns about honour were alive in all strata of social life throughout the Roman Empire, and could shape what was perceived as acceptable behaviour as well as relationships between people.

This ideology of honour is important for considerations of wealth and poverty. Those who made generous financial contributions to ancient associations, for example, were often praised for their φιλοτιμία or 'love of honour'.[34] G. E. M. de Ste. Croix has pointed out that when it comes to describing the wealthy:

> We have not only words which mean property-owning, rich, fortunate, distinguished, well-born, influential, but also, as alternatives for virtually the same set of people, words having a basically moral connotation and meaning literally the good, the best, the upright, the fair-minded, and so forth. On the other hand we find applied to the lower classes, the poor, who are also the Many, the mob, the populace, words with an inescapably moral quality, meaning essentially bad.[35]

Social-scientific studies of early Christian literature have shown that when we encounter words such as 'rich' πλούσιος (Jas 1.10, 11; 2.5, 6; 5.1) and 'poor' πτωχός (Jas 2.2, 3, 5, 6), these are not solely economic terms, but refer to the ability to maintain and gain honour and status, as in the case of the rich, or the loss of honour and status, as with the poor.[36] Indeed these terms can have economic dimensions to them, but they can also refer to the sick, to captives and mourners, among others.[37] The reasoning here is that economics was embedded in kinship and politics in antiquity; there

33. J. E. Lendon, *Empire of Honour: The Art of Government in the Roman World* (Oxford: Clarendon Press, 1997), p. 268.

34. Greek inscriptions regularly describe generous benefactors with such words. For example, see *IG* II² 1292 (Athens; ca. 250 BCE). See K. J. Dover, *Greek Popular Morality in the Time of Plato and Aristotle* (Oxford: Basil Blackwell, 1974), p. 230.

35. G. E. M. de Ste. Croix, *The Class Struggle in the Ancient Greek World* (Ithaca: Cornell University Press, 1981), pp. 423–24.

36. See Bruce J. Malina, 'Wealth and Poverty in the New Testament and Its World', *Int* 41 (1986), pp. 354–67. See also, Paul Hollenbach, 'Defining Rich and Poor Using Social Sciences', in *Society of Biblical Literature 1987 Seminar Papers* (ed. Kent Harold Richards; SBLSP, 26; Missoula: Scholars Press, 1987), pp. 50–63.

37. See Hollenbach, 'Defining Rich', p. 55.

was no notion that it was an identifiable sphere of activity that could be analysed independently. Thus, whenever we encounter references to rich and poor, we must be attentive to the social meanings of these terms. Moreover, this was a world of perceived limited good, including a limited amount of honour, and thus the gain of honour was usually at someone else's expense.

However, the bald pursuit of riches for the sake of increasing wealth itself was not admired, whether one looks at Jewish or Graeco-Roman sources.[38] Such persons were often considered to be greedy and wicked; in fact the tyrant was characterized as having an insatiable desire for wealth. Thus although honour and status went together, many literary sources indicate that those who pursued riches simply to increase their wealth, and not share it with others or put it to good use, were not deserving of praise. James is one of these sources.

4. *Ideological Strategies in James*

a. *James as a Rhetorical Text*

Although there continues to be great disagreement about the authorship, provenance and date of James, there is an emerging consensus among Jacobean scholars that James reflects structure and coherence, contrary to Martin Dibelius' influential commentary, in which he argued that the document was *paraenesis*, understood as a loose string of ethical admonitions. This is not to say that *paraenesis* has been thrown out as a descriptor for James, but that the notion of *paraenesis* itself has received reconsideration since Dibelius. More recent work argues that *paraenesis* can have rhetorical aims, and can address a social situation in order to promote a particular set of values.[39] Regarding James' status as a letter, I join scholars who claim that it is a literary letter with its address to the 'twelve tribes in the Diaspora' indicating its comparability to ancient

38. See Plutarch, *On Love of Wealth*. Plutarch was undoubtedly well off himself, but he sharply criticizes those obsessed with the pursuit of wealth for its own sake. Although Sirach has many positive things to say about wealth, the uncontrolled pursuit of wealth causes blindness (Sir. 27.1) See Victor Morla Asensio, 'Poverty and Wealth: Ben Sira's View of Possessions', in *Der Einzelne und seine Gemeinschaft bei Ben Sira* (ed. Renate Egger-Wenzel and Ingrid Krammer; BZAW, 270; Berlin and New York: Walter de Gruyter, 1998), pp. 151–78.

39. See Todd C. Penner, 'The Epistle of James in Current Research', *CRBS* 7 (1999), pp. 257–308 (esp. 270–71). Some scholars, such as Patrick J. Hartin (*A Spirituality of Perfection: Faith in Action in the Letter of James* [Collegeville, MN: Liturgical Press, 1999], pp. 45–49), prefer to think of James more as *protrepsis* than *paraenesis*, understanding the former as containing more sustained arguments than *paraenesis*, but there is still debate as to whether ancients really distinguished *paraenesis* and *protrepsis* from one another.

Jewish Diaspora letters,[40] such as the letters dispatched by members of the Gamaliel family,[41] or those preserved within 2 Maccabees (2 Macc. 1.1-9; 1.10–2.18). James also bears similarities to what Fred Francis calls 'secondary letters'. Such letters are found within historical narratives such as Josephus' *Antiquities* (8.50-54); they possess double opening statements, as James does,[42] and end abruptly, with no epistolary close, also a characteristic of James.[43] All of this is simply to say that the notion of James as a jumble of teachings, held together at best through catchwords, is no longer the dominant view of the text. James is a letter which deliberately seeks to convince its audience about what to think and what to do, and this persuasion clearly involves consideration of material concerns, as well as the relationship between ideas and practices. An ideological examination of such a text thus seems fitting.

b. *James 1.9-11*

Three sections of the letter that refer explicitly to rich and poor are Jas 1.9-11, Jas 2.1-13, and Jas 5.1-6. James 1.9-11 appears in the *exordium* (Jas 1.2–18), which introduces major themes, such as the notion of perfection or wholeness, that are then taken up later on. James 1.9-11 is an amplification on the pursuit of perfection, for part of being perfect is to resist the desire for riches.[44]

Many modern commentators on this passage agree that the words ταπεινός and πλούσιος refer to a lack or excess of material prosperity, status and honour. But the chief issue that perplexes interpreters is whether or not the rich person is representative of a community member

---

40. See Karl-Wilhelm Niebuhr, 'Der Jakobusbrief im Licht frühjüdischer Diasporabriefe', *NTS* 44 (1998), pp. 420–43.

41. See Dennis Pardee, *Handbook of Ancient Hebrew Letters* (SBLSBS, 15; Chico, CA: Scholars Press, 1982), pp. 186–89.

42. Fred O. Francis ('The Form and Function of the Opening and Closing Paragraphs of James and 1 John', *ZNW* 61 [1970], pp. 110–26) points out that in Jas 1.1-27, 'there is a presentation and representation of testing, steadfastness, perfect work/gift, reproaching/ anger, wisdom/words, and rich-poor/doer. In both cases these themes laid down in the opening verses are subsequently developed in the body of the epistle' (p. 111).

43. Embedded within Thucydides' historical narrative, for example, there are letters (7.10-15; 1.128.7) with neither opening nor closing formulae. See David E. Aune, *The New Testament in its Literary Environment* (LEC, 8; Philadelphia: Westminster, 1987), p. 169.

44. See Lauri Thurén, 'Risky Rhetoric in James', *NovT* 37 (1995), pp. 262–84 (esp. 272); John H. Elliott, 'The Epistle of James in Rhetorical and Social Scientific Perspective: Holiness-Wholeness and Patterns of Replication', *BTB* 23 (1993), pp. 71–81 (esp. 72); Wilhelm H. Wuellner, 'Der Jakobusbrief im Licht der Rhetorik und Textpragmatik', *LB* 43 (1978), pp. 5–66 (41). Ernst Baasland ('Literarische Form, Thematik und geschichtliche Einordnung des Jakobusbriefes', *ANRW* 2.25.5, pp. 3646–84 [esp. 3655]) includes Jas 1.5-15 within the exordium.

or an outsider. Some think that the most natural way to read the Greek text would be to supply ἀδελφός in v. 10, given that that verb for 'let him boast' refers both to the lowly and to the rich, thereby making the rich person a community member who will 'heroically' boast in his loss of wealth and dishonour.[45] However, the rest of the passage renders this interpretation difficult to accept. James states bluntly, with no trace of sentimentality, that the rich will pass away. The poor brother is offered hope for the future, for he will be exalted, while the rich person will be humiliated, with no second chance.[46] As such, I think that James is speaking ironically or derisively, indicating that like the flowers which last only a short while, the rich, who are not part of the community, will wither away.

What is particularly interesting here is how James has used pre-existing tradition. I am not suggesting that James necessarily had a Bible, but clearly he was familiar with portions of Jewish scripture, for he explicitly quotes from it from time to time. Perhaps as Wiard Popkes has hypothesized, James had a file, some sort of *Zettelkasten* or card index of Jewish, Christian (although James may not have perceived them as 'Christian' but as Jewish) and philosophical materials, from which he drew and then integrated into his letter.[47] Here James does not say that he is quoting Scripture but the re-expression of Isa. 40.6-8 (LXX) is 'unmistakable'.[48] James does not slavishly repeat the text, but creatively shapes it to suit his own purposes. Isaiah 40 speaks of humans whose constancy is like the flower of the field and the grass. The flower will fade and the grass will wither, but, says Isaiah, the word of God will stand forever.[49] James uses the same imagery but now the flower and the grass are compared to the rich person, or representative rich person, who will pass away and fade away in the midst of his pursuits. As Hartin points out, 'by using the words of the prophet Isaiah, James is in effect indicating

45. Patrick J. Hartin (*James* [SP, 14; Collegeville, MN: Liturgical Press, 2003], pp. 68–69) takes this position, for example.

46. See Sophie Laws, *The Epistle of James* (BNTC; London: A&C Black, 1980), p. 63.

47. Wiard Popkes, 'James and Scripture: An Exercise in Intertextuality', *NTS* 45 (1999), pp. 213–39.

48. Luke Timothy Johnson, *The Letter of James* (AB, 37A; New York: Doubleday, 1995), p. 191. See also the essay by Kloppenborg in this volume.

49. 1 Pet. 1.24 also uses the Isaiah passage here, but includes the reference to the 'word of the Lord abiding for ever' thus making a different point than James does, although 'the implanted word' of Jas 1.21 may be a reference to this notion of the word. Ephrem the Syrian's *Letter to Publius* 19 also seems to build upon Isaiah 40 here after he speaks of the decline of kings, nobles and generals: 'How long will you deceive yourself, thinking you are better than the grass of roof, grass which a single day's heat withers up'. Ephrem never explicitly quotes James, but he speaks of the apocalyptic destruction of the rich in images recalling Jas 5.1. See the translation and discussion of this letter by Sebastian Brock, 'Ephrem's Letter to Publius', *LM* 89 (1976), pp. 261–305.

that what the prophet had foretold now comes in fulfillment in the lives of the rich'.[50] James shapes the Isaiah passage to contrast the fate of the poor and the rich, then moves on to describe how blessed is the one who endures trial, a theme introduced in the first part of the chapter. Thus he does not *dwell* upon what will happen to the rich, nor describe them with any specificity.

How then might this passage work rhetorically, and what sorts of ideological strategies does it use? First, this notion of reversal is not new; rather it is a fairly traditional motif.[51] It seems likely that the audience would have recognized the Isaiah allusion as an important part of their tradition, given its widespread use in Jewish and early Christian literature. James can safely assume that the recipients would understand the weight of the reference, and thus be more likely to identify with his message. The reference thus *legitimates* James' point, for James has aligned himself with the *ethos* of Isaiah and built on an authority that is self-evident to his audience. The re-expression of the Isaiah language also functions rhetorically to establish the truth of the statement, as ancient rhetorical handbooks, such as the *Rhetorica ad Herrenium* (4.3.6), make clear. The text could also serve to *unify* the audience. As suggested earlier, those who received or heard this letter were not all of the same social status, although it is hard to imagine that there were any super-elites in their midst. Such communities experienced rivalries and struggles over resources and behaviour; and it is evident from elsewhere in James that the use of speech was a problem (Jas 3.1-12), as well as how to show concern for the needy (Jas 1.27). The passage therefore fosters solidarity within the group over against 'those rich' who will wither away. The pericope is also *action oriented*, for it links the practical of lived existence with the theoretical, or one might say, eschatological, insofar as it advocates being lowly, while it prophesies the destruction of the rich. This eschatological dimension of James, as Patrick Tiller writes, 'serves to explain and redefine experienced reality and the moral obligations of those who live in that reality'.[52] The text also *rationalizes* in that it gives reasons why the audience should adopt particular behaviours that might otherwise come under attack or question. In the immediate context, Jas 1.9-11 appears in the midst of calls

---

50. Hartin, *James*, p. 63. Interestingly, Donald Verseput ('Wisdom, 4Q185, and the Epistle of James', *JBL* 117 [1998], pp. 691–707), has found a comparison in the way that 4Q165 uses the same imagery from Isa. 40.6–8 to create 'an oracle of doom spoken against the adversaries of God's people' (p. 704). Here woe is pronounced upon the 'sons of man' and then the poem continues in language reminiscent of Jas 1.9-11.

51. Todd C. Penner, *The Epistle of James and Eschatology: Re-reading an Ancient Letter* (JSNTSup, 121; Sheffield: Sheffield Academic Press, 1996), p. 208.

52. Patrick A. Tiller, 'The Rich and Poor in James: An Apocalyptic Proclamation', in *Society of Biblical Literature 1998 Seminar Papers* (SBLSP, 37; Missoula: Scholars Press, 1998), pp. 909–20 (920).

to withstand trials and testing, to ask for wisdom from God, and not to argue with God.[53] Moreover, later in the letter there is a stress upon the need to care for the poor (e.g. Jas 1.27), and not to show partiality to the wealthy.

At this point, given the 'stylized' language that draws upon a prophetic tradition,[54] we need not conclude that the rich are a specific group of people. Rather, thus far they could simply function as an example of what James' listeners *are not* or *should not be*. Their projected demise serves as a contrast to the future of James' audience, and the letter writer does not dwell upon their fate with any specific detail.

This reversal of rich and poor also illustrates a clear challenge to the honour ideology. The contrast between the fates of the rich and the lowly indicates a status reversal of these two specific groups, who had economic, social and even moral identities in the eyes of many in the ancient world.[55] The lowly brother will boast in exultation while the rich will do the same in humiliation. This does not mean that the letter rejects honour, but it redefines who is honourable, reflecting the interests of a group who normally had little ascribed honour. In a world of limited good, someone had to lose in order for another to gain. In bringing low the rich, even if the author does not have specific individuals in view, James has effectively raised the status of 'the poor'.[56] Thus the identity of *being poor*, which included but was not solely based upon a socio-economic status, becomes comparatively more appealing. James has offered criticism of the rich, to be sure, but the focus of the text seems to be primarily positive and constructive in that it builds upon traditions that his audience would have taken for granted as important such as the prophetic tradition and the coming judgment, and shapes them to support a call to ask for wisdom from God who gives generously, and to withstand testing that leads to the receipt of the 'crown of life' (Jas 1.12). Thus James both reconceptualizes the honour ideology but also supplies a different set of beliefs and values that he shows to be deeply rooted and consistent with Jewish tradition.

---

53. Recently Peter Spitaler ('Diakrinomai in Mat 21.21, Mk 11.23, Acts 10.20, Rom 4.20, 14.23, Jas 1.6, and Jud 22 – The "Semantic Shift" that Went Unnoticed by Patristic Authors', *NovT* 48 [2006], forthcoming) has argued that a better translation for διακρίνομαι is 'to dispute' as opposed to 'to doubt' which also makes more sense given the focus upon speech in James.

54. Penner, *Epistle of James*, p. 271.

55. Indeed James may be alluding to a Jesus saying about status reversal here as well (Mt. 23.12; Lk. 14.11; 18.14). See Hartin, *James*, p. 83.

56. I would not go so far as to suggest that James challenges the *male* possession of honour, however, for in Jas 1.14-15 we see a typical characterization of 'desire' as a woman who lures a person, then conceives of and gives birth to sin, which grows up to produce death.

c. *James 2.1-13*

The next section referring explicitly to rich and poor is Jas 2.1-13. Here, as many scholars have suggested, James is probably making an argument to dissuade the audience from engaging in a patron–client relationship with a wealthy person with fine clothes and gold rings. This person need not be a specific individual, but serves as a stock character in a scenario that serves as an example of what the community should not do; they should not honour the rich man for that leads to dishonouring the poor one.[57]

Wesley Wachob and more recently John Kloppenborg have shown that Jas 2.5 is an example of James using a saying of Jesus from Q 6.20b (or a form of Q 6.20b), 'blessed are the poor', and adapting it to serve his own needs.[58] Richard Bauckham has also explored how James 're-expresses' things that he has learned, in this case some of the teachings of Jesus,[59] just as Sirach reformulates and creatively re-articulates previous traditions from Proverbs and elsewhere. Moreover, Wachob has demonstrated how Jas 2.5 takes over this saying of Jesus, which is epideictic in Q for there it reminds the audience that they belong to the kingdom, and transforms it into a deliberative saying that contributes to the overall exigence not to show partiality and not to dishonour the poor man. It does this by referring to Lev. 19.18 in Jas 2.8, which indicates that demonstrating partiality to the rich is actually violating the law, and through referring to the 'faith of our Lord Jesus Christ' in Jas 2.1 (assuming the reference to Jesus Christ in Jas 2.1 is not an interpolation, as various scholars have suggested in the history of interpretation of James)[60] which clinches the matter with its indication that showing partiality goes against the faith of Jesus, which is the faith of the 'poor in the world' who are said to be 'rich in faith' in Jas 2.5.[61] James wants his audience to identify with the poor of

---

57.   As John S. Kloppenborg ('Patronage Avoidance in James', *HvTSt* 55 [1999], pp. 755–94) has shown, James may be drawing upon caricatures of niggardly patrons who demean and humiliate their clients, such as Juvenal in *Sat.* 5 and Lucian in *Nigrinus*.

58.   Wesley H. Wachob, *The Voice of Jesus in the Social Rhetoric of James* (SNTSMS, 106; Cambridge and New York: Cambridge University Press, 2000); John S. Kloppenborg ('The Reception of Jesus Traditions in James', in *The Catholic Epistles and the Tradition* [ed. J. Schlosser; BETL, 176; Leuven: Peeters, 2004], pp. 93–141 [esp. 136–40]) has shown that James must have known the Q version, for Q and James are the only two texts that associate 'the poor' and 'kingdom' together, and Jas 2.6 shows familiarity with the larger context of Q 6.29 and Q 12.58-59 and Jas 2.7 seems to recall Q 6.22.

59.   Richard Bauckham, *James: Wisdom of James, Disciple of Jesus the Sage* (New Testament Readings; London and New York: Routledge, 1999), p. 91.

60.   For a recent discussion of parts of 2.1 as an interpolation see Dale C. Allison, 'The Fiction of James and Its *Sitz im Leben*', *RB* 108 (2001), pp. 529–70.

61.   Wachob, *The Voice of Jesus*, p. 192. Wachob shows how Jas 2.1-13 reflects 'an elaboration of a theme' exercise as developed by the *Rhet. Her.* 2.18.28. Jas 2.5 forms the beginning of the proof.

Jesus' saying. Moreover, as Kloppenborg has argued, if the addressees give the best seat to the patron and dishonour the poor man they are effectively violating Torah *and* acting against their own self-interest insofar as they *are* the poor.[62]

How might ideological strategies be manifest in James' rhetorical footwork here? The effort to *unify* the audience over against the rich again appears, for James wants the audience to identify as a whole with the 'poor in the world' who are 'rich in faith'. He is reinforcing a strong social identity. The passage is *action oriented* in that it seeks to persuade that audience that they must not show partiality to the rich, nor should they 'dishonour' the poor man, for indeed they share an identity with this poor man. It *legitimates* such behaviour through the reference to the Torah (Lev. 19.18), something which the audience was presumably trying to uphold. Returning to the work of Wachob and Kloppenborg on James' use of Q 6.20b, the argument is also *legitimated* through a paraphrase of Jesus' saying, what ancient rhetoricians termed *aemulatio*,[63] whereby James aligns himself with the *ethos* of Jesus, but also shows how Jesus' wisdom, which he shares, can apply to James' context. It also *rationalizes* for it gives reasons why not to show partiality. The rich are oppressive, says James, they drag people into court and they blaspheme the honourable name invoked over the audience (Jas 2.6-7).

Again, the passage does not dwell on what will happen to the rich, but uses them in an argument for how the addressees should treat the poor among them and for how they should understand themselves and the values that they should embody. There is nothing to indicate that identifiable wealthy people are in view; rather, the stereotypical rich function as a contrast to what James' audience should be. The characterization of the rich as exploitative, the reference to the Torah, and the reformulation of Jesus' teaching together support an argument to resist the patron and to care for the poor. It directly challenges the ideology of honour for the elites, but also offers an alternative ethical stance whereby the addressees, who are honourable and should honour one another, are exhorted to live differently, and to care for the poor among them. Again, just as James challenges the ideology of honour in his day, he also constructively replaces it with a different set of beliefs, values and actions that he shows to be consistent with the law, and consistent with the teachings of Jesus. He has not only offered a challenge, he has

---

62. As Kloppenborg ('The Reception', p. 141) puts it, this argument required a 'reframing of the (indicative) macarism [Q 6.20b] as a rhetorical question, parallel to the two other questions in 2.6b-7, and amplifying the saying so as to underscore the fact that the addressees identify themselves with the "poor" of the macarism'.

63. See Quintilian 10.5.5.

creatively refashioned tradition in a novel way; a creation which he hoped would motivate his audience to action.

d. *James 5.1-6*

Lastly, we turn to Jas 5.1-6, which contains the most biting critique of the wealthy in the entire letter. Here the rich are attacked not only because they store up treasures for themselves, but because they have held back the wages of the labourers, they have lived in luxury, fattened their hearts, and condemned and killed the righteous one (Jas 5.6).[64]

Prophetic and apocalyptic imagery reverberate throughout this section, but there does not seem to be a single LXX text that is quoted.[65] The language used recalls a 'prophetic funeral dirge and mourning cry'; in this case the funeral of the rich.[66] It is stereotypical language. For James the rich are wicked, and this characterization is not new, for in the Psalms, as Wachob has explained, the rich are wicked as well.[67] As in the case of Jas 1.9-11, this passage indicates a future reversal, albeit a more vivid and dramatic one, whereby the rich will be judged and face miseries, in contrast to James' audience which is encouraged to wait patiently, and not to grumble, lest they be judged as well.

James 5.2-3 could be another creative re-expression of a saying of Jesus, namely Mt. 6.19-20 // Lk. 12.33 [or: Q 12.33].[68] If so, James has transformed the teaching into part of a diatribe against the arrogant rich. Again, if the audience was familiar with the teaching of Jesus, then the letter's recipients would realize that the rich have done precisely the opposite of what Jesus advocated. As such, the passage functions as a way of illustrating that those who are wealthy; who store up treasures and exploit their workers, are not only doomed, they are violating Jesus' teaching.

The wealthy are also depicted in the most unflattering terms possible. They are greedy, they live in luxury, and they have 'stuffed their hearts for the day of slaughter' (Jas 5.5). Just as an animal is force-fed before it is killed, the rich are gorging themselves for the day of judgment.[69] They are hardly honourable.

---

64. There is no reason to interpret 'the righteous one' as Jesus, or as James the Just, for the 'righteous one' appears in Wis. 2.12 (τὸν δίκαιον) as the poor righteous one whom the rich murder. Similarly *1 Enoch* uses the imagery of the righteous person who is oppressed by the rich (*1 En.* 96.7-8).

65. For example, the 'day of slaughter' in Jas 5.5 recalls Jer. 12.3, which speaks of the divine judgment of evildoers.

66. Penner, *Epistle of James*, p. 175.

67. Wachob, 'The Epistle of James and the Book of Psalms'.

68. See, for example, Patrick J. Hartin, *James and the Q Sayings of Jesus* (JSNTSup, 47; Sheffield: Sheffield Academic Press, 1991), pp. 148–64.

69. Hartin, *James*, p. 230.

This passage reminds one of texts such as *1 Enoch* 97 which refers to the unjust storing up of gold and silver that will not remain (Jas 5.3).[70] But even though there is more elaboration of the rich people's activity here than earlier in the letter, James 5 does not provide a lengthy description of their downfall or visions of their suffering, as is depicted in *1 Enoch* 92–105. Certainly, the rich will not meet a pleasant fate, but Jas 5.7-20 moves immediately back into how the community members should behave, with an emphasis upon patience (5.7-11), not making oaths (5.12), and instructions for prayer, confessing sins (5.13-18), and preventing community members from wandering from the truth (6.19-20). Rather than dwelling upon the ruin of the rich, James may be using this prophetic denunciation and funeral dirge as a means of building a contrast in identity and behaviour between the rich and the poor, which reinforces the identity and actions that he wishes his audience to uphold and practise.

Pedrito Maynard-Reid has commented that the 'principal purpose of James' attack upon the rich is to give consolation and comfort to the poor and oppressed'.[71] I would go further and add that the purpose of this passage, comparable to the other two explored earlier, is to underscore what the addressees, who identify with the poor, should do. Jas 5.1-6 again serves to *unify* the audience in opposition to the rich, for who would want to be associated with such greedy, monstrous people? They are a clear contrast to James' audience. This is ideological in the sense that it renders the audience's identity as the poor as an 'of course'. Who among James' audience would venture to think that he or she had anything in common with the rich? The pericope's possible re-expression of a Jesus saying also *legitimates* James' moral teaching, for it demonstrates that the rich do precisely what Jesus teaches one *ought not* to do. This also undergirds the fact that the text is *action oriented*. Based upon what James says about the rich, no recipient in the letter would want to behave as they do. Moreover, James turns to positive exhortation in 5.7-11, in his stress to be patient for the coming of the Lord using the great figure of Job as an example, and assures his audience that the Lord is compassionate and merciful.

Again, James uses ideas such as the notion of a coming judgment, possibly a teaching of Jesus, and imagery from Jewish tradition to cement his argument that the audience should not behave as the rich do, but understand and comport themselves in contrast to the rich. James does not simply expose the negative dimensions of the dominant ideology of his

70. The reference to gold may recall the man with the gold ring who enters the assembly in Jas 2.2.

71. Pedrito U. Maynard-Reid, *Poverty and Wealth in James* (Maryknoll: Orbis, 1987), p. 97.

day, but supplies a different set of values and actions that, again, he shows to be consistent with tradition.

5. *The Ideology of the Letter of James*

This brief experiment in applying ideological strategies to James as they concern rich and poor illustrates aspects of the ideology of the letter as a whole. First, in each example the text is *oppositional* to the dominant honour ideology of the day. James reverses the notions of who is honourable and who is not, whether it is through an explicit statement of reversal, a criticism of showing partiality, or in a deeply unflattering and stereotypical description of what the rich have done, and their forthcoming judgment. James' ideology consists in part, therefore, of the notion of an honourable poor, a conclusion already reached by other interpreters.[72] This is not to suggest that every member of the community to which James writes is of identical social status, but that together as a unity – as 'the poor' – they are honourable in contrast to the rich. Thus James has not only exposed the ancient obsession with honour and wealth as corrupt and contrary to the traditions which his audience presumably shared; he has replaced it by stressing the poor as honourable, and shown how this notion of the honourable poor is the true understanding of the tradition (which would include some of Jesus' teachings).

James' ideology also challenges the practice of dependence upon wealthy patrons, as illustrated by the example from James 2. For James, God is the champion benefactor and depicted, as I have argued elsewhere, as a generous friend.[73] On the ground, it is not clear exactly what James imagines to be the best manner of managing socio-economically, but clearly he wants community members to care for one another materially (1.27; 2.1-7, 14-17) and morally, with the letter's emphasis upon proper use of speech (3.1-12; 4.11-12) and exhortation to avoid envy, fighting and arrogance (3.13–4.10). Perhaps James imagines that community members will act as benefactors and friends to one another, just as God does for the community. Moreover, if James' audience included some members of the retainer stratum of ancient society, who survived largely through their dependence upon the elites, James' call to resist patrons poses a serious test.

This resistance to patronage by the rich therefore challenges, or at least does not participate in, the dominant mode of production which served the interests of the more powerful. However, this is not an active or revolutionary challenge. James does not want his audience to go out and

---

72. See, for example, Wachob, *The Voice of Jesus*, pp. 178–85.

73. Alicia Batten, 'God in the Letter of James: Patron or Benefactor?' *NTS* 50 (2004), pp. 257–72.

change the world, but to remain unblemished by it. The world is depicted negatively in James (1.27; 3.15; 4.4); any hints of a missionary zeal to go out and transform it simply do not appear. In keeping with the ancient mindset, James imagines an apocalyptic transformation, not a worldly one.

Several have observed that the *Epistle of Enoch* (*1 En.* 92–105) shares many themes and images with James.[74] Both condemn the wealthy for their abuse of the poor (*1 En.* 94.7) and both indicate that any riches that are stored up will disappear (*1 En.* 97.8-10). Moreover, together these texts challenge the perspective of wisdom teachings found in such documents as Ecclesiastes (5.8-9, 17-19), which celebrates wealth as a gift from God, and Sir. 11.18-19, in which the sage ponders the man who has earned his wealth through hard work, but does not know how long he will have to live.[75] However, James, as we have seen, does not dwell on elaborate scenarios or visions of the destruction of the affluent. James is eschatological, and uses apocalyptic language, but the end times are not an obsession; rather they serve to motivate life in the present. As Hartin puts it, 'the traditional apocalyptic description of the destruction of the wicked is absent from James – in its place stands the positive challenge...to endure amidst the sufferings and persecutions of this age'.[76]

Thus although James may be representative of a group not aligned with the wealthy, just like the *Epistle of Enoch*, James is not, in my view, as aggressive nor particularly focused upon attacking the rich. Rather James uses the dishonourable depictions of the rich and their future demise as a contrast to his audience's identity as the honourable poor, who must continue to support one another and withstand the trials of carving out an existence without patronal support. James uses the negative portrayals of the rich, in other words, to aid in the construction of an identity of his audience and to exhort them to specific practices and social values.[77] In this sense the letter consists primarily of deliberative rhetoric. The rich are

74. See Patrick J. Hartin, '"Who is Wise and Understanding Among You?" An Analysis of Wisdom, Eschatology and Apocalypticism in the Epistle of James', in *Society of Biblical Literature 1996 Seminary Papers* (SBLSP, 35; Atlanta: Scholars Press, 1996), pp. 483–503; Penner, *Epistle of James*, pp. 221–23; John S. Kloppenborg, 'Response to "Riches, the Rich and God's Judgment in 1 Enoch 92–105 and the Gospel According to Luke" and "Revisiting the Rich and the Poor in 1 Enoch 92–105 and the Gospel According to Luke"', in *George W. E. Nickelsburg in Perspective: An Ongoing Dialogue of Learning* (ed. Jacob Neusner and Alan J. Avery-Peck; Leiden and Boston: E. J. Brill, 2003), pp. 572–85; Tiller, 'The Rich and Poor in James'.

75. See Kloppenborg, 'Response', pp. 574–75. For Sirach, wealth is only bad if it is earned unjustly. The wealthy person does have the obligation to give alms, however.

76. Hartin, '"Who is wise"', p. 495.

77. For an analysis of how the Gospels of Matthew and John use anti-Jewish rhetoric in order to establish the identity and communities of their respective audiences, see Sean Freyne, 'Vilifying the Other and Defining the Self: Matthew's and John's Anti-Jewish

a stereotype in James, and the letter draws upon what to him may be stock imagery to describe them. By grounding these ideas in the traditions of Judaism and the teachings of Jesus that are consistent with those of Judaism, James presents his audience with an ideology that is congruent with the past. In this sense, the Letter of James might be described as a creatively conservative letter, which imagines another way of being, but one which the author shows to be entrenched in the traditions and texts of Judaism.

In sum, the Letter of James manifests awareness that the temptation to link up with rich patrons is very real, and has perhaps even been yielded to by various members of James' audience, causing neglect of the poor. However the letter writer does not construct the document in order to target a particular historical wealthy person or group – probably no particular centre of affluence is in view – but uses various strategies to solidify the addressees with a communal identity as the poor who care for the poor among them. James, as we have seen, is not out to change society, but is '*introversionniste*',[78] and tries to preserve the community from the negative influence of wealth and all of the problems that such influence could bring. Unlike other NT texts which turn honour and shame upside down, such as 1 Peter, James does not invoke the suffering and death of Christ to support his ideology.[79] Rather, James constructs a positive ideology of an honourable poor through both a vilification of the wealthy and the havoc that an obsession with wealth can bring, and by presenting this ideology as continuous and consistent with Jewish tradition, and, it seems, some of the teachings of Jesus. The benefits of this ideology include a strong communal identity and presumably better material support in the form of mutual aid, the assurance of God's reliability, and the promise of salvation at the coming judgment. But whether James' efforts had a concrete impact upon his audience remains an open question.

Polemic in Focus', in '*To See Ourselves as Others See Us': Christians, Jews and 'Others' in Late Antiquity* (ed. Jacob Neusner and Ernest S. Frerichs; Scholars Press Studies in the Humanities; Chico, CA: Scholars Press, 1985), pp. 117–43.

78. See Pierre Antoine Bernheim, 'La mort de Jacques, l'épître de Jacques et la dénonciation des riches', in *The Catholic Epistles and the Tradition* (ed. J. Schlosser; BETL, 176; Leuven: Peeters, 2004), pp. 249–61.

79. On 1 Peter's manipulation of honour and shame, see the excellent article by John H. Elliott, 'Disgraced Yet Graced: The Gospel According to 1 Peter in the Key of Honour and Shame', *BTB* 25 (1996), pp. 166–78.

NATIVISM IN JAMES 2.14-26: A POST-COLONIAL READING

K. Jason Coker

The faith/works binary in Jas 2.14-26 has received a tremendous amount of attention since the Reformation due to the anti-Pauline rhetoric that James employs. Although many scholars downplay the oppositional nature of Jas 2.14-26 with Romans 3–4 and Galatians 2–3, I will highlight the differences and argue that James and Paul are in direct opposition to each other. The conflict between James and Paul, however, has less to do with a faith/works binary than with the issue of identity. The faith/works binary simply functions as the site for James' and Paul's politics of identity. This issue of identity politics in both James' and Paul's polemic, specifically Jas 2.14-26, is ripe for a post-colonial reading. Through the post-colonial lens, James takes a nativist position over against a hybrid position, which Paul represents in Romans 3–4 and Galatians 2–3. The polemical nature of this dialogue between James and Paul is then set in the context of anti-imperial discourse. James takes a very conservative position and argues that the identity of believers should come from a pure form of piety that is set in opposition to surrounding cultural norms and has continuity with that which is old, that is, Abraham and Rahab. Paul, on the other hand, argues for an identity that is based on something new and, to use a post-colonial term, hybrid. James and Paul's argument can then be seen as an argument between nativist resistance to colonial power, which is characterized by reproducing colonial representations in order to resist colonial influence, and hybrid resistance, which is characterized by blurring the boundaries of colonizer/colonized in order to renegotiate a new set of power relations. Before I attempt a post-colonial reading of Jas 2.14-26, however, I will briefly introduce important post-colonial scholars and thoroughly identify key concepts in post-colonial studies that will be essential for this essay.

Broadly conceived, post-colonial studies encompasses all that is colonial and the effects that colonialism had and continues to have on the colonized and on the imperial powers. The three dominant figures in post-colonial studies are Edward W. Said, Homi K. Bhabha and Gayatri Chakravorty Spivak. Said's charter document, *Orientalism*, critiqued

western representations of 'the Orient' as 'other'. Said's main critique was
that western knowledge of the Orient gave the West power to dominate/
colonize the oriental. He argues: 'The Orient that appears in Orientalism,
then, is a system of representations framed by a whole set of forces that
brought the Orient into Western learning, Western consciousness, and
later, Western empire'.[1] Said's analysis was critiqued and appropriated by
Bhabha and Spivak in such a way as to define the field of post-colonial
studies. Bhabha argues that colonial discourse is not and has never been
as unambiguous as Said affirms. Bhabha understands colonial discourse
as fundamentally unstable to the degree that instead of representing the
colonial proper, it is appropriated and interpreted by the native and
becomes something different altogether. This transformation of colonial
discourse in the contact zone of colonialism is always ambivalent and
hybrid. Bhabha reiterates: 'Hybridity represents that ambivalent "turn"
of the discriminated subject into the terrifying, exorbitant object of
paranoid classification – a disturbing questioning of the images and
presence of authority.'[2] The display of this ambivalent hybridity, Bhabha
continues, 'terrorizes authority and the *ruse* of recognition, its mimicry, its
mockery'.[3] Hybridity, mimicry, and ambivalence can then be used by the
colonized as a space for resistance to colonial power. Bhabha, however,
overstates his reasoning by universalizing the hybrid. The colonized/
subaltern are not simply a single homogenous group. Spivak warns
against this type of universalizing and homogenizing of the subaltern. She
argues: 'Certain varieties of the Indian elite are at best native informants
for first-world intellectuals interested in the voice of the Other. But one
must nevertheless insist that the colonized subaltern *subject* is irretrievably
heterogeneous.'[4] Bhabha's concepts of hybridity, mimicry and ambivalence would, then, be exceptionally different based on each subaltern
subject.

One of the many critiques levied against Said, Bhabha and Spivak is
that they are more concerned with texts – that is, colonial discourse – than
with the materiality of the subaltern. In response to the arcane writings of
Said, Bhabha and Spivak, Stephen Slemon writes:

> I believe that post-colonial studies needs always to remember that its
> referent in the real world is a form of political, economic, and discursive
> oppression whose name, first and last is *colonialism*... But, wherever a

1.   Edward W. Said, *Orientalism* (New York: Vintage Books, 1978), pp. 202–203.
2.   Homi K. Bhabha, *The Location of Culture* (London and New York: Routledge, 1994),
p. 113.
3.   Bhabha, *Location of Culture*, p. 115.
4.   Gayatri Chakravorty Spivak, 'Can the Subaltern Speak?', in *The Post-Colonial Studies
Reader* (ed. B. Ashcroft, G. Griffiths and H. Tiffin; London and New York: Routledge,
1995), pp. 24–28 (26).

globalised theory of the colonial might lead us, we need to remember that resistances to colonialist power always find material presence at the level of the local, and so the research and training we carry out in the field of post-colonialism, whatever else it does, must always find ways to address the local, if only on the order of material applications.[5]

Slemon's remarks attempt to ground post-colonial theory, like that of Said's, Bhabha's and Spivak's, in local situations of the colonized. Slemon argues that colonialism impacts the materiality of the colonized as much as or more than it impacts the ideation of the colonized. In other words, post-colonial studies should, according to Slemon, have as much to do with the material liberation of the colonized as with the theoretical foundations for liberation. This is a move from theory to praxis.

Three crucial concepts that have already made their way onto the pages of this essay deserve more explanation. Hybridity, mimicry and ambivalence have become somewhat of a holy trinity in post-colonial studies. This is the case, in part, because all three concepts are intimately connected. To his credit, Bhabha has mainly been responsible for the popularization of these terms in the field. For Bhabha, hybridity can be liberating for the colonized because it 'intervenes in the exercise of authority not merely to indicate the impossibility of its identity, but to represent the unpredictability of its presence'.[6] As colonial discourse attempted to constrain the native, both the colonizer and the colonized were changed by their interaction to the degree that the identities of both were compromised. Through this ambivalent relationship, the colonized native began to take on the characteristics of the colonizer, which performed as mimicry. Hybridity is then not simply the interaction between the colonizing and colonized cultures, but it is an identity that threatens the authority of the colonizer as one who controls representations. The colonizers' (authoritative) representation of the native as something *other* begins to disseminate as the native mimics/mocks the identity of the colonized. Ania Loomba reiterates this point, saying: 'The converted heathen and the educated native are images that cannot entirely or easily be reconciled to the idea of absolute difference. While at one level they represent colonial achievements, at another they stand for impurity and the possibility of mixing, or to use a term that has become central to postcolonial theory, "hybridity".'[7] Hybridity, in this case, not only threatens the colonizers' identity and authority, but also notions of 'pure' native identity. Later she adds: 'Identity is a matter of "becoming" as well

5. Stephen Slemon, 'The Scramble for Post-colonialism', in Ashcroft *et al.* (eds), *The Post-Colonial Studies Reader*, pp. 45–52 (52).

6. Bhabha, *Location of Culture*, p. 114.

7. Ania Loomba, *Colonialism/Postcolonialism* (London and New York: Routledge, 1998), p. 119.

as "being".[8] Identity in the colonial interactions between the colonizer and the colonized, then, is constantly shifting. There is neither a pure imperial identity nor a pure native identity because both become intermingled in each other and become something altogether different. As an intermingled identity, hybridity poses a problem or threat to both the imperial power and the native nationalist. Since both the cultural centre and the margins are blurred, *othering* becomes nearly impossible. The colonized can no longer be categorized as the ultimate other; therefore, a space is opened for manipulating the socio-cultural systems established by imperial power by means of mimicry that slips into mockery. Mimicry and mockery, however, still function within colonial discourse thereby not allowing full dismissal of imperial power. In this way, hybridity not only threatens imperial rule, it also threatens any sense of native identity that is free of imperial influence.

If hybridity characterizes post-colonial identity, then mimicry characterizes post-colonial action. Specifically, it is the action taken by the colonized, yet initiated by the colonizer, where the colonized imitates the life and culture of the colonizer. This action is most pronounced through language, that is, when the colonized begins to speak/write the language of the colonizer. The problem with this action is that the mimetic product is never a perfect reproduction of the imperial power. The eventual product is a hybrid that is incapable of being an identical twin. At best, it is a mirror image – almost the same, but not quite.[9] By means of manipulation, mimicry becomes mockery and can function as resistance to colonial authority. Ashcroft, Griffiths and Tiffin make this point abundantly clear: 'This is because mimicry is never very far from mockery, since it can appear to parody whatever it mimics. Mimicry therefore locates a crack in the certainty of colonial dominance, an uncertainty in its control of the behaviour of the colonized.'[10] This slippage in mimicry reveals the limited power of the colonizer to control the colonial subject. In Bhabha's view, this slippage is always already present in colonial discourse. In other words, the colonial endeavour 'inevitably embodies the seeds of its own destruction'.[11] This mimetic action that Bhabha outlines only exists in an ambivalent relationship between the colonizer and the colonized. Ambivalence, then, is the context for mimicry and hybridity.

Hybridity, as the state of identity flux and interchange, and mimicry, as the resistant actions of the hybrid that destabilize the colonial power, are both characterized, for Bhabha and Loomba, as ambivalent. Bhabha

8. Loomba, *Colonialism/Postcolonialism*, p. 181.

9. Bhabha, *Location of Culture*, p. 86.

10. Bill Ashcroft, Gareth Griffins and Helen Tiffin (eds), *Post-Colonial Studies: The Key Concepts* (London and New York: Routledge, 1998), p. 139.

11. Ashcroft *et al.*, *Post-Colonial Studies*, p. 140.

explicitly states: 'Consequently, the colonial presence is always ambivalent, split between its appearance as original and authoritative and its articulation as repetition and difference.'[12] In another chapter, Bhabha describes this ambivalent relationship of love and hate, compulsion and revulsion:

> Two contradictory and independent attitudes inhabit the *same place*, one takes account of reality, the other is under the influence of instincts which detach the ego from reality. This results in the production of multiple and contradictory belief. The enunciatory moment of multiple belief is both a defense against the anxiety of difference, and itself *productive* of differentiations. Splitting is then a form of enunciatory, intellectual uncertainty and anxiety that stems from the fact that disavowal is not merely a principle of negation or elision; it is a strategy for articulating contradictory and coeval statements of belief.[13]

In this paragraph Bhabha deals specifically with the deep psychological impact that post-colonial ambivalence has on the post-colonial hybrid. Based on Bhabha's definition, ambivalence can only always exist in hybrid identities. Ambivalence characterizes both the colonizer and the colonized as *less than one and double*.[14] The colonized do not fit into tight boxes of those who desire colonial comfort and those who resist colonial rule. This desire and disgust happens simultaneously in everyone involved in the colonial project. Post-colonial ambivalence, then, 'describes this fluctuating relationship between mimicry and mockery, an ambivalence that is fundamentally unsettling to colonial dominance'.[15] Bhabha also points out that ambivalence has the capacity to subvert imperial power: 'The ambivalence at the source of traditional discourses on authority enables a form of subversion, founded on the undecidability that turns the discursive conditions of dominance into the grounds of intervention.'[16] This post-structuralist subversion of hierarchy to which Bhabha alludes provides the foundation for his concept of ambivalence as resistance. This resistance, however, is problematic in the same way hybridity and mimicry are, that is, it is firmly within the boundaries of colonial discourse. In other words, ambivalence as a form of resistance and subversion is always a part of the colonial authority that is being resisted and subverted. In short, ambivalence describes the psychological state of being or attitude of the post-colonial hybrid, which continually mimics and mocks colonial power as a means of resistance.

The concepts of hybridity, mimicry and ambivalence are controversial

12. Bhabha, *Location of Culture*, p. 107.
13. Bhabha, *Location of Culture*, p. 132.
14. Bhabha, *Location of Culture*, pp. 102–22.
15. Ashcroft *et al.*, *Post-Colonial Studies*, p. 13.
16. Bhabha, *Location of Culture*, p. 112.

not simply because they do not seem to take the materiality of the subaltern into consideration, but because they also destroy the clear distinction of colonizer and colonized – a distinction that nativist/ nationalist resistance needs in order to legitimate its stand against the colonialists. The nature of the relationship between the colonizer and colonized is always one of oppressor and oppressed. In other words, it is characterized by violence. Said speaks to the seriousness of this violence: 'There is no minimizing the discrepant power established by imperialism and prolonged in the colonial encounter.'[17] Although Bhabha argues that ambivalent hybridity provides a space for the colonized to resist, Said's comment emphasizes the massive power difference between the colonizer and the colonized. Indeed, hybridity only comes about by means of violent conflict between two different cultures hierarchically organized. In colonialism, one culture dominates another and imposes its own sensibilities onto the dominated/oppressed culture. This is always an act of violence and usually poorly masked in hegemonic language. Rasiah S. Sugirtharajah helpfully shows how Bhabhan hybridity lacks 'real' political impetus to subvert authority:

> Hybridity in the postmodern lexicon is defined as possessing emancipatory potential and an antidote to the virulent form of nativist thinking. While nativism seeks to eradicate any form of impurity in the indigenous culture, postmodern notions of hybridity tend to sweep under the carpet the cultural and political impact of colonialism. Such a notion of hybridity is oblivious to the economic hardship, helplessness, and marginalization which are ongoing realities.[18]

Although the colonized can use these concepts as a means of resistance, the colonizer can also use them to further dominate. If the colonizer can use ambivalent hybridity to keep the colonized in a state of *always not quite*, then the colonized could remain in a subjugated position relative to the colonizer. As stated earlier, Bhabha argues that the internal logic of colonial representation of the native always has the capacity to implode and is always unstable; however, this *capacity* to implode and its instability does not necessarily weaken the power of the colonizer. The continual subjugation of the oppressed/colonized is always violent. Said addresses this violence when he says: 'For the victim, imperialism offers these alternatives: serve or be destroyed.'[19] Franz Fanon also exposes the violence in the power discrepancy between the colonizer and the colonized:

---

17. Edward W. Said, *Culture and Imperialism* (New York: Vintage Books, 1993), p. 166.
18. Rasiah S. Sugirtharajah, *Postcolonial Criticism and Biblical Interpretation* (Oxford: Oxford University Press, 2002), p. 194.
19. Said, *Culture and Imperialism*, p. 168.

Their first encounter was marked by violence and their existence together – that is to say the exploitation of the native by the settler – was carried on by dint of a great array of bayonets and cannons. The settler and the native are old acquaintances. In fact, the settler is right when he speaks of knowing 'them' well. For it is the settler who has brought the native into existence and who perpetuates his existence.[20]

It is clear from Fanon's comment that he was very cognizant of the intricacies of the relationship between the colonizer and the colonized. Just as the settler brought the native into existence, so also has the native brought the settler into existence:

We are not blinded by the moral reparation of national independence; nor are we fed by it. The wealth of the imperial countries is our wealth too. On the universal plane this affirmation, you may be sure, should on no account be taken to signify that we feel ourselves affected by the creations of Western arts or techniques. For in a very concrete way Europe has stuffed herself inordinately with the gold and raw materials of the colonial countries: Latin America, China, and Africa. From all these continents, under whose eyes Europe today raises up her tower of opulence, there has flowed out for centuries toward that same Europe diamonds and oil, silk and cotton, wood and exotic products. Europe is literally the creation of the Third World. The wealth which smothers her is that which was stolen from the underdeveloped peoples.[21]

Indeed, the contact zones where the colonizer and colonized interact are always places of violence as illustrated by Fanon. Bhabha never emphasizes the actual violence that helped create his notions of hybridity, mimicry and ambivalence. Said's words can caution against such apolitical usage of these concepts: 'In modern times, however, thinking about cultural exchange involves thinking about domination and forcible appropriation: someone loses, someone gains.'[22]

The nativist/nationalist resistance takes seriously the devastation wreaked by colonizers and seeks to overturn this devastation. Ania Loomba, however, rightly says: 'Colonial identities – on both sides of the divide – are unstable, agonised, and in constant flux. This undercuts both colonialist and nationalist claims to a unified self, and also warns us against interpreting cultural difference in absolute or reductive terms.'[23] The drive for resistance that underpins nativist/nationalist movements is in direct relation to the drive that underpinned colonialism. In this sense,

20. Franz Fanon, *Wretched of the Earth* (trans. Constance Farrington; New York: Grove Press, 1963), p. 36.
21. Fanon, *Wretched of the Earth*, p. 102.
22. Said, *Culture and Imperialism*, p. 195.
23. Loomba, *Colonialism/Postcolonialism*, p. 178.

nativism/nationalism reproduces colonial power in its attempt to resist it. For this reason, nativism or nativist resistance comes under the same threat as colonialism based on the concepts of hybridity, mimicry and ambivalence. Nativism's desire for purity with the exclusion and expulsion of colonial influence is made impossible exactly because of the post-colonial hybrid. These theoretical concepts, then, are at odds with one another and when theoretical concepts become material reality, there is serious conflict between the involved parties. This conflict between the post-colonial concepts of ambivalence, mimicry and hybridity, on the one hand, and nativism/nationalism on the other is the main lens through which I will read Jas 2.14-26.

Since the Reformation, the Epistle of James has been read in the shadow of the Pauline Epistles in most Protestant churches and in the academy. This has happened due to the startling differences between James and Paul on the issue of faith and works. This difference, however, did not simply arise during the Protestant Reformation, but existed in the first century CE when the documents were first written. Scholars disagree about the extent to which James and Paul disagreed, agreed and/or even knew each other. This has more to do with scholarship concerning the Epistle of James than with the Pauline Epistles. Historical-critical scholars simply have not come to a consensus regarding the author of James, the date of James, the genre of James, the audience of James, etc. Because of the elusive nature of the Epistle of James, scholars have reached various conclusions about all these issues.

When considering the authorship and the date of the Epistle of James, Brevard S. Childs rightly claims that there are basically two positions held by scholars:

> One group of scholars dates the letter early, from 40–60 CE, at times even claiming it to be the earliest writing of the New Testament. Another group of scholars, who perhaps now form the majority opinion, dates it much later, from the last quarter of the first century or the early second... Those holding the first position argue that the letter was written by James, the brother of Jesus who was leader of the Jerusalem church and representative of Jewish Christianity... Conversely, those defending the second position argue that the letter reflects a later Hellenistic period both in its use of polished Greek and of Hellenistic literary conventions, and its familiarity with the Old Testament in its Greek rather than Hebrew form.[24]

In either case, however, the obvious referent of James is James the brother of Jesus and leader of the Jerusalem church. Childs agrees, saying: 'There

---

24. Brevard S. Childs, *The New Testament as Canon: An Introduction* (Valley Forge, PA: Trinity Press International, 1994), p. 434.

can be little doubt that the canonical editors identified this James with the brother of Jesus and the leader of the Jerusalem church. James, more than any other person in the early church, was the representative figure of Jewish Christianity.'[25] What is most important is not whether the actual James of Jerusalem wrote the epistle, but that it was, at the very least, attributed to him or was written by someone in his theological lineage. The attestation of the epistle to James of Jerusalem is important because of the textual evidence outside of the epistle that indicates an uneasy relationship between this James and Paul. The tenuous relationship between James and Paul is attested in Galatians 2–3 and Acts 15.

Both Galatians 2–3 and Acts 15 recount the events that happened at what scholars call the Jerusalem Council or the Apostolic Council. In both accounts, Paul meets James and there is a discussion about how Gentiles are to be incorporated into the church. The central issue is circumcision. Hans Conzelmann comments on the Acts account: 'It is the great turning point, the transition from the primitive church to the "contemporary" church. From this point on the apostles disappear, even in Jerusalem itself. In Jerusalem continuity is represented by James, in the Gentile Christian church by Paul.'[26] Conzelmann divides the formation of the church in two. James represents the traditional Jewish formation and Paul represents the newer/liberal Gentile formation. Luke Timothy Johnson, however, emphasizes the apparent unity that resulted from the meeting:

> But we must observe now that the decision by James emphatically agrees with the perception of Peter, Paul, and Barnabas, that God was at work in the Gentile mission that the Church must respond obediently to God's initiative. The Pharisaic position is emphatically rejected. The equal status of the Gentiles in the messianic community is confirmed by the head of the Jerusalem community.[27]

Johnson's analysis of Acts 15 seems strangely informed by his commentary on James, or vice versa. For Johnson, there is absolutely no indication of any dispute between James and Paul in Acts 15. According to Acts 15.6-7, however, the apostles and elders considered the matter of circumcision for the Gentiles *at length*. After a speech from Peter (Acts 15.7-11) and a report from Barnabas and Paul (Acts 15.12), James finally spoke. His speech ended the debate and brought the meeting to a close with these words: 'Therefore I have reached the decision that we should

25. Childs, *New Testament as Canon*, p. 435.

26. Hans Conzelmann, *Acts of the Apostles: A Commentary on the Acts of the Apostles* (ed. E. J. Epp and C. R. Matthews; trans. J. A. Limburg, A. T. Kraabel and D. H. Juel; Hermeneia; Philadelphia: Fortress, 1987), p. 115.

27. Luke Timothy Johnson, *The Acts of the Apostles* (SP, 5; Collegeville, MN: Liturgical Press, 1992), p. 272.

not trouble those Gentiles who are turning to God, but we should write to
them to abstain only from things polluted by idols and from fornication
and from whatever has been strangled and from blood' (Acts 15.19-20).
Although James decrees that Gentiles do not have to be circumcised, he
does insist that they observe the food laws prescribed in the Torah (see
Lev. 17.8–18.30). Barnabas and Paul are then sent to the Antioch church
with a letter describing the results of the meeting. In the Acts story, James
is *the* authority figure at the Jerusalem Council and Paul is characterized
as someone under James' authority. Although there is no narration in
Acts that James and Paul had any quarrels, it is clear from 1 Cor. 8.8-10
that Paul disagreed with the outcome of the meeting in Acts.[28] Paul's
comments in 1 Cor. 8.8-10 fall within his broader argument concerning
the consumption of meat that had been sacrificed to idols.

Although Acts was written many years after most of Paul's epistles, the
Apostolic Decree – to tell Gentile believers to 'abstain only from things
polluted by idols and from fornication and from whatever has been
strangled and from blood' – seems to have influenced some of Paul's
thought in 1 Corinthians. The specific issues in 1 Corinthians that relate
both to the Acts version of the Apostolic Decree and the Epistle of James
is eating meat that was sacrificed to idols. This practice had some
significant effect on how believers – Jews and Gentiles – related to the
'world' and each other. In 1 Cor. 8.7-13, Paul tells the Corinthians that
there is nothing wrong with eating meat sacrificed to idols, but that they
should abstain anyway because it may make another believer stumble in
his/her faith:

> It is not everyone, however, who has this knowledge. Since some have
> become so accustomed to idols until now, they still think of the food
> they eat as food offered to an idol; and their conscience, being weak, is
> defiled. 'Food will not bring us close to God.' We are not worse off if we
> do not eat, and no better off if we do. But take care that this liberty of
> yours does not somehow become a stumbling block to the weak. For if
> others see you, who possess knowledge, eating in the temple of an idol,
> might they not, since their conscience is weak, be encouraged to the
> point of eating food sacrificed to idols? So by your knowledge those
> weak believers for whom Christ died are destroyed. But when you thus
> sin against members of your family, and wound their conscience when it
> is weak, you sin against Christ. Therefore, if food is a cause of their
> falling, I will never eat meat, so that I may not cause one of them to fall.

Paul's interesting position with regard to eating food sacrificed to idols
warns believers to abstain not because there is something wrong with the

---

28.   Since Acts was written after 1 Corinthians, this may indicate that the writer of Acts, if
he was familiar with 1 Corinthians, was using the authority of James to combat and/or
correct certain Pauline teachings.

food, but because it may lead to another believer stumbling. Conzelmann, summarizing this passage, rightly says: 'The neutrality of food does *not* mean neutrality of *conduct*.'[29] By the end of the passage, Paul takes a very strong stand against eating this type of food, which would bring him into compliance with the Apostolic Decree in Acts. As Paul continues in 1 Corinthians, however, he begins to add conditions to this rigorous position. In a commonly quoted passage, 1 Cor. 9.19-23, Paul tells his readers/listeners that he becomes all things to all people in order to convince them of the message that he preaches. He says this in relation to his apostleship and his right to eat the food that he just warned the Corinthians not to eat. In 9.20, Paul says: 'To the Jews I became as a Jew, in order to win Jews'; and later in v. 21, he says: 'To those outside the law I became as one outside the law (though I am not free from God's law but am under Christ's law) so that I might win those outside the law.' He finishes in v. 23 saying: 'I do it all for the sake of the gospel, so that I may share in its blessings.' In other words, Paul will become anybody he needs to be in order to win others for Christ. To Paul's opponents, this simply seems wishy-washy as Gordon D. Fee acknowledges, 'On the matter of marketplace food he had been known to be of two minds. He ate such food in Gentile settings, but declined when among Jews (vv. 19-22). Such vacillation does not seem worthy of an apostle.'[30] Although James never speaks about food sacrificed to idols explicitly, there are multiple occasions when he speaks of the evil generated from a double mind (Jas 1.8; 4.8). Paul's hybrid response to this issue gives his opponents a nice opportunity to ridicule him as being hypocritical. Later in 1 Cor. 10.23– 11.1, Paul will explicitly tell his readers/listeners to eat such meat during certain times. Again, this reveals Paul's hybrid nature and clearly distinguishes him from someone like James. Besides the faith/works binary, one needs only to read 1 Cor. 5.9-10 over against Jas 4.4:

> I wrote to you in my letter not to associate with sexually immoral persons – not at all meaning the immoral of this world, or the greedy robbers, or idolaters, since you would then need to go out of the world. (1 Cor. 5.9-10)

> Adulteresses! Do you not know that friendship with the world is enmity with God? Therefore whoever wishes to be a friend of the world becomes an enemy of God. (Jas 4.4)

29. Hans Conzelmann, *1 Corinthians: A Commentary on the First Epistle to the Corinthians* (ed. G. W. MacRae; trans. J. W. Leitch; Hermeneia; Philadelphia: Fortress, 1975), p. 148.
30. Gordon D. Fee, *The First Epistle to the Corinthians* (NICNT; Grand Rapids: Eerdmans, 1987), p. 393.

Commenting on 1 Cor. 5.9-10, Conzelmann makes an interesting point. One cannot ascertain if Conzelmann is commenting on or preaching this passage. In any case, I wonder what James would have to say to Conzelmann with remarks such as:

> The community practices not an ascetic ideal, but that freedom which includes freedom to separate itself from vice. It is of the very essence of the community to manifest its freedom from sin *in* the world, not alongside of it. We do not have to depart from the world in order to be able to believe. On the contrary, the world is the place of faith, because it belongs to God and, as his creation, is not abandoned.[31]

Paul's own account of the Jerusalem Council in Galatians portrays a much more hostile encounter between Paul and James. Paul tries not to address his subservient position in relation to James, but slips in Gal. 2.2: 'Then I laid before them (though only in a private meeting with the acknowledged leaders) the gospel that I proclaim among the Gentiles, in order to make sure that I was not running, or had not run, in vain.' In other words, these leaders – James in particular – had the power to authorize or deny the legitimacy of Paul's message. After authorizing Paul's message, Paul says that they only gave him one command: 'Remember the poor' (Gal. 2.10). In Paul's own words, his position in relation to the Gentiles prevailed. This 'prevailing' is exactly why he was so upset with Peter in Antioch. Peter, in Paul's view, reneged on the agreement reached in Jerusalem when he refused to eat with Gentiles in Antioch after certain men from James visited him (2.11-14). These 'men from James' and those like them formed Paul's opposition in Galatia. This opposition had enough persuasion/authority to sway believers in Galatia to follow certain deeds prescribed by the law. Circumcision was the main issue, but the observance of certain religious holidays may have also been an item (see Gal. 4.10). Paul systematically attacks these men and their rigorous position on the law with the faith/works binary. Paul says: 'We ourselves are Jews by birth and not Gentile sinners; yet we know that a person is justified not by the works of the law (οὐ δικαιοῦται ἄνθρωπος ἐξ ἔργον νόμου) but through faith (διὰ πίστεως) in Jesus Christ, so that we might be justified by faith in Christ, and not by doing the works of the law, because no one will be justified by the works of the law' (Gal. 2.15-16). In v. 21, Paul reaches the pinnacle of his argument saying: 'I do not nullify the grace of God; for if justification comes through the law, then Christ died for nothing.' After directly addressing the Galatians in 3.1 (You foolish Galatians!), Paul then turns to a figure in Israelite history that would function as his proof-text, Abraham. Paul says of Abraham in 3.6-9:

---

31. Conzelmann, *1 Corinthians*, p. 100.

> Just as Abraham 'believed God, and it was reckoned to him as righteousness,' so, you see, those who believe are the descendants of Abraham. And the scripture, foreseeing that God would justify the Gentiles by faith, declared the gospel beforehand to Abraham, saying, 'All the Gentiles shall be blessed in you.' For this reason, those who believe are blessed with Abraham who believed.

After using Abraham as his proof-text, Paul goes on to criticize the law and then provide his readers/listeners with the reason why God gave the law to the Jews in the first place (3.19-29). The whole episode of faith/works with Abraham as a proof-text functioned as Paul's argument against his opponents in Galatia, who he described as false believers at the Jerusalem Council (Gal. 2.4), men from James (Gal. 2.12) and those who were more law observant (Gal. 3.1-5).

Although the purpose of Paul's Epistle to the Romans was different from Galatians, he uses the same faith/works argument. The similarity between Romans 3–4 and Galatians 2–3 cannot be overstated. In Rom. 3.28, Paul says: 'For we hold that a person is justified by faith apart from works prescribed by the law' (δικαιοῦσθαι πίστει ἄνθρωπον χωρὶς ἔργων νόμου). In the following verses, Paul uses Abraham as his example of how believers are justified by faith and not by works: 'For what does the scripture say? "Abraham believed God, and it was reckoned to him as righteousness"' (Rom. 4.3). The faith/works binary with the use of Abraham as an example was central to Paul's gospel as James D. G. Dunn rightly affirms:

> Here [Rom. 3.28] again, as in 3.20, the train of thought comes so close to that of Paul's argument in Galatians that the phrasing of the earlier letter is closely reproduced: Gal. 2.16 - εἰδότες ὅτι οὐ δικαιοῦται ἄνθρωπος ἐξ ἔργων νόμου ἐὰν μὴ διὰ πίστεως. Since it was also Gal. 2.16 which was paralleled in 3.20, and since Paul was hardly writing Romans with a copy of Galatians at hand, the obvious conclusion is that the theological assertions formulated in Gal. 2.16 were a fundamental part of Paul's understanding of the gospel, and fundamental in these terms.[32]

Not only should the faith/works binary be understood as central to Paul's message, it should also be understood as his central argument against his opponents at the Jerusalem Council and in Galatia. When James picks up the faith/works binary in Jas 2.14-26, then, one has to understand it in relation or reaction to Paul's message.

In light of this argument, the Epistle of James represents a type of nativist rejection of hybridity, mimicry and ambivalence found in Galatians 2–3 and Romans 3–4. The hybridity that Paul espouses blurs

---

32. James D. G. Dunn, *Romans 1–8* (WBC, 38A; Dallas: Word Books, 1988), p. 187.

the boundaries between believers and non-believers, which James inter-
prets as assimilation and compromise. James criticizes Paul for not
considering the severe and brutal effects of the empire on the native soul/
soil (see Jas 1.9-11; 2.1-13; and 5.1-6). James writes in order to promote a
pure native piety. In his commentary on Galatians, J. Louis Martyn says
this of Paul's opponents:

> In addition to identifying themselves and their Law-observant Gentile
> converts as 'descendants of Abraham,' the Teachers [Paul's opponents
> in Galatia] speak of Jerusalem as their 'mother,' referring thereby to the
> Jerusalem church. We cannot say with great confidence that the
> Teachers have come to Galatia from Jerusalem, but there are grounds
> for thinking that they claim to be the true representatives of the
> Jerusalem church, and that, in making that claim, they are confident of
> the support of a powerful group in that church.[33]

Martyn comes very close to saying that Paul's opponents were sent from
James. Later in his commentary, however, Martyn makes the connection:
'We can be sure, however, that the total impact of the Antioch episode left
Paul feeling suspicious of James.'[34] Hans Dieter Betz also makes this
connection between Paul's opponents and James, saying:

> The gospel which the opponents proclaimed was, in Paul's view,
> 'another gospel.' In some way, this gospel was associated with
> observance of the Jewish Torah and with the ritual of circumcision.
> The opponents had, in Paul's words, 'confused' the churches. Paul also
> puts the opponents in a historical perspective. He names as their
> historical predecessors the dissenting faction at the Jerusalem confer-
> ence, 'the men from James,' and the Cephas group at Antioch.[35]

It is clear from Galatians and these commentators that there existed a
deep conflict between Paul and James. The nature of this conflict is found
in the polemical passage of Jas 2.14-26.

James 2.14-26 is flanked by two passages that indicate James' insistence
on law observance and his attempt to silence his opponents. In Jas 2.8-13,
which introduces the faith/work binary, James refers to the law as the
royal law (v. 8, νόμον βασιλικὸν) and the law of liberty (v. 12, νόμου
ἐλευθερίας). What follows in Jas 2.14-26 can hardly refer to anything
other than works (ἔργα) of the law (νόμος).[36] The opening questions in v.

---

33. J. Louis Martyn, *Galatians: A New Translation with Introduction and Commentary*
(AB, 33A; New York: Doubleday, 1997), p. 126.

34. Martyn, *Galatians*, p. 244.

35. Hans Dieter Betz, *Galatians: A Commentary on Paul's Letter to the Churches in
Galatia* (Hermeneia; Philadelphia: Fortress, 1979), p. 7.

36. Other commentators do not account for Jas 2.8-13 as an introduction to 2.14-26.
Because of this, they conflate James and Paul and argue that James and Paul are saying the
same thing or that James and Paul are addressing different problems. Childs argues: 'Thus,

14 not only champion works, but also seriously doubt the effectiveness of faith by itself: 'Faith is not able to save you, is it?' (μὴ δύναται ἡ πίστις σῶσαι αὐτόν;). James 2.14-26 ends with an emphatic, 'So also, faith without works is dead' (οὕτως καὶ ἡ πίστις χωρὶς ἔργων νεκρά ἐστιν). Following the faith/works binary, he quickly silences any opposition with his negative concentration on speech acts. He effectively tells his audience and his opponents to bite their tongues (3.1-12); although, James never practises what he preaches.

In Jas 2.14-26, James attempts to 'undo' and undermine Paul's usage of the faith/works binary. It is clear in Galatians that Paul and James had met and spoken to each other. It is also clear from the textual evidence above that the faith/works binary was central to the gospel Paul preached. James, then, most likely heard Paul's faith/works binary during the Jerusalem Council. This being the case, the reaction that we read in Jas 2.14-26 does not necessarily need to be a reaction to Galatians or Romans proper. It could be James' reaction to what he heard from Paul at the Jerusalem council and which Paul continued to preach afterward – as is the case with both Galatians and Romans. In any case, James uses Paul's faith/works binary as a means to undermine Paul's own argument. In v. 14, James asks two rhetorical questions: 'What good is it, my brothers and sisters, if you say you have faith (πίστιν) but do not have works (ἔργα)? Can faith save you?' The answer to the first question is: 'faith without works is good for nothing', and the answer to the second is: 'no, such a faith cannot save you'. By opening with these two rhetorical questions, posed immediately following a passage concerning the law, James directly attacks Paul's message in Galatians and Romans. James argues that the faith that Paul promotes is not mutually exclusive of the law, but absolutely dependent on it, that is, they cannot be separated. Instead of having a negative view of faith, however, James speaks about the necessity of faith elsewhere in the epistle: 'But ask in faith (πίστει), never doubting, for the one who doubts is like a wave of the sea, driven and tossed by the wind' (Jas 1.6). This first verse of James' letter functions to remind readers/listeners of Paul's message and then James proceeds to turn it upside down.

---

an apparently minor shift in vocabulary from Paul's "apart from works of law" (χωρὶς ἔργων νόμου) to "apart from works" in James (χωρὶς ἔργων) is actually of major significance, and reveals that an entirely different understanding of faith and works is operative. Paul is defending the sufficiency of faith in Christ's salvation against claims of the law, whereas James is calling for a true faith which is demonstrated by concomitant deeds of charity. James' polemical adversary emerges as a caricature of Pauline theology' (*New Testament as Canon*, p. 440). In his commentary on James, Luke Timothy Johnson argues: 'I underline the point: James' usage concerning "works" is both unconnected to "law" and is entirely consistent with the dominant NT usage concerning moral effort as an expression of convictions' (*The Letter of James* [AB, 37A; New York: Doubleday, 1995], p. 60).

The next two verses, vv. 15-16, relate James' concern for the poor and his disdain for a faith that does not specifically address such poverty. This passage, along with other passages concerning the poor in James, directly addresses Paul. Throughout the epistle, James concentrates on the relationship between the rich and the poor. This preoccupation indicates that the community to which James is writing is probably poor. James 1.9-11; 2.1-7; and 5.1-6 all address the rich as seriously flawed if not altogether unredeemable. James 1.9-10 says: 'Let the believer who is lowly boast in being raised up, and the rich in being brought low, because the rich will disappear like a flower in the field.' At the beginning of ch. 2, James chastises his readers/listeners for showing favouritism to the rich. Verses 6-7 read: 'But you have dishonoured the poor. Is it not the rich who oppress you? Is it not they who drag you into court? Is it not they who blaspheme the excellent name that was invoked over you?' Finally, the most condemnatory passage against the rich in the entire epistle is found in 5.1: 'Come now, you rich people, weep and wail for the miseries that are coming to you.' This passage shows tremendous disdain for the rich. It is important to notice that at the very beginning of James' faith/works binary, he brings up the poor again. At this point, the poor are brought into dialogue with those whose faith has no action. Does James consider Paul one of these rich people that does not take care of the poor? In Gal. 2.10, Paul says that the only command that James, Peter and John gave him was to 'remember the poor'. Many scholars see this as a command to take up an offering from all of his churches and bring it to the Jerusalem church. Indeed, in many of Paul's epistles he says that he is taking up a collection for the church in Jerusalem (Rom. 15.25-27; 1 Cor. 16.1-4; 2 Cor. 8.12-14; 9.6-12; and Gal. 2.9-10).[37] If Paul is indeed taking up an offering for the 'poor among the saints in Jerusalem' (Rom. 15.26), one wonders if they every received it based on James' comments. Paul's collection activities may be the direct address of Jas 2.15-16: 'If a brother or sister is naked and lacks daily food, and one of you says to them, "Go in peace; keep warm and eat your fill," and yet you do not supply their bodily needs, what is the good of that?'

Verse 17 acts as a bridge from the first part of James' faith/works binary to the second part, which will conclude in the exact same way. James' interesting construction, 'So faith by itself, if it has no works, is dead' (οὕτως καὶ ἡ πίστις, ἐὰν μὴ ἔχῃ ἔργα, νεκρά ἐστιν καθ' ἑαυτήν), is seriously close to Paul's construction in Gal. 2.21, 'if justification comes through the law, then Christ died for nothing' (εἰ γὰρ διὰ νόμου δικαιοσύνη, ἄρα Χριστὸς δωρεὰν ἀπέθανεν). In both of these constructions, there is a conditional sentence and there is something that is dead. In James, if works does not accompany faith, then that faith is dead. In

---

37. See also Acts 24.17.

Galatians if someone can be justified by the law, then Christ died for nothing.

Verse 18 reiterates James' position that faith with works is the ideal. This introduces the second half of James' faith/works binary. After this introduction, James uses the Shema (Deut. 6.4) in his argument, but in a very unusual manner. In v. 19, he says: 'You believe that God is one (εἶς ἐστιν ὁ θεός); you do well. Even the demons believe – and shudder.' The way in which James employs this line of argument is that he puts the Shema on the lips of his adversary. Interestingly enough, Paul uses the Shema in his faith/works binary in Rom. 3.29-30: 'Or is God the God of Jews only? Is he not the God of Gentiles also? Yes, of Gentiles also, since God is one (εἶς ὁ θεός); and he will justify the circumcised on the ground of faith and the uncircumcised through that same faith.' Instead of arbitrarily using the Shema, he is here appropriating Paul's message in a way to undermine it.

As in the case with Paul's faith/works binary, James also uses Abraham as a proof-text. For James, Abraham is the example that shows how faith cannot exist apart from works (vv. 20-24). In vv. 20-21, James speaks to a single rhetorical individual saying: 'Do you want to be shown, you senseless person, that faith apart from works is barren? Was not our ancestor Abraham justified by works when he offered his son Isaac on the altar?' In the same way that Paul used the Akedah (Gen. 22.1-19) to prove his point, James now uses it to make the opposite point and, by doing so, he attempts to make Paul's message impotent. Just before James concludes his faith/works binary, he uses another figure from scripture. Rahab. This may be an attempt to twist Paul's use of Sarah and Hagar in Gal. 4.21-31, but there is little evidence that this is James' purpose. Rahab simply exists in James' argument to provide another scriptural proof for his polemic. James finally concludes his faith/works binary by reminding his readers/listeners of what he had said before: 'So faith without works is also dead' (v. 26).

Because of this bitter polemic one is tempted to ask James a question: what is at stake? Throughout the epistle, James exhorts his readers/ hearers to follow a rigorous practice in an attempt to maintain purity and attain perfection. In this small epistle, James uses *perfect* (τέλειος) five times[38] (twice in 1.4 and once in 1.17, 25, and 3.2) and *pure/purify* (καθαρίζω in 4.8, καθαρός in 1.27, ἁγνίζω in 4.8, and ἁγνός in 3.17) four times. The culmination of ch. 1 acts as a conclusion to the chapter and the theme for the entire epistle: 'Piety that is pure (καθαρά) and undefiled before God, the Father, is this: to care for orphans and widows in their distress, and keep oneself unstained by the world' (v. 27). In 4.4, James emphasizes the need to separate from the world: 'Adulterers! Do

---

38. Perfect (τέλειος) is used only eighteen times in the entire NT.

you not know that friendship with the world is enmity with God? Therefore whoever wishes to be a friend of the world becomes an enemy of God.' These verses act to clearly define the boundaries between believers and non-believers. James 2.14-26 identifies the praxis of the *inside*. This functions as nativist/nationalist rhetoric that supports James' ideology of otherness. Musa Dube grasps the impact of this nativist/ nationalist rhetoric saying:

> New Testament texts, written under the domination of the Roman Empire, resisted the imperial oppression in their own ways but also articulated the right to propagate their own version of imperialism. Consequently, from Constantine's conversion, Christianity became 'unique in its imperial sponsorship' because its texts have always harbored an ideology of geographical expansion to foreign lands.[39]

James, however, sees a very real threat from imperial assimilation – Paul – that would render his piety impotent. James reaches out to his diasporic (1.1) audience, exhorting them to maintain their boundaries with the world. Bill Ashcroft, Gareth Griffiths and Helen Tiffin describe this nativist desire to maintain colonial boundaries:

> The descendants of the diasporic movements generated by colonialism have developed their own distinctive cultures which both preserve and often extend and develop their originary cultures... It also questions the simpler kind of theories of nativism which suggest that decolonization can be effected by a recovery or reconstruction of pre-colonial societies.[40]

James understands works as a way to display faith and this display would demarcate a believer from the 'world'. Faith that did not manifest itself in works, such as not giving a collection to the people that needed it, would indicate that that type of faith would make a believer indistinguishable from a non-believer. The main threat James confronts is the compromising attitude found in statements like: 'Yet we know that a person is justified not by works of the law but through faith in Jesus Christ' (Gal. 2.16). For James, *works* (ἔργα) are constitutive of his religious identity.

Paul, on the other hand, understood *faith* as constitutive of his religious identity. Paul's faith could appropriate colonial culture as a way to transform it from within. Paul's gospel is, then, a hybrid that accepts diasporic identity as contradictory and ambivalent, which makes claims of cultural/religious 'purity' untenable. R. S. Sugirtharajah describes this type of hybridity:

---

39. Musa Dube, *Postcolonial Feminist Interpretation of the Bible* (St. Louis: Chalice Press, 2000), p. 18.
40. Ashcroft *et al.*, *Post-Colonial Studies*, p. 70.

The postcolonial notion of hybridity is not about the dissolution of differences but about renegotiating the structure of power built on differences. It is not synonymous with assimilation. Assimilation is something that the colonialists, and later the nativists advocated. Hybridity is a two-way process in which both parties are interactive so that something new is created.[41]

Paul, at times, accepts the status quo of the world (empire) and his own ethno-religious practices and at other times rejects both. He will appropriate Graeco-Roman household codes (1 Corinthians 7), yet will reject them in another setting (Gal. 3.28). Paul's religious identity mimics and mocks the Roman Empire, and at the same time, Paul's religious identity refuses nativist/nationalist purity. Bhabha describes the threat of this type of mimicry/mockery:

> It is from this area between mimicry and mockery, where the reforming, civilizing mission is threatened by the displacing gaze of its disciplinary double, that my instances of colonial imitation come. What they all share is a discursive process by which the excess or slippage produced by the *ambivalence* of mimicry (almost the same, *but not quite*) does not merely 'rupture' the discourse, but becomes transformed into an uncertainty which fixes the colonial subject as a 'partial' presence. By 'partial' I mean both 'incomplete' and 'virtual'. It is as if the very emergence of the 'colonial' is dependent for its representation upon some strategic limitation or prohibition *within* the authoritative discourse itself. The success of colonial appropriation depends on a proliferation of inappropriate objects that ensure its strategic failure, so that mimicry is at once resemblance and menace.[42]

Ultimately, the hybrid is 'uncontainable because it breaks down the symmetry and duality of self/other, inside/outside. In the productivity of power, the boundaries of authority – its reality effects – are always besieged by "the other scene" of fixations and phantoms.'[43] Paul's ability to become 'all things to all people' makes him a threat to the purity that James is trying to uphold. Paul claims that his ability to transform into whatever he needs to in order to share his message is a direct result of his faith in Christ. Paul is a hybrid *because* of his faith in Christ. He uses his hybridity in order to transform the world. Paul's hybridity breaks down the distinctions constructed by his culture and begins to threaten both colonizer and native: 'There is no longer Jew or Greek, there is no longer slave or free, there is no longer male and female; for all of you are one in Christ Jesus. And if you belong to Christ, then you are Abraham's offspring, heirs according to the promise' (Gal. 3.28-29).

41. Sugirtharajah, *Postcolonial Criticism*, p. 191.
42. Bhabha, *Location of Culture*, p. 86.
43. Bhabha, *Location of Culture*, p. 116.

The destruction of the duality, inside/outside, disrupts James' religious identity/ideology. James takes more seriously the effect of the empire on his (and his audience's) subaltern position. In three different sections of his epistle (1.9-11; 2.1-13; 5.1-6), he condemns those who are in positions of power and also condemns anyone that colludes with or shows partiality to those in power. Ania Loomba sympathetically narrates this nativist/ nationalist reaction/resistance to the colonial power:

> Nationalist struggles as well as pan-nationalist movements such as Negritude were fuelled by the alienation and the anger of the colonized, and cannot be understood, according to this view, within the parameters of current theories of hybridity. As mentioned earlier, many nationalists and anti-colonialists passionately, and often poetically appropriated the notion of a binary opposition between Europe and its others. Liberation, for them, hinged upon the discovery or rehabilitation of their cultural identity which European colonialism had disparaged and wrecked.[44]

Loomba's statement cannot be overstated. Throughout the Epistle of James and at least once in Rom. 15.26, the believers in Jerusalem are considered poor. Out of this poverty, James confronts a hybridity that threatens to coalesce with the power that made James' poverty what it was. For James, his religious identity cannot partake in any way with Roman imperial power that so dominated the world. Religious identity could not be characterized as being friendly at all with the 'world'. Paul represents everything that James stands against, that is, a religious identity that is thoroughly hybridized. Seeing the poverty of his community, James exhorts his readers/listeners to separate. In this case, Elsa Tamez is correct when she writes about the author of the epistle:

> He [James] is a person concerned about the well-being of the oppressed Christian communities and about the poor in general. What matters is not so much the true identity of this man, but rather his message for us today. When did he write the letter? At a time when there was suffering and oppression. Where did he write it? Any place in the world where the Christian communities needed it. This is one of the so-called universal, or catholic, epistles.[45]

The dangers of this type of nativist/nationalist reaction/resistance, however, are made clear by Bill Ashcroft and others: 'The dangers of a national bourgeoisie using nationalism to maintain its own power demonstrates one of the principal dangers of nationalism – that it frequently takes over the hegemonic control of the imperial power, thus

---

44. Loomba, *Colonialism/Postcolonialism*, p. 181.
45. Elsa Tamez, *The Scandalous Message of James: Faith Without Works Is Dead* (trans. Mortimer Arias; New York: Crossroad, 2002), p. 7.

replicating the conditions it rises up to combat.'[46] This danger is extremely potent in nativism. The rhetoric that James employs throughout the epistle simply does not allow room for any opposing position. James attacks his opponent, Paul, with such vigour that he undermines his own call for ethics/works that should characterize faith. Indeed, if James actually practised what he preached in Jas 3.1-12, a passage concerning how a believer should handle his or her tongue, he could hardly be so bold as to call people adulteresses (4.4). In other words, the polemical rhetoric James uses simply makes his argument about works and faith improbable. The way in which he addresses the threat of hybridity destroys his own call for faith with actions.

James' nativist desire for purity is nostalgic for a time in the past. Robert Young describes this innate nostalgia in nativism:

> Those who evoke the 'nativist' position through a nostalgia for a lost or repressed culture idealize the possibility of that lost origin being recoverable in all its former plenitude without allowing for the fact that the figure of the lost origin, the 'other' that the colonizer has repressed, has itself been constructed in terms of the colonizer's own self-image. The 'nativist' argument thus simply reproduces a Western fantasy about its own society now projected out onto the lost society of the other and named 'the Third World'... Nationalist resistance to imperialism, for example, itself derives its notion of nation and of national self-determination from the Western culture that is being resisted.[47]

The nativist position of James wants to maintain imperial distinctions in such a way as to have the native destroy the empire by maintaining pure religious identity: 'The testing of your faith produces endurance' (1.3). The distinctions are maintained by the material works found in James' epistle. This vision of a pure native piety that James espouses, however, is simply a projection of the Roman imperial ideal. Although empire and in-between places of hybridity repulse James, he nevertheless reproduces the colonial dream in his epistle in an attempt to fight against it. In other words, James wants his community to be the empire.

James' notion of 'pure' piety, although admirable, simply could not resist the onslaught of empire. Paul's more hybridized form of religious identity, however, only gained in popularity as a viable way to exist and resist in a colonial context. What is good about having both of these contentious texts in the Bible is that we, as modern readers, can combine the nativist/nationalist awareness of the violence innate in empire with the mode of resistance found in ambivalence, mimicry and hybridity. The combination of this type of awareness with this type of resistance may/

46. Ashcroft *et al., The Post-Colonial Studies Reader*, p. 151.

47. Robert Young, *White Mythologies: Writing History and the West* (London and New York: Routledge, 1990), p. 168.

could/should lead to ethical readings of these passages. Through a post-colonial lens the argument between James and Paul provides fertile ground for the church and the academy to reconceptualize the effects of colonialism on the biblical authors as well as modern readers. James' nativist approach recognized the plight of the poor, but failed for two reasons: (1) it simply overturned the binary of colonized/colonizer and desired to oppress the oppressors and (2) the vision of pure piety was actually a colonial concept in the first place. The hybrid, on the other hand, found a place in-between colonizer and colonized and manipulated that existence through ambivalent mimicry that turned into mockery. Paul's hybrid concept of *faith* literally changed the Roman world. Christianity became empire and utterly forgot about the Epistle of James. This post-colonial reading, then, not only forces one to understand the polemic between Paul and James in a different light, it also gives one the opportunity to reconceptualize the sordid relationship between empire and Christianity.

'Unstained by the World': Purity and Pollution as an Indicator of Cultural Interaction in the Letter of James

Darian Lockett

Maps, like texts, consist of a set of symbols 'governed by a set of conventions that aim to communicate a certain sense of place. Fully to understand a map requires one to be able to use it in the way it was intended, and this means in turn being conversant with its conventions.'[1] Like a map, the Letter of James marks out a particular ideological territory its readers should inhabit. In order to read the lines of this map the reader of James must become conversant with the text's particular conventions, or rules for line drawing.

The function of purity language, as a type of line drawing, has not been explored as it relates to the Letter of James. This state of affairs might be justified because, in the assessment of Scot McKnight, purity is not a central or controlling theme of the letter.[2] In this case the relative silence on the part of scholars concerning purity language in James may be justifiable. Yet, if purity does not mark the cartographic lines of ideology in James, why does the author use terms of purity and pollution to map out particular areas within his composition? The author describes 'piety' (1.27), 'the world' (1.27), improper use of the tongue (3.6), 'wisdom' (3.17), and return to God/resistance of the devil (4.7-8) in terms of purity and pollution. It will not do to claim that purity is not a major category in the Letter of James merely because it does not appear to take up the concerns modern scholarship assumes such language is usually associated with, namely table fellowship, clean and unclean foods, and issues of the temple. Rather, in order to read the map of James competently, one must

---

1. Kevin Vanhoozer, *The Drama of Doctrine: A Canonical-Linguistic Approach to Christian Theology* (Louisville: Westminster John Knox, 2005), p. 296.
2. McKnight concludes: 'I do not see "purity" as a central theme of the letter. Though we might be able to extract features of his view of purity and do so in a seemingly coherent manner, we should not at the same time think that purity was a central category of James' ('A Parting Within the Way: Jesus and James on Israel and Purity', in *James the Just and Christian Origins* [ed. B. Chilton and C. A. Evans; NovTSup, 98; Leiden: E. J. Brill, 1999], pp. 83–129 [117 n. 84]).

view the function of such language as a means to understand the
perception of reality embedded in the text itself. I propose that the
language of purity serves as a helpful vantage point from which to
correctly view James' cartographic depiction of reality – the social and
ideological concerns of the text.

To date the lines of purity language have not been systematically drawn
together, nor have they been appreciated as part of James' overall
geographical presentation. In the main commentators have been satisfied
to point out that: (1) James does not make any reference to specific Jewish
practices of ritual purity and therefore (2) purity language in James must
metaphorically refer to moral behaviour usually of the individual (the
moral behaviour of the community is not entirely, but often, over-
looked).[3] Only two short studies directly address purity in James with one

---

3. Most commentators understand purity in James as a metaphor of individual or
corporate morality: Joseph B. Mayor, *The Epistle of St. James* (London: Macmillan, 3rd edn,
1913), p. 146; James H. Ropes, *A Critical and Exegetical Commentary on the Epistle of St.
James* (Edinburgh: T&T Clark, 1916), pp. 170, 183, 249; Martin Dibelius, *James: A
Commentary on the Epistle of James* (ed. H. Koester; rev. Heinrich Greeven; trans. Michael
A. Williams; Hermeneia; Philadelphia: Fortress, 1976), pp. 121–22; James B. Adamson, *The
Epistle of James* (NICNT; Grand Rapids: Eerdmans, 1976), pp. 85, 154, 174–75; Bo Reicke,
The Epistles of James, Peter, and Jude (AB, 37; Garden City, NY: Doubleday, 1978), p. 25;
Sophie Laws, *The Epistle of James* (BNTC; London: A&C Black, 1980), pp. 81, 163, 183–84;
Peter H. Davids, *The Epistle of James: A Commentary on the Greek Text* (NIGTC; Grand
Rapids: Eerdmans, 1982), pp. 102–103; Ralph P. Martin, *James* (WBC, 48; Waco, TX:
Word, 1988), pp. 52, 153; James B. Adamson, *James: The Man and His Message* (Grand
Rapids. Eerdmans, 1989), pp. 73–75, 382, 442; Luke Timothy Johnson, *The Letter of James*
(AB, 37A; New York: Doubleday, 1995); Robert W. Wall, *Community of the Wise: The
Letter of James* (Valley Forge, PA: Trinity Press International, 1997), pp. 14–15, 101, 105–
106; Douglas J. Moo, *The Letter of James* (PNTC; Grand Rapids: Eerdmans, 2000); Patrick
J. Hartin, *James* (SP, 14; Collegeville, MN: Liturgical Press, 2003), p. 74; William F. Brosend
II, *James and Jude* (NCBC; Cambridge: Cambridge University Press, 2004), pp. 54–55, 97–
99. Several recent monographs hint at the importance of purity language yet do not offer a
full discussion of its function: Patrick J. Hartin, *A Spirituality of Perfection: Faith in Action in
the Letter of James* (Collegeville, MN: Liturgical Press, 1999), p. 68; Richard J. Bauckham,
James: Wisdom of James, Disciple of Jesus the Sage (New Testament Readings; London:
Routledge, 1999), pp. 146–47, 165, 180; Luke L. Cheung, *The Genre, Composition and
Hermeneutics of James* (Paternoster Biblical and Theological Monographs; Carlisle:
Paternoster, 2003), p. 177. Several works fail to mention purity language at all. Peter H.
Davids, 'The Epistle of James in Modern Discussion', *ANRW* 2.25.5, pp. 3621–45; Andrew
Chester and Ralph P. Martin, *The Theology of the Letters of James, Peter, and Jude* (New
Testament Theology; Cambridge: Cambridge University Press, 1994); and in a more recent
summary of research on James, Todd C. Penner ('The Epistle of James in Current Research',
CRBS 7 [1999], pp. 257–308) only mentions purity as it pertains to John H. Elliott's 1993
article on the subject (pp. 294–95).

concluding that purity is not an important category[4] and the other conflating James' use of purity with the notion of perfection.[5]

It is insufficient to assume that purity language in James is merely 'metaphorical' without properly arguing for such a position. And even if it is metaphorical, such language should be understood as an integral part of the author's construction and perception of reality – a distinct means of charting social and theological territory. Clearly one has not accounted for the ideological significance and function of the language by labelling purity/pollution language as a metaphor for morality. Therefore I propose that purity language is an important concept for James and that it is distinct, yet related to the epistle's major theme of perfection. In this essay purity and pollution are viewed as a worldview forming language that maps out key boundaries for James' readers. Though purity language is not the only, nor the primary, cartographic symbol used to chart James' worldview, it is a neglected component of this text. Concentrating on these particular lines in James allows for a new perspective on the ideological and social realities of the text – especially how the text envisions its audience(s) should position themselves with respect to their surrounding culture.

1. *Methodology: Purity/Pollution and Ideology*

Mary Douglas pioneered the study of purity and pollution in biblical texts with her 1966 work *Purity and Danger*.[6] Though some of her initial ideas have come under critique[7] (she has amended some of her initial ideas),[8] four of her conclusions have stood the test of time. First, Douglas's work fundamentally challenged the notion that pollution-based systems along with notions of defilement are 'primitive', and thereby separating purity

4. McKnight quoted above in note 2.

5. John H. Elliott, 'The Epistle of James in Rhetorical and Social Scientific Perspective: Holiness-Wholeness and Patterns of Replication', *BTB* 23 (1993), pp. 71–81.

6. Mary Douglas, *Purity and Danger: An Analysis of the Concepts of Pollution and Taboo* (1966; repr., London: Routledge, 1991).

7. Jonathan Klawans (*Impurity and Sin in Ancient Judaism* [Oxford: Oxford University Press, 2000]) notes: 'One error made in *Purity and Danger* is the assumption that Israelites considered all that exudes from the body to be ritually defiling (see p. 121). In reality...the biblical purity system problematizes only certain bodily substances' (p. 24). For other critiques of Douglas see Howard Eilberg-Schwartz, *The Savage in Judaism: An Anthropology of Israelite Religion and Ancient Judaism* (Indianapolis: Indiana University Press, 1990), pp. 177–79, 189–90, and 218–19; and Jacob Milgrom, *Leviticus 1–16* (AB, 3; New York: Doubleday, 1991), pp. 704–42, 720–21.

8. See especially Mary Douglas, *In the Wilderness: The Doctrine of Defilement in the Book of Numbers* (Sheffield: JSOT Press, 1993).

and impurity from supposedly 'higher' pieties which rely upon moral notions such as sin.[9]

A second lasting contribution is the recognition that any given culture's conception of defilement or impurity is systemic in nature. For Douglas, 'where there is dirt, there is a system', and consequently, 'this idea of dirt takes us straight into the field of symbolism and promises a link-up with more obviously symbolic *systems* of purity'.[10] Famously, she states that 'dirt' should be understood as 'matter out of place'.[11]

> The idea of dirt implies a structure of idea. For us dirt is a kind of compendium category for all events which blur, smudge, contradict, or otherwise confuse accepted classifications. The underlying feeling is that a system of values which is habitually expressed in a given arrangement of things has been violated.[12]

The key insight here is that when a text uses the terminology of purity, labelling something dirty or impure, this is evidence of an underlying system of classification at work ordering the author's perception of the world. Following from this observation is the recognition that impurity is a structure, 'whose individual components are not to be analysed as if they were freestanding'.[13] Thus, the idea is not to rely upon a mere descriptive comparison of the different impurities or defilements but to examine the entire system of impurity – the sum total of entities they pollute, and the ways in which pollution can be communicated.[14] Beyond mere historical description, Douglas seeks to understand the function and meaning of the entire system.

Third, having established the systemic nature of impurity, Douglas posits that such impurity systems should be understood symbolically. The reason why particular animals, ritual practices or acts are impure can only be understood when seen as functioning within a system of symbols. For Douglas, 'the body is a model which can stand for any bounded system. Its boundaries can represent any boundaries which are threatened or

---

9. See Klawans, *Impurity and Sin*, p. 8. This is one of the primary concerns of Eilberg-Schwartz's *The Savage in Judaism*.

10. Douglas, *Purity and Danger*, p. 36 (emphasis added).

11. Douglas, *Purity and Danger*, pp. 29–40, especially 35. But not all have been convinced of this definition of 'dirt'. Milgrom (*Leviticus 1–16*, p. 729), for example, argues that ancient Israelites did not view all misplaced objects as sources of impurity. However, Klawans (*Impurity and Sin*, p. 165 n. 30) helpfully insists that Douglas' notion has been pushed too far by the opposition: 'Her definition, I believe, was never meant to be reversible, not all matter out of place is to be understood as defiling! Douglas's point, as I understand it, is simply that impure things fall outside the category patterns of the system in question.'

12. Douglas, *Purity and Danger*, p. 51.

13. Klawans, *Impurity and Sin*, p. 8.

14. Klawans, *Impurity and Sin*, p. 8.

precarious'.[15] Thus boundaries of the individual body marked by the rules
of purity correspond to boundaries within and between societies. In her
fieldwork, Douglas identifies four kinds of precarious boundaries that
threaten a society's ordered system and which evoke purity rhetoric as a
response: (1) danger pressing on the external boundaries, (2) danger from
transgressing the internal lines of the system, (3) danger in the margins of
the lines and (4) danger from internal contradiction.[16]

Finally, Douglas connects the symbolic interpretation of the impurity
system to social function. That is to say, purity beliefs affect or shape
human behaviour and social interaction. Crucially there are two levels at
which the symbolic system of ritual purity may work for Douglas –
instrumental and expressive. At the instrumental level the system of
impurity maintains a unified experience within society. Specifically,
normed moral values and defined social roles are upheld along with the
broader structures of society. Colleen Conway helpfully observes that this
is the level at which the historian views the function of ancient impurity
systems.[17] At the expressive level the impurity system carries a 'symbolic
load' serving as analogies for expressing a particular view of social order
or a 'worldview'. Douglas states:

> For I believe that ideas about separating, purifying, demarcating and
> punishing transgressions have as their main function to impose system
> on an inherently untidy experience. It is only by exaggerating the
> difference between within and without, above and below, male and
> female, with and against, that a semblance of order is created.[18]

Thus purity language functions not only to maintain order but it also
creates order in a previously undefined situation.

Fundamentally the language of purity and pollution separates one
sphere from another. It is boundary language distinguishing differences
and encircling similarities. Purity language, in this way, functions like the
lines of a map upon which the core values of an ancient society are
charted. Yet these lines of purity, as all such boundaries in antiquity, are
perhaps more like frontiers, not representing 'fixed lines so much as zones
of influence or areas of control'.[19] The metaphor of map-making is apt
because maps, as purity lines, are interpretative frameworks – 'every map
reflects specific perspectives and serves specific purposes'.[20] Though

15. Douglas, *Purity and Danger*, p. 115.

16. Douglas, *Purity and Danger*, p. 122.

17. Colleen M. Conway, 'Toward a Well-formed Subject: the Function of Purity
Language in the Serek ha-Yahad', *JSP* 21 (2000), pp. 103–20 (107).

18. Douglas, *Purity and Danger*, p. 4.

19. Judith Lieu, *Christian Identity in the Jewish and Graeco-Roman World* (Oxford:
Oxford University Press, 2004), p. 98.

20. Vanhoozer, *Drama of Doctrine*, p. 296.

aiming for geographical accuracy, maps are subjective in that they reflect the map maker's interests. As mapped lines, the terms of purity and pollution encircle specific areas upon this map distinguishing different regions or frontiers marking off areas of 'safety' and 'danger', or indicating danger pressing on the external boundaries of a particular ideology. Purity language then becomes an important way to order or 'label' objects, places, actions, individuals and ideologies. The language of purity bounds a particular 'world' in a text. Readers of such texts are encouraged to equate the textually constructed 'world' with objective reality.[21] The 'world' as used here is similar to Clifford Geertz's description of 'worldview':

> The picture...of the way things in sheer actuality are, [a culture's] most comprehensive ideas of order. In religious belief and practice a group's ethos is rendered intellectually reasonable by being shown to represent a way of life ideally adapted to the actual state of affairs the world view describes, while the world view is rendered emotionally convincing by being presented as an image of an actual state of affairs peculiarly well-arranged to accommodate such a way of life.[22]

Thus purity and pollution must be understood as significant labels functioning as building blocks of a textually created worldview, even a particular identity with respect to broader culture.[23]

The lines of a 'worldview map' are drawn in terms of purity and impurity, and through the analysis of purity language in a text one may discover some of the primary boundaries between 'safe' and 'dangerous' ideological territory. This is especially interesting in the case of James because McKnight insists: 'I do not see "purity" as a central theme of the letter. Though we might be able to extract features of his view of purity and do so in a seemingly coherent manner, we should not at the same time think that purity was a central category of James.'[24]

I contend, however, that not only is purity an important category to James, it is an indication of the text's worldview and cultural stance. The goal of the following section is to identify the uses of purity language in James and ask whether there is a consistent concern articulated by such language. From this exegesis I demonstrate that 'the world' is consistently labelled impure which in turn indicates James' understanding of purity as

---

21.   Peter L. Berger, *The Sacred Canopy: Elements of A Sociological Theory of Religion* (1967; repr. New York: Anchor Books, 1990), p. 9; see also pp. 22–28.

22.   Clifford Geertz, *The Interpretation of Cultures* (New York: Basic Books, 1973), pp. 89–90.

23.   See Conway, 'Toward a Well-Formed Subject', pp. 103–20. Conway specifically takes up Douglas's idea of purity and pollution to show the rhetorical function of purity/pollution in creating a 'worldview' that readers of the Community Rule should accept.

24.   McKnight, 'A Parting Within the Way', p. 117 n. 84.

separation from or resistance to the 'worldview' of 'the world'. Furthermore, because the emphasis upon separation raises the question of how purity relates to other themes in James, I will argue that, despite claims to the contrary, purity and the key theme of perfection are related yet distinct concepts in the text.

2. *Exegesis of Purity Language in James*

a. *James 1.26-27*

The function of 1.2-27 is to introduce the controlling contrasts and associations woven throughout the main body of the letter (chs 2–5). Significantly, vv. 26-27 are placed at the end of this introductory prologue to draw the section to a close. Aptly placed then, this aphorism has been carefully crafted and given priority as a concluding distillation of James' wisdom. Therefore the thematic importance of these two verses within the framework of James cannot be over-emphasized.

Here true piety is defined first in negative ('worthless') then positive terms ('pure and unblemished'). Key to understanding the passage is the term 'piety' (θρησκεία) which only occurs four times each in the LXX and the NT. θρησκεία appears twice in the Wisdom of Solomon (14.18, 27) where it refers to idol worship (cf. 11.15; 14.17) and twice in 4 Maccabees where Antiochus refers to the 'piety' of the Jews (5.7, 13). There are two occurrences of the term in the NT outside of James. In Col. 2.18 it is used to describe the 'worship of angels' or 'worshipping of angels' (θρησκεία τῶν ἀγγέλων) and Luke attributes the use of the term to Paul with reference to Jewish worship of God (Acts 26.5).[25] Thus the term can be used positively and negatively depending upon the context.[26] The NT passages may be divided between both negative and positive uses of the term and Schmidt asserts that one must emphasize that 'the bad sense is not intrinsically necessary'.[27] The objective genitive following the term is what gives it either a positive or negative meaning. It is a more plastic term that can be used to describe either the negative or positive aspects of devotion to a deity. Thus the emphasis is not on 'piety' but its description as 'worthless' or 'pure and undefiled'.

'Worthless' piety is linked in 1.26 to speech ethics: 'If any one thinks he is pious (θρησκός), and does not bridle his tongue but deceives his heart, this man's piety (θρησκεία) is worthless.' Thus, for the author,

25. The term appears in later Christian literature comparing Jewish and Christian worship: 'We have written enough to you, brothers, about the things which pertain to our piety (θρησκεία)' (*1 Clem.* 62.1).

26. For example, Philo, *Spec.* 1.315; *Det.* 21; Wis. 11.15; 14.17, 18, 27; and Col. 2.18 which describes an attack on worship of angels as the wrong worship.

27. K. L. Schmidt, 'θρησκεία, κτλ.', *TDNT* vol. 3, p. 157.

uncontrolled speech and self-deception are related to improper or defiled piety. Piety that fails to result in the control of the tongue is deemed 'worthless' (μάταιος). θρησκεία is here used in an ironic sense for those who fail to 'bridle' the tongue (χαλιναγωγῶν), or are deceitful, and demonstrate they do not possess real piety at all. The one who is faultless in speech, bridling his tongue (not being deceitful), is later described by James as a 'perfect person' (τέλειος ἀνήρ) who is able to keep the entire body in check (3.2). Uncontrolled, deceitful speech, which the speaker begins to believe, disrupts group cohesion and is deemed 'worthless' piety rather than 'pure and undefiled'. The author declares that this individual is not aligned with the correct construal of the 'world', his piety is 'worthless'.

That this kind of piety is 'worthless' is significant. The term μάταιος is used in the LXX to describe idols and idol worship (Jer. 2.5; 10.3). Jeremiah's point is that rendering service to idols, things fundamentally not God, is worthless or not 'pure and undefiled' piety at all. Here the line is drawn between the one in v. 26 who 'thinks he is pious' and really is not at all because his 'piety' is worthless, and 'pure and undefiled piety' in v. 27. The one deceitful and undisciplined in speech is implicitly on the impure side of a line marking what is and is not 'real' piety. This individual is in danger because his 'worthless' piety is likened unto the idolatry of worshipping stones as the 'world' does. This is tantamount to the idolatrous alliance with the world (1.27; 4.4) that James refers to later. Identifying the alliance between 'worthless piety' and the 'staining' influence of the world reinforces the implicit impurity of this so-called 'piety' in 1.26. One who thinks himself to be pious in this wrong sense 'deceives his own heart'.

In v. 27, the author conveys the heart of his concern for writing as 'piety that is pure and undefiled before God, the Father'. Here the line is clearly drawn between true or 'pure and undefiled' piety and 'worthless' piety or, by implication, impure piety in 1.26. Both in the LXX and the NT, καθαρός refers to ritual purity[28] and to moral purity.[29] Hauck notes that in Diaspora Judaism there is a trend toward 'spiritualizing' the older concept of ritual purity in favour of the ethical and spiritual connotations thus highlighting its metaphorical use.[30] This 'metaphorical' use is evident in Josephus where there is an emphasis upon the purity of the soul and conscience (*B.J.* 6.48), a concern also present in Philo (*Deus* 132; *Ebr.* 143; *Plant.* 64). Likewise, the term 'undefiled' (ἀμίαντος) is used in the LXX

---

28. See, Lev. 7.19; 10.10; 13.17, etc.; Mt. 23.26, 35; Heb. 10.22.
29. See, Ps. 51.10; Hab. 1.13; Prov. 12.27; Job 8.6; 33.9; Tob. 3.14; *T. Ben.* 8.2; Mt. 5.8; 1 Pet. 1.22; 1 Tim. 1.5; 3.9; 2 Tim. 2.22.
30. Friedrich Hauck and Rudolf Meyer, 'καθαρός, κτλ.', *TDNT* vol. 3, p. 417.

with reference to the ritually undefiled temple[31] and to moral purity.[32] The related term μιαίνω is frequently used in the LXX for rendering someone or something ritually impure[33] but can also refer to moral aspects of purity as well.[34] Yet, in the present context using the terms 'pure' and 'undefiled' to describe piety specifically sets out a contrast (or draws a line) between this kind of 'piety' and the 'worthless' piety in 1.26.

It is important to note that what James calls 'pure and undefiled' piety is qualified as such 'before God and the Father' (παρὰ τῷ θεῷ καὶ πατρί). Here παρα in this context suggests a sphere, 'in the sight/ judgment of God',[35] indicating the ultimate standard by which all aspects of piety should be assessed and will, in the end, be judged. Thus piety here is 'pure and undefiled' 'with reference to God's scale of measurement'.[36] The author insists that it is God's perspective that functions as the key indicator separating worthless piety from 'pure and undefiled piety'. Opposed to this pure piety in the sight of God is the staining influence of the world. The prepositional phrase παρὰ τῷ θεῷ ('in the sight of God') along with the similar phrase in verse 27, ἀπὸ τοῦ κόσμου ('from the world'), 'clearly suggest an opposition between God and the world'.[37] This rhetoric effectively demonstrates that the author does not wish to cast the two types of piety as equal and opposite, but rather he refers to God as the only one who approves pure piety effectively demonstrating that there is only one way to construe the ordered 'world'.

Acceptable piety in the sight of God first includes looking after orphans and widows in their affliction (1.27) and secondly, keeping oneself 'unstained' (ἄσπιλον) from 'the world' (τοῦ κόσμου). James' audience is to keep ἄσπιλος with respect to 'the world', that is, to maintain a particular purity boundary between themselves and 'the world'. The term ἄσπιλος is not found in the LXX and only appears four times in the NT. Two of these NT occurrences pair the term with ἄμωμος 'unblemished' (1 Pet. 1.19, with reference to Christ as an 'unblemished' lamb; 2 Pet. 3.14),[38] while in 1 Tim. 6.14 ἄσπιλος appears with τηρέω: 'I charge you to keep

---

31. 2 Macc. 14.36; 15.34.
32. Wis. 3.13; 4.2; 8.20; Heb. 7.26; 13.4; 1 Pet. 1.4.
33. Lev. 5.3; 11.24; 13.3; Deut. 21.23.
34. Gen. 34.5, 13, 27; Lev. 18.24-28; LXX Ps. 105.39.
35. As in Rom. 2.13; 1 Cor. 3.19; 7.24; 1 Pet. 2.20.
36. Johnson, *James*, p. 212.
37. Wesley H. Wachob, *The Voice of Jesus in the Social Rhetoric of James* (SNTSMS, 106; Cambridge: Cambridge University Press, 2000), p. 83.
38. In Jude 24, several manuscripts read ασπιλους either beside αμωμους or earlier in the verse (see 𝔓[72], codd. 945, 1243, 1505) and thus may add weight to understanding the two terms as commonly being used together.

the commandment unstained and free from reproach until the appearing of our Lord Jesus Christ.'

In order to correctly determine the context of ἄσπιλος one must first understand what James means by 'world'. In challenging his readers with the incongruity of believing in Jesus Christ and practising favouritism, James rhetorically asks in 2.5: 'Has God not chosen the poor in the world (τῷ κόσμῳ) to be rich in faith?' The phrase τῷ κόσμῳ should be read as a dative of advantage[39] and thus 'poor in the eyes of the world'. The syntactical construction here emphasizes that it is from the perspective or valuation of the world that these people are counted poor or low in social and economic status. Rather than humanity in general, 'the world' is the system of order contrary to the heavenly order, 'a measure distinguishable from God's'.[40] In 3.6 James identifies the tongue as a 'world of wickedness' (ὁ κόσμος τῆς ἀδικίας), or taken adjectivally, 'a wicked world' which 'stains (σπιλοῦσα) the whole body'. Though the issues of translation and interpretation in this passage are complex, James understands κόσμος with the nuance of the sinful world-system[41] that 'stains' the body. Finally, in 4.4 James uses κόσμος twice in conjunction with friendship. 'You adulteresses, do you not know that friendship with the world (τοῦ κόσμου) is hostility toward God? Therefore whoever wishes to be a friend of the world (τοῦ κόσμου) makes himself an enemy of God.' The notion of friendship (φιλία) in the Graeco-Roman world meant above all to share, that is, to have the same mindset, the same outlook, the same view of reality.[42] To be a friend of the world is to live in harmony with the values and logic of the world in the context of Jas 4.1-10, namely envy, rivalry, competition and murder. Friendship language is the language of alliance or coalition and here in 4.4 those allying themselves with 'the world' are labelled 'adulteresses', or those unfaithful to covenant relationship. These references to 'the world' in James refer to something more than the material world or humanity in general, but rather the entire cultural value system or world order which is hostile toward what James frames as the divine value system.

Thus, the context in which to place the meaning of ἄσπιλος in 1.27 is precisely its relationship to 'the world' as a system of values. For Peter Berger and Thomas Luckmann the highest level of legitimation for a

---

39. Or *dativus commode*. Many understand the dative in this way: Luke Timothy Johnson, *Brother of Jesus, Friend of God: Studies in the Letter of James* (Grand Rapids: Eerdmans, 2004), p. 212; Ropes, *St. James*, pp. 193–94; Dibelius, *James*, p. 138; Davids, *James*, pp. 111–12; Martin, *James*, pp. 64–65; Moo, *James*, p. 107; *pace* Laws, *James*, p. 103, who takes it as a dative of respect.

40. Johnson, *Brother of Jesus*, p. 212.

41. There is evidence of the pre-Christian use of 'world' with this nuance, see *1 En.* 48.7; 108.8; *T. Jos.* 4.6.

42. See Johnson, *James*, pp. 243–44.

society is the 'symbolic universe'.[43] This symbolic universe is the 'all-embracing frame of reference' within which all human experience can be conceived as taking place.[44] Symbolic universes serve as 'sheltering canopies over the institutional order as well as over individual biographies' and 'set the limits of what is relevant in terms of social interaction'.[45] Berger and Luckmann's concept of symbolic universes corresponds to Geertz's notion of 'worldviews' mentioned above. Edward Adams has helpfully demonstrated how Paul's use of κόσμος functions as 'world-building' language.[46] He argues from ancient Greek sources that the term κόσμος bears a 'natural relation between the social order and the cosmic order... The conviction that the order of the universe is analogous to the civic order runs through Presocratic philosophy from Anaximander onward.'[47]

For James, κόσμος bears a similar function – the term refers to a cultural system which organizes language and behaviour. James actually presents two different worldviews. One worldview he refers to as ὁ κόσμος, namely the system of valuation and organization of language and behaviour which has the ability to 'stain', and another worldview which the readers are to embrace as 'pure and undefiled' in the sight of God. Readers are to keep themselves 'unstained' from the contagious pollutant of ὁ κόσμος, 'from a society regulated by the polluted values of [ὁ κόσμος]'.[48] It is the worldview of the world, an alien scale of measurement from that of God's, which radiates a polluting influence upon James' audience.

b. *James 3.6*

The section consisting of 3.1-12 begins with an address to the 'brothers' warning them of the improper use of the tongue, with special reference to those aspiring to be teachers (3.1).[49] After illustrating the disproportionate influence of the tongue upon the body with the common Graeco-Roman metaphors of the horse's bit and ship's rudder (3.3-4), James

43. Peter L. Berger and Thomas Luckmann, *The Social Construction of Reality: A Treatise in the Sociology of Knowledge* (Harmondsworth: Penguin, 1967), pp. 110–46. Berger (*Sacred Canopy*, p. 25) refers to the act of religious 'world-building' as constructing a sacred cosmos: 'Religion is the human enterprise by which a sacred cosmos is established.'

44. Berger and Luckmann, *Social Construction of Reality*, p. 114.

45. Berger and Luckmann, *Social Construction of Reality*, p. 120.

46. Edward Adams, *Constructing the World: A Study in Paul's Cosmological Language* (SNTW; Edinburgh: T&T Clark, 2000).

47. Adams, *Constructing the World*, p. 69.

48. Elliott, 'Holiness-Wholeness', p. 73.

49. The unity of this passage has often been recognized. See Martin, *James*, p. 103; Duane F. Watson, 'Rhetoric of James 3.1-12 and a Classical Pattern of Argumentation', *NovT* 35 (1993), pp. 48–64 (52); William R. Baker, *Personal Speech-Ethics in the Epistle of*

declares the tongue an 'unrighteous world' set among our members, 'staining the whole body' (ἡ σπιλοῦσα ὅλον τὸ σῶμα). It is important to note that the last phrase 'the whole body' appears in both vv. 2 and 6 and reinforces the primary contrast in this passage between the one who 'does not stumble in what he says' and the one stained or defiled by the tongue.[50] On the one hand, according to 3.2, one who controls the tongue, the one who 'does not stumble in what he says', also controls the whole body, and thus is a 'perfect man' (τέλειος ἀνήρ). On the other hand, the one unable to control both tongue and, by extension, the whole body has been affected by the staining power of the tongue. Furthermore, the text indicates that the author expects his audience to be familiar with this contrast, due to the fact that he uses the phrase 'for you know' in 3.1.[51] Interestingly the defiling tongue is described as a 'world of iniquity' or an 'unrighteous world'. Note again the connection between κόσμος, the 'world', and pollution, which is mediated here through the tongue.

The phrase 'unrighteous world' (ὁ κόσμος τῆς ἀδικίας) describes the tongue, the agent of pollution. Though the understanding of this phrase has been one of the more intensely debated complexities of this passage, a slim consensus has begun to form. Mayor seems to have had the best feel for the phrase saying: 'In our microcosm, the tongue represents or constitutes the unrighteous world.'[52] With Mayor most take τῆς ἀδικίας as an attributive genitive and thus render the phrase, 'unrighteous world' as does the RSV. As noted above, every occurrence of ὁ κόσμος in James carries the negative connotation of an evil and unrighteous system in opposition to God. Therefore, just as ὁ κόσμος is the agent of contamination the readers are warned to avoid (1.27), so too the tongue is likened to the 'unrighteous world' that is able to pollute 'the whole body' (3.6).[53] In both 1.26-27 and 3.6 the polluting effects of the world stain the entire body by means of the unchecked tongue.

James (WUNT, 2.68; Tübingen: J. C. B. Mohr [Paul Siebeck], 1995), ch. 4; Johnson, *James*, pp. 253–55; Bauckham, *James*, pp. 63–69; Moo, *James*, pp. 146–48; *pace* Dibelius, *James*, pp. 181–82.

50.   Duane Watson notes the importance of the repeated phrase ὅλον τὸ σῶμα, and notes that this is an indication that rhetorically the author is returning to the main or strongest point under consideration. See Watson, 'Rhetoric of James 3.1-12', p. 60.

51.   Davids, *James*, p. 137; followed by Baker, *Personal Speech-Ethics*, p. 123.

52.   Mayor, *St. James*, p. 115; cf. Ropes, *St. James*, p. 233; Laws, *James*, p. 91; Johnson, *James*, p. 259; Cheung, *Genre, Composition and Hermeneutics*, p. 203. Here the genitive is a substitute for the adjective as elsewhere in James (see 2.4, κριταὶ διαλογισμῶν πονηρῶν – 'judges with evil motives'; see *1 En.* 48.7; Mk 16.14; Lk. 16.9).

53.   With reference to the dangerous force standing behind the tongue (and the world) as a staining influence, many have taken the reference to ἡ γέεννα in 3.6 as referring to the devil or the forces of evil (see Moo, *James*, p. 126; Baker, *Personal Speech-Ethics*, p. 128). However, the recent study by Bauckham ('The Tongue Set on Fire by Hell [James 3.6]', in

c. *James 3.13-17*

James 3.13-17 not only contrasts two types of wisdom with respect to their origin, namely 'from above' versus 'earthly, unspiritual, demonic', but also with respect to their consequent external behaviours, 'pure' versus 'jealousy and selfish ambition'. The characteristics of 'wisdom from above' and 'earthly, unspiritual, demonic' wisdom are given as a response to the rhetorical question posed in 3.13: 'Who is wise and understanding among you? By his good life let him show his works in the meekness of wisdom (ἐν πραΰτητι σοφίας).' As Dibelius observed, first one demonstrates his wisdom by a good life and second the wise individual proves his wisdom in 'meekness' (πραΰτητι, cf. 1.21).

Though implicit, the contrast between two kinds of wisdom draws readers to choose between them. He affirms that if the group has 'bitter jealousy' and 'selfish ambition' in their hearts then they do not have wisdom that comes down from above (3.14).[54] 'Jealousy' and 'selfish ambition' or 'rivalry' indicate that individuals within the audience are seeking higher-status positions within the group and thus creating internal dissension and disorder. This so-called wisdom which animates such self-seeking is 'earthly' (ἐπίγειος), 'unspiritual' (ψυχική), and 'demonic' (δαιμονώδης), each adjective indicating an ever decreasing reality[55] and thus further alienation from God. The first term, 'earthly', is not attested in the LXX and in the NT it is often used for what is characteristic of the earth as opposed to the heavenly.[56] With this implicit contrast in mind, 'earthly' denotes not only what is inferior to the heavenly, but also that which is in opposition to the heavenly. Acknowledging that James consistently uses ὁ κόσμος to denote the sinful, polluting system of values that stands in opposition to God, the term 'earthly' certainly reinforces and parallels the notion of κόσμος. The second adjective, ψυχική is used in the NT to oppose something that is πνευματικός, 'of the spirit'.[57] The final adjective, δαιμονώδης, does not appear in the LXX and only here in the NT. Several commentators note that the suffix -δης suggests the term

---

Fate of the Dead: Studies on the Jewish and Christian Apocalypses [NovTSup, 93; Leiden: E. J. Brill, 1998], pp. 119–31) has convincingly argued that Gehenna refers not to the force behind the world or tongue, but rather to the place of just punishment for the one who errs with the tongue. Thus, as the tongue is a fire, so one sinning with the tongue will be punished by fire.

54.   Hartin notes how James is unique in beginning with the list of 'vices' as opposed to a list of 'virtues' (*A Spirituality of Perfection*, p. 72 n. 34). However, it does not seem that these are proper lists of virtues and vices; rather in 3.15, we are offered the animating principle behind that which is not 'wisdom' at all.

55.   Ropes, *St. James*, p. 248.

56.   Jn 3.12; 1 Cor. 15.40; 2 Cor. 5.1; Phil. 2.10.

57.   E.g., of an 'unspiritual' person, 1 Cor. 2.14; 15.46; Jude 19.

means 'demon-like', that is, performing deeds similar to demons,[58] which ultimately demonstrates that this wisdom originates not from God but from the devil.

The next verse carries through on the logic of this so-called 'wisdom', for James states that: 'where jealousy and selfish ambition exist, there will be disorder (ἀκαταστασία) and every vile (φαῦλον) practice' (3.16).[59] This 'earthly' wisdom traffics in jealousy and ambition, the external qualities indicative of one motivated by self-interest viewing others as rivals because they possess what one lacks.[60] James has already noted that the 'double-minded' man is ἀκατάστατος ('unstable'; 1.8) in all his ways, which is thematically and lexically similar to the idea here that 'earthly' wisdom produces social 'disorder' (ἀκαταστασία) by means of jealousy and ambition. The term ἀκαταστασία in classical Greek has the nuance of political disorder, anarchy or confusion that come from a variety of disruptions of the state.[61]

In sharp contrast to the wisdom characterized as 'earthly, unspiritual and demonic' and issuing in social disorder, is the 'wisdom coming down from above' (3.17). The origin of this wisdom is highlighted as coming down from God and thus the only real wisdom. The δέ in 3.17 signals a contrast with what has come before. The rhetoric betrays the author's view that 'earthly' wisdom is really only such by name, and that the wisdom coming down from above, that is from God (see Jas 1.5, 17), is the only real wisdom by which one may demonstrate he is 'wise and understanding' (3.13). Rather than 'earthly', this wisdom is from God and, as wisdom from God, it is 'pure' (ἁγνή). Like 'pure and undefiled piety' (1.26-27), wisdom is pure with respect to its origin from God and thus is 'real' wisdom over against 'earthly' wisdom. It is significant that wisdom is labelled 'pure'. Whereas the author uses τέλειος with emphasis elsewhere (1.2-4; 3.2), here wisdom is not 'perfect' but 'pure'. The syntax of the phrase singles out the quality of purity from the other character-istics of wisdom in 3.17. This wisdom 'is first pure' (πρῶτον μὲν ἁγνή ἐστιν), which the NIV renders 'is first of all pure'. The use of μέν without δέ appears in Luke for emphasis (3.18; 8.5; 22.22; 23.56), and in Paul as an anacolouthon (Rom. 1.8; 3.2). Here the πρῶτον μέν emphasizes that 'pure' is the first, or head, quality of the succeeding list, as Moo notes: 'the

58. Hort, *St. James*, p. 84; Laws, *James*, pp. 161, 163; Davids, *James*, p. 153; Martin, *James*, p. 132.

59. In 3.14 James identifies the characteristic of 'earthly wisdom' as 'bitter jealousy' (ζῆλον πικρὸν). Note that the similar phrase ῥίζα πικρίας ('root of bitterness') in Heb. 12.15 has the potential to 'defile' (μιανθῶσιν).

60. The term ζῆλος is negatively defined by Aristotle (*Rhet.* 1387B-1388A) as the sorrow one feels because someone else possesses what one wants.

61. See Dionysius of Halicarnassus, *Ant. Rom.* 6.31.1; Lk. 21.9, 'insurrection'; 1 Cor. 14.33.

seven qualities that follow in the list are specific dimensions of this overall purity'.[62] So here, ἁγνή denotes that 'wisdom from above' is free from moral pollution and, therefore, entails total sincerity or devotion. This is very much like the central notion of wholehearted, undivided commitment to God conveyed by the idea of τέλειος introduced in 1.2-4.[63] Hartin suggests:

> This pure wisdom is such that it has come down from above (3.17) as opposed to the wisdom from the earth, which is 'demonic' (3.15). This provides the backdrop to the search for wholeness and purity: it comes from having access to God, from being in a wholehearted relationship with God. When one is separated from this source of wholeness and holiness one is divided, like a wave of the sea that is tossed about in the wind (1.6).[64]

However, though communicating similar concepts, it is crucial to note that the author did not describe wisdom from above as τέλειος. I will return to this distinction below.

'Wisdom from above' is a key component in building the worldview associated with God and it animates the social behaviours of the distinctively pure groups associated with it. This wisdom is first pure, that is 'wisdom from above' is aligned with God and thus produces the qualities and characteristics deemed 'safe' and appropriate by the author. By contrast wisdom that is not from God is labelled 'earthly', again indicating that which is inferior or polluted is associated with the worldview of ὁ κόσμος.

d. *James 4.8*

Though the two sections may stand on their own, 3.13-18 and 4.1-10 have been linked together through lexical and thematic connections.[65] Johnson has noted that 3.13–4.10 progresses by means of rhetorical questions (3.13, 4.1 [2 ×], 4.4, 4.5 [2 ×]), the first two formulated by ἐν ὑμῖν. 3.13 inquires regarding the 'wise and understanding among you' and 4.1 asks about the source of conflict 'among you'.[66] These rhetorical questions raise the fundamental issue of wisdom's connection with behaviour. Those among the community who are truly 'wise', animated by 'wisdom from

---

62. Moo, *James*, p. 175.

63. Both Cheung (*Genre, Composition and Hermeneutics*, p. 143) and Hartin (*Spirituality of Perfection*, p. 73) make this connection independently of one another.

64. Hartin, *James*, p. 74.

65. The thematic and lexical connections are most convincingly argued by Johnson (*Brother of Jesus*, pp. 182–201; *James*, pp. 268–69, 286–89). See also Cheung, *Genre, Composition and Hermeneutics*, pp. 76–79; and Moo, *James*, pp. 167–68, who draws together 3.12–4.6.

66. Johnson, *Brother of Jesus*, p. 188.

above', will demonstrate such by their good life-style in 'meekness of wisdom', yet the rhetoric of the letter clearly demonstrates that readers are not acting according to such wisdom. Marked by the second ἐν ὑμῖν (4.1), the rhetorical question sharply raises the issue that the community members have not lived in keeping with 'wisdom from above' because there is strife and battles raging 'among them'. The connected passages serve as an indictment against incorrect wisdom/perception (3.15-16) and action (4.1-4), both which are associated with 'the world' (3.15, wisdom is 'earthly' [ἐπίγειος]; 4.4, 'friendship with the world [τοῦ κόσμου]').

The indictment of desire and passion as the cause of social disorder in 4.1 comes to a climax in v. 4: 'Adulteresses! Do you not know that friendship with the world is enmity with God? Therefore whoever wishes to be a friend of the world becomes an enemy of God.' The label 'adulteresses' (μοιχαλίδες) symbolically refers to the covenant relationship between God as a groom and Israel as his bride found in the Torah.[67] Edgar notes that the 'metaphor depicts God's people as disobedient to God's order, expressed in the covenant relationship... They dishonor God through their unfaithful behaviour.'[68] This address is followed by the climactic indictment of the letter, stated first as a rhetorical question then as a direct statement. The use of οὐκ οἴδατε ('do you not know') indicates the author assumes the readers refuse to act upon the shared knowledge that 'friendship' with the world is incompatible with relationship with God.[69] As noted above, the use of 'friendship' in the first century was much more restrictive and had deeper connotations than today. One of the most common uses of friendship in ancient literature applied to alliances, cooperation or non-aggression treaties among peoples.[70] The alliance between friends referred to the fact that friends shared similar vision and values. Euripides referred to a friend as 'one soul with mine' (καὶ ψυχὴν μίαν)[71] and Cicero considered a friend as a 'second self' referring to the friendship between Laelius and Scipio: 'we shared the one element indispensable to friendship, a complete agreement in aims,

67. Johnson, *James*, p. 278.

68. David Hutchinson Edgar, *Has God Not Chosen the Poor? The Social Setting of the Epistle of James* (JSNTSup, 206; Sheffield: Sheffield Academic Press, 2001), p. 103.

69. This shared base of knowledge is assumed elsewhere in the letter ('knowing [γινώσκοντες] that the testing of your faith produces endurance', 1.3; 'let not many become teachers, my brethren, knowing [εἰδότες] that as such we will incur a stricter judgment', 3.1; 'you should know [γινωσκέτω]', 5.20).

70. See Homer, *Il.* 3.93, 256; 4.17; 26.282; Virgil, *Aen.* 11.321; Demosthenes, *On the Navy Boards* 5; *On the Embassy* 62; *Letters* 3.27; Josephus, *C.Ap.* 1.109; 2.83b. See also, Alicia Batten, 'Unworldly Friendship: The "Epistle of Straw" Reconsidered' (unpublished doctoral dissertation, University of St. Michael's College, 2000).

71. Euripides, *Orest.* 1046.

ambitions, and attitudes'.[72] He goes on to say: 'Now friendship is just this and nothing else: complete sympathy in all matters of importance.'[73] Though overstating the case, M. Heath asserts that friendship in Greece 'is not, at root, a subjective bond of affection and emotional warmth, but the entirely objective bond of reciprocal obligation; one's *philos* is the man one is obligated to help, and on whom one can (or ought to be able to) rely for help when oneself is in need.'[74] Furthermore, this ancient concept of friendship included a particular kind of social relationship within the pervasive social structure of honour and shame. Alicia Batten comments: 'Closely related to other political uses of friendship is the relationship between patrons and clients, often defined as friendship.'[75]

The indictment of alliance with the world in 4.4 is completed by a quotation from Prov. 3.34. The citation from Prov. 3.34 ('God opposes the proud [ὑπερηφάνοις], but gives grace to the humble [ταπεινοῖς]') does not merely add ornamentation to the passage but serves as the founding principle which the author builds his call to repentance upon[76] and constitutes the subject of an extended *midrashic* interpretation in verses 4.7–5.6. In the verses following the quotation of Prov. 3.34, James, in reverse order, first expounds the second half of the quotation in 4.7-10, and then considers the first phrase of the citation in 4.11–5.6. Alonso Schökel argued this position specifically asserting that the thematic refrain of 'humble yourselves' (ταπεινώθετε) in 4.10 recalls the 'lowly' (ταπεινοῖς) in 4.6 and thus frames James' exposition on the second half of the citation: 'God gives grace to the lowly'.[77] This lexical link ties the following commands to the promise of God's grace in the text citation in 4.6. Furthermore, the first half of the citation, 'God resists the proud', is considered in 4.11–5.6. This is signalled by the connection between 4.6 and 5.6 in the repetition of the rare verb ἀντιτάσσω in both verses.[78] Whether or not 4.11–5.6 should be viewed as commentary on the first half of the Prov. 3.34 citation, the lexical connection between ταπεινοῖς/ταπεινώ-θετε (4.6/4.10) and the related theme of humble submission and

72. Cicero, *Amic.* 21.80; 4.15 (see Aristotle, *Eth. Nic.* 9.4.5, 9.1, 9.10).
73. Cicero, *Amic.* 6.20.
74. M. Heath, *The Poetics of Greek Tragedy* (Stanford: Stanford University Press, 1987), pp. 73–74, as quoted in David Konstan, *Friendship in the Classical World* (Cambridge: Cambridge University Press, 1997), p. 2.
75. Batten, 'Unworldly Friendship', p. 27.
76. Davids, *James*, p. 165; Martin, *James*, p. 152; Bauckham, *James*, pp. 152–55; Moo, *James*, p. 192; *contra* Laws, *James*, pp. 180–81.
77. Luis Alonso Schökel, 'James 5.2 and 4.6', *Bib* 54 (1973), pp. 73–76.
78. Read in light of this lexical connection the subjectless phrase in 5.6 'he does not resist you' (οὐκ ἀντιτάσσεται ὑμῖν), which could either be a statement or a question, may be read in light of the text citation in 4.6. Therefore the subject of the verb in 4.6 may be supplied in 5.6 and rendered as a question rounding off James' exposition of God's judgment against the proud. Thus 5.6 would read 'does he [God] not resist you?'

repentance clearly draws the citation to the following verses (4.7-10). These second person plural imperatives mark off and state the topic of the section, namely submitting to God in repentance. God's 'grace' is given to the 'humble' (4.6); therefore, the readers must 'submit' to God (4.7), a notion that is expanded in the rest of the passage (4.7-10).

The first steps in submitting to God are to 'resist the devil' (4.7b) and 'draw near to God' (4.8a). They are to 'resist the devil', because, if the community does, James says, 'he will flee from you'. If the associations hold throughout this section, 'the devil' (διαβόλω) is certainly connected to 'earthly, unspiritual, demonic' (δαιμονιώδης) wisdom (3.16) that produces 'disorder' which manifests itself in the community through conflicts and disputes (4.1), and is ultimately associated with alliance with ὁ κόσμος (4.4).[79] Johnson comments: 'The devil personifies the negative side of James' cosmic dualism, the force that influences the *kosmos* resistant to God's kingdom.'[80] True enough, but what Johnson fails to note is the apt designation of ὁ κόσμος as polluted, ultimately by means of the devil himself. If strife and dissension are the devil's work, then, in the author's worldview, it would make reasonable sense to highlight 'purity' rather than 'perfection'. The devil is much more a pollutant than an 'imperfection' in this instance. Thus, drawing near to God necessarily entails resisting the devil and the consequent wisdom and alliances associated with him. Significantly the author describes drawing near to God and resisting the devil in terms of purification. The verb ἐγγίζω is often used in the LXX to refer to the priest 'drawing near' to God in cultic worship.[81] And this image is reinforced by the parallel command: 'Cleanse your hands, you sinners, and purify your hearts, you double-minded' (4.8b).

The parallelism may be shown in this way:

καθαρίσατε χεῖρας, ἁμαρτωλοί, καὶ
ἁγνίσατε καρδίας, δίψυχοι.

The verb 'cleanse' (καθαρίζω) is used for priestly removal of defilement in Lev. 16.19-20 and specifically with reference to 'sins' in Lev. 16.30 and

79. Failing to resist the devil is associated with being 'double-minded'. 'Those who are two-faced are not of God, but they are enslaved to their evil desires, so that they might be pleasing to Beliar and to persons like themselves' (*T. Ash.* 3.2).

80. Johnson, *James*, pp. 283–84.

81. See Exod. 19.21, where the people could not 'draw near' to God but in 19.22 the priests could; Lev. 21.21, 23; Deut. 16.16; Isa. 29.13; 58.2; Ezek. 40.46; and in the NT once with this sense in Heb. 7.19: Davids, *James*, p. 166; Martin, *James*, p. 153; Johnson, *James*, p. 284. Moo argues that the cultic metaphor is not in view because later in the same verse God 'will draw near (ἐγγιεῖ)' to humans, an idea which disrupts the cultic image (*James*, p. 195); however the following image of cleansing and purifying again calls attention to the cultic image.

Sir. 23.10 (also Heb. 9.14, 22, 23; 1 Jn 1.7, 9; 2 Cor. 7.1). Likewise ἁγνίζω is associated with cultic purity (Exod. 19.10; Num. 8.21; 19.12; 31.23). The command is to 'cleanse your hands' and 'purify your hearts'. The reference to both parts of the body is reminiscent of Ps. 24.4 (LXX 23.4) where the one who may ascend the hill of the Lord and stand in his holy place is 'he who has clean hands and a pure heart' (ἀθῷος χερσὶν καὶ καθαρὸς τῇ καρδίᾳ). In Jas 4.8 'hands' and 'heart' refer to both external behaviour and internal attitude and should not be conflated into a single command to 'purify yourselves'.[82] There was concern for maintaining purity of the hand in the Second Temple period as both the Gospels (Mt. 15.2; Mk 7.2-5) and later rabbinic (m. Yad. 1.1–4.8) discussion indicate. Often the hands could represent one's actions in general. For example, the phrase 'from your hand' in Gen. 4.11 refers to Cain's immorality; God stretches out his hand to strike Egypt in Exod. 3.20; and in Deut. 2.7 literally 'in the work of you hands' is translated 'in all your undertakings' in the NRSV. Similarly, the heart is often referred to as the seat of the affections (Gen. 6.5; Deut. 8.2) and the 'pure heart' represents a right relationship with God (Ps. 50.10, 12 LXX). In this way James is addressing both the inward disposition ('purify your hearts') and the outward moral and social concern ('cleanse your hands').

Thus part of resisting 'the devil' and drawing 'near to God', is cleansing/purification. The first line, 'cleanse your hands', makes reference to ritual practice but applies it to the social and moral context. The cultic requirements for approaching Israel's God which were fiercely debated among Jews in the Second Temple period are now figuratively applied to moral and ideological purification required of the one approaching God in spirit.[83] The 'sinners', those treasonous to God's covenant and the people of God, are to 'cleanse' themselves. The author's rhetoric implicitly labels the actions (hands) of these 'sinners' as impure (associated with both the devil and ὁ κόσμος), and thus in danger. The second line, 'purify your hearts', interestingly may refer to the unmixed quality of the heart's devotion in worship. The stains of the world and the devil affect the readers internally and therefore they must be purified. The logic of the entire passage suggests that the means by which one 'repents' or turns from the inappropriate alliance ('friendship') with the world is to 'cleanse' the hands and 'purify' the heart. Again purity, here in the action of cleansing and purification, is set alongside an inappropriate relationship with the world.

82. *Contra* Davids, *James*, pp. 166–67.
83. Bauckham, *James*, p. 146.

e. *Observations*

The composition uses purity language eight times and makes one clear allusion to the purity concept of 'mixed kinds'.[84] Though purity references are not numerous (nine references in 108 verses) they appear in key passages of the text. First, there is a compelling cluster of purity terms in the important concluding and transitional aphorism in 1.26-27. Here the author distils the primary wisdom contained in the themes of the prologue by offering an aphorism regarding 'pure and undefiled' piety; piety in which one must keep 'unstained' from ὁ κόσμος. Second, in the pivotal section regarding two kinds of wisdom and their consequent behaviours, the first and most important characteristic of 'wisdom from above' is that it is 'pure' (3.17). It is important to note that the author chose not to use 'perfect' (τέλειος) to describe this wisdom. Because this is a favourite term for the author elsewhere, his choice of words here is all the more significant. Finally, in arguably the sharpest call to repentance in the letter, the author chooses to characterize such repentance as cleansing and purification from alliance with ὁ κόσμος and the devil (4.1-10).

The exegesis above suggests that James outlines two competing worldviews or culturally constructed systems which order language and behaviour. The author equates one worldview with ὁ θεός (1.27; 2.5; 4.4) and the other he equates with ὁ κόσμος (1.27; 2.5; 3.6; 4.4 [2 x]), or ἐπίγειος ('earthly'; 3.14-17). Each time James uses ὁ κόσμος it is antithetically contrasted with ὁ θεός as a counter system of order. And in these very contexts, where two systems of order are set in opposition, purity language is frequently used.[85] For example, in 1.27 'pure and undefiled piety' is such in 'the sight of God' (as opposed to the world) and maintaining such piety entails keeping oneself 'unstained from the world'.[86] Though there is no reference to ὁ θεός, in 3.6 the tongue is an 'unrighteous world' able to 'stain the whole body'. Here the staining influence of the tongue is associated with the unrighteous κόσμος. Wisdom appears in one of two forms; it is either 'earthly' (thus associated with ὁ κόσμος) and 'demonic' (3.15) creating disorder and instability (3.16), or it comes from God ('wisdom from above' [3.17] is, by association, the perfect gift 'from above' [1.17] freely given by God when asked in faith [1.5]) and produces peaceableness and mercy (3.17).

---

84. 'Filthiness', 2.21; 'pure and undefiled' and 'unstained', in 1.27; 'stains', 3.6; 'pure', 3.17; 'cleanse' and 'purify', 4.8. The allusion to 'mixed kinds', arguably a category of purity (see Darian Lockett, *Purity and Worldview in the Epistle of James* [LNTS; London: T and T Clark, forthcoming], ch. 2), is found in 3.11-12.

85. The only instance of ὁ κόσμος appearing without reference to purity/impurity in the larger context is 2.5.

86. See Hartin's comments regarding 1.27: 'he is using the imagery and language of purity in order to capture the essential understanding of separation between those who belong to God and those who belong to the world' (*James*, p. 109).

The 'wisdom from above' is 'first of all pure' (3.17) in contrast to 'earthly' wisdom which creates 'disorder' (3.16). 'Sinners' and the 'double-minded' are told to 'cleanse your hands' and 'purify your hearts' in order to 'draw near to God' (4.8). And in context, this purification is from the staining alliance with ὁ κόσμος (4.4).

The composition is not addressed to 'the world' but to James' specific readers, and as such the readers are challenged with regard to particular cultural values of ὁ κόσμος. Bauckham recognizes that the reversal of status in James explicitly challenges contemporary Graeco-Roman values:

> Since material goods and social status were connected with honour (e.g. Aristotle, *Rhet*. 2.5.7), the poor were generally treated with contempt in the ancient world ... Patronage (of inferiors by superiors in the social scale) was a pervasive part of the social system, a relationship which forged links of mutual benefit up and down the social hierarchy, benefiting most people except the really poor. Thus the special attention shown to the rich man, as a potential patron of the community, and the contemptuous attitude shown to the poor person, in James' hypothetical example (2.2-4), are the attitudes to rich and poor which could be expected of ordinary people in the normal social mores of the time. James' accusation that they are dishonouring or shaming the poor (2.6) reverses the evaluations of the dominant social values.[87]

In this respect, the readers are condemned as lawbreakers when they show preferential treatment toward the rich at the expense of the poor (2.2-9). James' rhetoric challenges this notion of status (1.9-11; 4.10) indicating the inversion of social stratification associated with the values of ὁ κόσμος. James elevates the poor and lowly along with the attitude of meekness despite their lack of social status and economic power. What Bauckham does not point out is that the sharp contrast between the values of the surrounding culture and James' readers is mapped by the 'worldview language' of purity and pollution.

Purity language rhetorically marks the 'danger' associated with crossing the line between the two worldviews, or put another way, the danger of not maintaining a distinct boundary between the readers, who are to associate with God, and ὁ κόσμος, the values of the surrounding culture. The composition consistently uses the notion of purity to mark the boundary between two different worldviews: the worldview associated with God and worldview of ὁ κόσμος. As a means of labelling these different worldviews the language of purity is taken up with the rhetorical intent to legitimate one view of reality over against another, which has the effect of bringing the readers to a decision as to which worldview they will adhere to. The concern is to maintain a pure community (with respect to

---

87. Bauckham, *James*, p. 189. See also, Chester and Martin, *Theology*, pp. 33–34; *contra* Johnson, *Brother of Jesus*, p. 232.

their internal constitution and external boundaries) in the midst of a dominant, contaminating culture. The cartographic line drawn by purity is integral to James' concern to challenge the counter-cultural community to adhere to God's measure of reality by strengthening the boundary between them and the values of the ambient culture which are infiltrating their thinking and behaviour and thus is a call to separate from the polluting 'world' (ὁ κόσμος). However, this observation alone is not enough to situate the purity language in James. It remains to be demonstrated how the concern for purity, or separation from ὁ κόσμος, is related to another, perhaps the, major theme of the text.

3. *Purity as Integral to Perfection*

I noted above that purity is neither the only nor the primary lens through which to view James' worldview. A growing group of scholars have identified perfection as a key theme running through James.[88] There are several terms that denote the idea of perfection/wholeness in the Epistle of James. Most important of these is the τέλ- word group. The foremost term denoting perfection or wholeness that appears in the epistle is the adjective τέλειος ('perfect') which appears five times in the text (1.4a, b; 1.17; 1.25; 3.2).[89] It is suggestive that in the short 108 verses of James this adjective occurs 5 times out of the total 19 in the rest of the NT. The term is used 3 times in both Matthew and 1 Corinthians, books more than twice the size of James, which again illustrates the significance of the frequent use of the term in such a relatively short work. Strategically, τέλειος appears with other key terms in James: ἔργον (1.4; 2.22), πίστις (2.22), and νόμος (1.25; 2.8; cf. 2.10 ὅλον τὸν νόμον).[90] In addition to the adjective τέλειος, the text contains 2 τέλ-related verbs: τελέω ('complete', or 'fulfil'; 2.8) and τελειόω ('accomplish', or 'carry out'; 2.22), both of which are common verbs appearing several times in the NT. The concentration of τέλ-related words in James is suggestive of the concept's importance to the theme of the letter. In addition to the concentration of the τέλ-based word group, James contains other terms that denote the

---

88. Most recently and comprehensively Cheung identifies 'perfection' as the major theme of James (*Genre, Composition and Hermeneutics*); see also, Martin Klein, *'Ein vollkommenes Werk': Vollkommenheit, Gesetz und Gericht als theologische Themen des Jakobusbriefes* (BWANT, 7/19; Stuttgart: Kohlhammer, 1995); Moo, *James*, p. 46; Hartin, *Spirituality of Perfection*; Bauckham, *James*, pp. 177–85; Martin, *James*, pp. lxxix–lxxxii; Josef Zmijewski, 'Christliche "Vollkommenheit": Erwägungen zur Theologie des Jakobusbriefes', *SNTU* 5 (1980), pp. 50–78; Elliott, 'Holiness-Wholeness'; Laws, *James*, pp. 28–32.

89. The term appears a total of 19 times in the NT: 5 time in James, 5 times in the undisputed Pauline epistles (Rom. 12.2; 1 Cor. 2.6, 13.10, 14.20; Phil. 3.15), the term also appears in Mt. 5.48 (2×); 19.21; Eph. 4.13; Col. 1.28; 4.12; Heb. 5.14; 9.11; 1 Jn 4.18.

90. See also the connection of τέλειος with σοφία in the section 1.2-5, 17.

idea of completeness or wholeness. In the important opening passage of 1.2-4, the author of James not only uses τέλειος twice but he also uses the synonym ὁλόκληρος ('whole' or 'intact') which conveys the idea of being complete or meeting every expectation. This term is paired with the participial phrase 'lacking nothing' (ἐν μηδενὶ λειπόμενοι),[91] and both concepts relating wholeness or completeness in every respect are applied directly to the individual (as τέλειος in 3.2). The entire complex of terms which convey wholeness or perfection stand in opposition to terms relating imperfection or lack of wholeness. The epistle expresses this antithesis with the adjectives δίψυχος ('double-minded'; 1.8; 4.8) and ἀκατάστατος ('unstable', or 'restless'; 1.8; 3.8; cf. 3.16 where the substantive ἀκαταστασία is used).

John Elliott understands that the purity/pollution language replicates the wholeness/dividedness, or τέλειος language in James, a notion largely followed by Hartin. Elliott asserts: 'concepts of pollution and purity...are used to summarize the exhortations regarding incompleteness and integrity, division and wholeness', and furthermore: 'concepts of pollution and purity, division and wholeness, may be merged in an effort to address the issues of distinctive Christian identity, responsibility, social cohesion, and social boundaries'.[92] Yet, predicated upon the exegesis above, should one conclude that the perfection language in James, like the purity language, is calling for separation from ὁ κόσμος? Are, as Elliott's thesis claims, wholeness/perfection replicated by purity/pollution or are these related yet distinct concepts? I contend that Elliott is correct in identifying the important relationship between perfection and purity; however, I contend that one cannot understand the 'call to perfection', as Cheung has called it, without a proper understanding of James' concern for purity. Elliott's claim that purity language replicates the perfection blunts our understanding instead of sharpening it.

Rather than conflating these concepts, as Elliott does, perfection and purity are distinct, yet dynamically related conditions. The primary concern for purity in James focuses upon the audience's relationship with the surrounding culture (ὁ κόσμος) and their internal coherence. Interaction (1.27) and alliance (4.4, 8) with ὁ κόσμος is deemed a source of defilement for James' readers. The overall notion of perfection in James is that of resolute devotion to God, the opposite of 'double-mindedness'. The contrast between τέλειος and δίψυχος refers to the relationship between James' readers and God; they either may be wholehearted, single-minded in devotion, or irresolute, double-minded in their relationship

---

91. Zmijewski ('Christliche Wollkommenheit', p. 52) adds ὅλος to the list of key words denoting perfection/wholeness.

92. Elliott, 'Holiness-Wholeness', p. 74.

with God.[93] Perfection, as it were, renders the readers wholly unto God and thus makes them holy. On the other hand, double-mindedness is an indication of lack of devotion, the consequence (not condition) of maintaining an alliance with the world. Note that the composition uses the notion of δίψυχος not 'impurity' in direct contrast with perfection. Thus, it is only when James' readers maintain a degree of separation from ὁ κόσμος (thus achieving purity) that they are able to begin to achieve perfection. It is only when readers 'cleanse' their hands and 'purify' their hearts that they are able to start down the road to perfection (4.8). Where the readers align themselves with the world, in James' view, there can only be imperfection (= 'double-mindedness') and ultimately eschatological 'death' (1.15; 5.20). Whereas separating from ὁ κόσμος, *by means of* 'pure' wisdom, leads to perfection and wholeness (1.4) and ultimately eschatological 'life' (1.12). There is no indication in the text that one can ally with ὁ κόσμος and expect to be τέλειος. Yet one must do more than separate from ὁ κόσμος to be τέλειος. Thus purity is the necessary, yet not sufficient, condition for achieving perfection. Where it is true that to be wholeheartedly devoted to God entails that one is separated from 'the world', the converse, that separation from the world necessarily entails that one is wholehearted in devotion to God, is not true. Mere separation from the surrounding culture without respect to one's devotion to God is hardly James' concern.

It is only as separation from ὁ κόσμος serves the objective of wholehearted devotion to God (perfection), that James' antagonism toward the world is understood. Here, unlike Elliott, I claim that perfection is not replicated by the notions of purity and pollution, which rather are related yet separable concepts working together in the text. Rather than wholeness (perfection) language being 'replicated' in purity/ pollution, the evidence indicates that purity in James' understanding is a necessary condition for perfection.

Closer to the point are Bauckham's comments regarding the relationship between perfection and purity. The use of purity 'belongs to this aspect of wholeness as exclusion: purity must be preserved by removing and keeping untainted by anything that would defile'.[94] Bauckham also adds a decisive comment regarding the particular function of purity language:

> But it is important to notice that [purity] does not seem to be used to draw a sociological boundary around the community, distinguishing

---

93. Bauckham notes: 'The overarching theme of James is "perfection" or "wholeness" (1.4). Wholeness requires wholehearted and single-minded devotion to God, and its opposite is that half-heartedness in devotion to God and that divided loyalty, vacillating between God and the world, which James calls double-mindedness (1.8; 4.8)' (*James*, p. 146).

94. Bauckham, *James*, p. 180.

insiders from outsiders in order to reinforce the community's sense of self-identity. Self-identity, as we shall see, is secured with reference to God as the focus and integrating point of the community's wholeness, rather than by a negative delineating of themselves over against others. As a counter-cultural community, the church is distinctive, but is not at pains to secure this distinctiveness in social separateness.[95]

The specific issue of how purity functions to encircle James' readers and thereby gives them a particular identity, namely what James means by purity as separation from ὁ κόσμος, is an issue I cannot take up fully here. However, I will say that though purity in James does envisage a boundary which strengthens (or calls forth) a 'countercultural' stance toward the reader's ambient culture, it is not at all clear that this is indicative of a sectarian line of separation.[96] Furthermore, elsewhere I have argued that James' call to create or maintain boundaries does not entail that the identity of James' readers is secured by delineating themselves over against enemies or 'outsiders'.[97] Based upon the exegesis above it is clear that James' call to separation (the call to 'purity') is distinct from, yet integrally related to, the call to perfection in the text. It is insufficient to view their relationship in terms of replication because a significant segment of James' worldview is obscured from view – if purity merely replicates perfection the call to separate from the values and worldview of ὁ κόσμος is eclipsed.

4. *Conclusion*

James employs the line-drawing language of purity/pollution to map out a proper construal of reality – labelling the values associated with ὁ κόσμος as impure or 'dangerous'. Where the worldview associated with God is labelled 'pure and undefiled', the worldview of ὁ κόσμος is the source of pollution ('stain', 1.27; 3.6). The call to cleanse and purify (4.8) is a call to create or maintain a boundary between James' readers and surrounding culture. The community's proximity to ὁ κόσμος has been seen to directly impact their ability to attain perfection, or wholehearted devotion to God. Thus one cannot understand the concern for perfection in James without a proper understanding of purity.

While the purity concern in James specifically calls forth some kind of separation from ὁ κόσμος, the purity language alone does not indicate the *kind* or *degree* of separation. Does the call to cleanse oneself from ὁ

95. Bauckham, *James*, p. 180.
96. *Contra* Wall, *Community of the Wise*, pp. 14–15; Elliott, 'Holiness-Wholeness'; and Ben Witherington, *Jesus the Sage: The Pilgrimage of Wisdom* (Minneapolis: Fortress, 1994), p. 246.
97. Lockett, *Purity and Worldview*, ch. 5.

κόσμος demand sectarian separation or partial separation? And what specifically are readers to separate from when they refuse alliance with ὁ κόσμος? These follow-on questions must be considered in order to complete James' purity geography. Though there is hardly space to take up these questions here, I have argued elsewhere that James' purity lines do not chart a defensive community blindly separating itself from the rest of the world. The overall stance toward the surrounding culture need not, as others have argued, be indicative of sectarian separation. I have observed that where James highlights particular points of separation from the world (significantly mapped by purity language), there are indications of broader cultural accommodation. Taking up the specific alien values of patron–client relationships and the misuse of the tongue are the only two cultural values clearly plotted as 'dangerous' upon James' map. Thus James ought not be read as promoting sectarian separation from the world but only the specific separation from particular alien values embodied in the ambient culture.[98]

It is telling that James' readers need such a strong note of warning to renounce alliance with the world and maintain (or create) a sense of boundary between themselves and the values, attitudes and actions derived from the world. Failing to take note of purity and pollution as line-drawing language – or 'worldview' language – results in a distorted vision of the contours of James' overall map of reality. Thus the analysis of the purity language in James provides a helpful vantage point on the text's cultural stance. James' theo-centric map draws human behaviour in terms of 'perfect' relationship to God, which, as a consequence, calls for separation from ὁ κόσμος – namely, to strengthen the too loosely defined lines marking off the values and actions which are 'pure and undefiled before God' from those originating from a polluting 'friendship with the world'.

---

98. Lockett, *Purity and Worldview*.

THE LETTER OF JAMES AS A DOCUMENT OF PAULINISM?

Margaret M. Mitchell

1. *Thesis and Context*

At this moment – and in this collection of essays – I find myself paddling upstream. I seek to reopen precisely the question that many are relegating to the margins these days – the relationship between James and Paul. There has for a couple of decades been a rising tide of opinion that James be read 'on its own terms' or 'on its own merits' apart from the refracted light of the Pauline sun, which appears unfairly to diminish James and his contribution to Christian theology.[1] This appeal, cast as a bid for simple justice on James' behalf, undoubtedly has keen rhetorical force.[2] As a modern, text-immanent or canon-critical reading strategy, it can certainly be granted, even commended. But as a move in historical research it merely begs the question by assuming, rather than proving, that there was no intersection between Paul and his letters and the author of James. In other words, in historical research, 'to read James on his own terms' *must include grappling with Paul if Paul was one of those terms.*[3] Yet although I find myself waving to my contemporaries as they canoe down the opposite

---

1. Recent reviewers speak of this movement as James' 'rehabilitation' (Luke Timothy Johnson, 'Review of Luke Leuk Cheung, *The Genre, Composition and Hermeneutics of the Epistle of James*', CBQ 66 [2004], pp. 641–43; Matthias Konradt, 'Review of Patrick Hartin, *A Spirituality of Perfection: Faith and Action in the Letter of James*; David Hutchinson Edgar, *Has God Not Chosen the Poor? The Social Setting of the Epistle of James*; and Matt A. Jackson-McCabe, *Logos and Law in the Letter of James: The Law of Nature, the Law of Moses and the Law of Freedom*', JBL 122 [2003], pp. 182–89). See also Luke Timothy Johnson, *The Letter of James* (AB, 37A; New York: Doubleday, 1995), p. 114 on how 'breaking the Pauline fixation' will 'liberate James to be read...in terms of its own voice rather than in terms of its supposed muting of Paul's voice'.

2. The rhetorical power of this appeal was well testified to in the SBL session, when my friend William Brosend's stirring exhortation to read James outside of Paul's shadow was greeted by a spontaneous and loud 'Amen!' from one of the members of the audience.

3. The problem may be illustrated in this statement by Brosend: 'what happens when one reads the letters of James and Jude on their own merits and not in light of any *real or*

side of the river, I spy ancient exegetes like Augustine headed the same direction as I (if paddling different kinds of water craft!). The great North African certainly did not wish to read James apart from Paul, or Paul apart from James, but understood James as playing the essential role of steering the reading of Paul's letters in the right direction: *locus iste hujus Epistolae* [Jas 2.14-26] *eumdem sensum Pauli apostoli, quomodo sit intelligendus, exponit.*[4] The intent of the present paper is to ask whether that ancient view of the invaluable function of James – as providing a corrective to a reading of Paul deemed problematic – might not correspond to its original purpose.[5]

In modern scholarship, broadly speaking, seven different logical options for the literary-historical relationship between James and Paul are on the table:[6]

---

imagined relationship to the letters of Paul and Peter?' (William F. Brosend II, *James and Jude* [NCBC; Cambridge: Cambridge University Press, 2004], p. 3). But surely if that relationship is *real*, the historian cannot simply ignore it!

4.   The full context of the passage reads as follows: *De eo quod apostolus Jacobus dicit* [quotes 2.20]. *Quoniam Paulus apostolus praedicans justificari hominem per fidem sine operibus, non bene intellectus est ab eis qui sic acceperunt dictum, ut putarent, cum semel in Christum credidissent, etiamsi male operarentur, et facinorose flagitioseque viverent, salvos se esse posse per fidem: locus iste hujus Epistolae [Jas 2.14-26] eumdem sensum Pauli apostoli, quomodo sit intelligendus, exponit* ('On that which the apostle James said [2.20]. Seeing that the apostle Paul, in preaching that a man is justified by faith without works, is not rightly understood by those who received this statement such that they supposed they could be saved by faith when once they had believed in Christ, even if they were wickedly engaged and lived in a criminal and disgraceful manner, this very passage [2.14-26] of [the apostle James'] letter [Jas 2.14-26] explains in what way the precise meaning of the apostle Paul is to be understood') (Augustine, *Div. quaest. LXXXIII* 76 [*PL* vol. 40, cols. 37–38]).

5.   The essay by Robert W. Wall, 'A Unifying Theology of the Catholic Epistles: A Canonical Approach', in *The Catholic Epistles and the Tradition* (ed. J. Schlosser; BETL, 176; Leuven: Peeters Press, 2004), pp. 43–71 (I regret not having seen this before the SBL session) sees so well the unifying role of James in its 'eventual canonization' at the head of the Catholic Epistles which balance Paul (as known in *Praxapostolos* form), but eschews consideration that it was composed for this very reason ('Without proposing a theory of the book's composition as a pseudepigraphy ...' [p. 48]). The placement of the Catholic Epistles (with James at their head) between Acts and the Pauline Epistles in the Byzantine manuscript tradition does indeed enshrine this canonical function (Bruce M. Metzger, *The Canon of the New Testament: Its Origin, Development, and Significance* [Oxford: Oxford University Press, 1987], pp. 295–96). A striking illustration of my proposal is Gregory-Aland ms 1780 (ca. 1200; Duke University Kenneth Clark Manuscript #1), which has James (alone) between Acts and Romans, and hence having readers come to Paul directly through James. But can we really imagine that the Letter of James was just waiting in the wings for centuries until this serendipitous hermeneutical fit be noticed?

6.   Compare the list of five positions on literary dependency laid out by Andrew Chester (Andrew Chester and Ralph P. Martin, *The Theology of the Letters of James, Peter, and Jude* [New Testament Theology; Cambridge: Cambridge University Press, 1994], p. 47) and the accent on the question of whether the author understood or misunderstood Paul in the list of

1. James and Paul were completely independent (any alleged overlaps are mere coincidence).[7]
2. James and Paul both reflect 'Hellenistic Judaism' or 'first generation Jewish [Christianity]' (without direct connection to one another).[8]
3. Paul knew the Epistle of James and wrote against it in his letter(s), especially Galatians (and/or Romans).[9]
4. James did not know Paul's letters but had heard something (accurate) about Paul.[10]
5. James did not know Paul's letters but had heard something (inaccurate) about Paul.[11]
6. James depends on the Pauline letters (especially Galatians, perhaps Romans) and writes against them because he understands how

---

three positions outlined in Andreas Lindemann, *Paulus im alten Christentum: Das Bild des Apostels und die Rezeption der paulinischen Theologie in der frühchristlichen Literatur bis Marcion* (BHT, 58; Tübingen: J. C. B. Mohr [Paul Siebeck], 1979), p. 243.

7. I do not know of anyone who has argued this recently, but I include it here as a logical possibility.

8. Richard J. Bauckham, *James: Wisdom of James, Disciple of Jesus the Sage* (New Testament Readings; London and New York: Routledge, 1999), pp. 127–31: ('the best explanation is that both are dependent on a Jewish tradition of discussion of Abraham' (p. 130); '[this] accounts for the parallels and differences between them more satisfactorily than postulating a direct relationship between them' (p. 131)); Johnson, *James*, p. 120: ('Rather than place Paul and James in direct conversation or polemical conflict, the best way to account for the combination of similarity and difference in their language is to view them both as first generation Jewish Christians deeply affected by Greco-Roman moral traditions yet fundamentally defined by an allegiance to the symbols and story of Torah'. There is, however, a problem with this view, because if the Letter of James was written by the historical brother of the Lord, he and Paul *did* meet face to face (according to Gal. 1.19), so 'direct conversation' must be allowed in some fashion. This appears to be acknowledged in Luke Timothy Johnson, *Brother of Jesus Friend of God: Studies in the Letter of James* (Grand Rapids: Eerdmans, 2004): 'Although James is influenced by Hellenism, Judaism, Jesus, *Paul*, and the early Christian movement...' (p. 31, emphasis added). If so, then is not Paul one of James' terms?

9. Joseph B. Mayor, *The Epistle of St. James* (London: Macmillan, 3rd edn, 1913), p. xcii: 'while St. James has no reference to St. Paul, St. Paul on the contrary writes with constant reference to St. James'.

10. James B. Adamson, *James: The Man and His Message* (Grand Rapids: Eerdmans, 1989), p. 225: 'the connection need not be direct but due rather to oral reminiscences behind the written passages'.

11. James Hardy Ropes, *The Epistle of St. James* (ICC; Edinburgh: T&T Clark, 1916), p. 35: '[James'] language is probably capable of explanation on the assumption that he had not read [Paul's epistles], and his entire failure to suggest that Paul's formula could be dissociated from its misuse shows at least that he had paid surprisingly little attention to Romans and Galatians.' Also Sophie Laws, *The Epistle of James* (HNTC; San Francisco: Harper & Row, 1980), pp. 15–18; Franz Mussner, *Der Jakobusbrief* (HTKNT, 13; Freiburg: Herder, 1964), pp. 14–21.

radical Paul's teaching on justification was and wishes to combat it.[12]

7. James depends on the Pauline letters (especially Galatians, perhaps Romans) and writes against them, but 'misunderstands' Paul's true teaching on justification and wishes to combat it.[13]

I am myself convinced (along with the proponents of options 6 and 7) that the resemblances between Jas 2.14-26 and Gal. 2.16–3.29 (and Romans 3–4)[14] defy coincidence and point to a literary relationship – that is, that the author of the Letter of James knew one or (likely, because of Jas 1.3-4 and Rom. 5.3-5) both of these Pauline letters.[15] Yet despite this fundamental agreement, there are I think two major flaws in options 6 and 7.

Those who have argued for or allowed some direct literary connection between James and the letters and/or person of Paul have misconstrued the question when they ask if James was 'anti-Pauline', or whether James had 'correctly or incorrectly understood' Paul.[16] This way of formulating the question assumes that the construct 'Paul' (as operative for 'James') is unambiguously clear, uniform, and self-evident to the critic. In particular, it must assume that the 'Paul' James had contact with was mainly

12. Martin Hengel, 'Jakobusbrief als antipaulinischen Polemik', in *Tradition and Interpretation in the New Testament* (ed. G. F. Hawthorne and O. Betz; Grand Rapids: Eerdmans, 1987), pp. 248–78; Lindemann, *Paulus im ältesten Christentum*, pp. 250–52. However, Lindemann belongs also in category 5, since he is on the whole extremely cautious about direct literary dependence on Paul's letters, finding it more probable only in the case of Jas 2.21-24 and Romans 3–4, though even there he thinks an oral knowledge of a Pauline sentence as a kind of slogan ('einen gewissen Parole-Charakter') is feasible (see p. 247).

13. Famously Martin Dibelius, *James: A Commentary on the Epistle of James* (ed. H. Koester; rev. Heinrich Greeven; trans. Michael A. Williams; Hermeneia; Philadelphia Fortress, 1975), p. 180: 'But the criticism which James offers does not go against the experience of Paul at all, since *the depth of Paul's experience was closed to James.* And not only to him. The full titanic power of the Pauline slogan, "apart from works, faith" has hardly ever in the course of Christian history been grasped by the masses.' See also Gerd Luedemann, *Opposition to Paul in Jewish Christianity* (trans. M. Eugene Boring; Minneapolis: Fortress, 1989), pp. 140–49, 146: 'James caricatures the key sentences from Galatians and Romans.'

14. The parallel phrasing of Gal. 2.16 and Rom. 3.28 makes it impossible to decide between Galatians and Romans as an influence (I regard knowledge of Romans likely because of Rom. 5.4-5 and Jas 1.3-4), and we should not try. The reason I focus on Galatians as the Pauline influence is that it, unlike Romans, names James the brother of the Lord (1.19; 2.9), and, as I shall show below, its angry invective against the Jerusalem pillars made it a problematic text for early interpreters. But I do not think there is a dichotomy to be drawn (Galatians *or* Romans, but rather *both* are in view).

15. I shall present the arguments for direct dependency on Galatians and 1 Corinthians below.

16. Dibelius, *James*, pp. 179–80: 'But also he could be thinking of people who advocate the genuine ideas of Paul, and whom Jas misunderstands. Yet the existence of such true disciples of Paul is very doubtful. In fact, it was Paul's fate to be misunderstood within the church.'

concerned with the issue echoed in Jas 2.21-26, and that 'Paul' was himself consistent on the issue of 'faith' and 'works' and clearly saw the two as 'opposed'. Such a line of thought seems to assume the 'true Paul' is to be found in Gal. 2.16, read as a sentence apart from the full argument of that letter, including Gal. 5.13–6.10 (or especially perhaps 5.6: πίστις δι' ἀγάπης ἐνεργουμένη).[17] Secondly, such an approach arbitrarily or artificially isolates Galatians (and/or Romans) among the Pauline letters in the quest to form a single letter-to-letter comparison between Paul and James. Consequently, the intense focus on Jas 2.14-26 when asking about James' relationship to Paul has obscured the equally strong evidence that the author of James also knew at least one other Pauline letter – 1 Corinthians (as I shall show below). This also stands to reason, for there is no evidence in ancient Christianity of individual letters, such as Galatians, circulating beyond their recipient communities in published form outside of some collection of the *corpus Paulinum*. The logical consequence of this deserves more attention: if this author knew some collection (four letters, or letters to seven churches), then he – like all readers of the Pauline corpus – was already faced with multiple 'Pauls' and a complicated and tensive Pauline legacy he sought to steer in a particular direction. Taking this into account, I would like to propose an eighth option for consideration:

8.   The author of the Letter of James knows some collection of Paul's letters, and writes *from within Paulinism* (rather than in opposition to Paul), creating a compromise document which has as one of its purposes reconciling 'Paul with Paul' and 'Paul with the pillars'.[18]

In my view, the author's dependence on Paul's letters shows that he largely approves of them and presumes they are authoritative, but draws upon them in such a way as to tip the interpretation of them (as a canonical collection and on-going source of theological teaching) away from polarization (around faith and works, the proper role of the law, rich versus poor, or Paul versus the Jerusalem 'pillars') and toward concord. In doing so the author wishes to confront a legacy of the earliest collection[19] that juxtaposed Galatians and 1 Corinthians in close proximity, revealing tensions or potential contradictions within Paul (esp. Gal. 2.13 and 1 Cor. 9.20-23 on ὑπόκρισις, and Gal. 2.16 and 1 Cor. 13.2 on πίστις), and

17.   See, e.g.: 'The two things which are opposed are not faith and works (as with Paul) but a living faith and a dead faith' (Ropes, *James*, p. 207). But does Paul always oppose faith and works, as this statement assumes?

18.   I would like to stress that the present essay deals only with the Pauline influences on James. I need not and do not deny that James also had other literary influences, including Jesus sayings in some form.

19.   In whichever form: no posited early *corpus Paulinum* does not contain both Galatians and 1 Corinthians (see n. 24 below for literature).

between Paul and the Jerusalem leaders and his relationship to their authority (Gal. 2.11-14; cf. 1 Cor. 3.22; 15.1-11). As such, this document written in the name of James is of a piece with other late-first- and early-second-century documents of Paulinism, such as *1 Clement*, the pseudepigraphical Paulines, 1 Peter, Acts, and the *Letter of Polycarp*, which, adopting the epistolary form themselves, interpret Paul toward the centre and away from extremes, and attempt to show that the church had a concordant apostolic foundation, rather than an isolated maverick Pauline cornerstone.[20] Like 1 Peter (with which many see a direct literary relationship) and Acts 15, the Letter of James could be seen as a conscious attempt to include all parties at the notorious 'Antioch incident' as actually (despite Gal. 2.10-14) on the same page, all tilting toward a reasonable middle.

2. *Methodological Approach*

My proposal, which seeks to set James within the history of Paulinism, is based on a network of sensibilities that all cohere under the umbrella of reception history. In the oral version of this paper I remarked off the cuff, 'what is methodology anyway, but who you've been hanging out with?' While admittedly an insufficiently rigorous statement of method, that remark does point to some truths about how I have come to the present position, even as the principle that one's autobiography and reading partners affect one's interpretive work is probably one that would fit other interpreters as well (without assuming that these considerations constitute a *sufficient* explanation in any of our cases). My thinking about James has been heavily influenced by the convergence of four channels of my research, each of which has supported one plank of the current argument: early study of 1 Corinthians and its wide-spread and early dissemination;[21] investigation of the history of Pauline interpretation in the early church, especially much time spent with John Chrysostom, an eastern devotée of Paul for whom 'justification by faith' was never viewed as incompatible with 'works';[22] exploration of the key role of Paul as the inaugurator of an early Christian literary culture in the first century, and the pervasive influence of his letters in fashioning a movement that

20. Cf. also the pseudepigraphic Eph. 2.21.
21. Margaret M. Mitchell, *Paul and the Rhetoric of Reconciliation: An Exegetical Investigation of the Language and Composition of 1 Corinthians* (HUT, 28; Tübingen: J. C. B. Mohr [Paul Siebeck], 1991; Louisville: Westminster John Knox, 1993).
22. Margaret M. Mitchell, *The Heavenly Trumpet: John Chrysostom and the Art of Pauline Interpretation* (HUT, 40; Tübingen: Mohr/Siebeck, 2000; Louisville: Westminster John Knox, 2002).

conspicuously employed textual means;[23] and increasing awareness of the importance of the *corpus Paulinum* as interpretive context for any Pauline utterance already in antiquity.[24] At the same time as I have focused in my scholarship on the history of Pauline interpretation in the early church I have been a creature of my own age, much influenced by the work of such scholars as Krister Stendahl and E. P. Sanders on breaking down the 'Augustinian–Lutheran' paradigm of reading Paul that so acutely formed many earlier proponents of the unequivocal view that James was 'anti-Pauline',[25] and by such authors as Dennis MacDonald on the Pastoral Epistles, and Christopher Mount on Acts,[26] whose studies have helped me to see 'Paulinism' in a broader perspective that calls into question the simplistic formulation of the 'anti-Paulinism' of James. Out of this nexus of concerns and influences on my interpretive perspective, I have come to think it worth asking if we should turn the 'anti-Pauline' thesis on its head, and ask if James might not be seen as a document of Paulinism. I see now that a few others have looked also in this direction, in whole or in part,[27] so perhaps I am on less of a lonely path than first I

23.   Margaret M. Mitchell, 'The Emergence of the Written Record', in *The Cambridge History of Christianity*, vol. 1 *Origins to Constantine* (ed. Margaret M. Mitchell and Frances M. Young; Cambridge: Cambridge University Press, 2006), pp. 103–24. It bears emphasizing here that arguing for the centrality of Paul in the history and development of the Christian literary culture that was to develop is not the same as maintaining that in his historical context of the early decades of the movement Paul was the most significant figure. See Johnson, *Brother of Jesus*, p. 10: 'A first impulse for those who have not, as good historians, been seduced by the importance accorded Paul in the canon of the New Testament into thinking that Paul's historical importance must have been equally central to the early Christian movement ...'. As a historian I think James the brother of the Lord must have been a major figure, but that does not mean I am sure we have any literary texts from him (in fact I think we do not).

24.   Here I have learned much from the important work of Harry Y. Gamble, 'The Pauline Corpus and the Early Christian Book', in *Paul and the Legacies of Paul* (ed. W. Babcock; Dallas: Southern Methodist University Press, 1990), pp. 265–80; Harry Y. Gamble, *Books and Readers in the Early Church* (New Haven: Yale University Press, 1995), pp. 58–66; and David Trobisch (though I am less sure of the latter's hypothesis that Paul himself crafted the first four-letter collection) (see *Paul's Letter Collection: Tracing the Origins* [Minneapolis: Fortress, 1994]; idem, *Die Entstehung der Paulusbriefsammlung. Studien zu den Anfängen christlicher Publizistik* [NTOA, 10; Göttingen: Vandenhoeck & Ruprecht, 1989]).

25.   E. P. Sanders, *Paul and Palestinian Judaism* (Philadelphia: Fortress, 1977); Krister Stendahl, 'The Apostle Paul and the Introspective Conscience of the West', in *Paul Among Jews and Gentiles and Other Essays* (Philadelphia: Fortress, 1976), pp. 78–96. The literature on the 'new perspective' on Paul is now legion.

26.   Dennis R. MacDonald, *The Legend and the Apostle: The Battle for Paul in Story and Canon* (Philadelphia: Westminster, 1983); Christopher N. Mount, *Pauline Christianity: Luke-Acts and the Legacy of Paul* (NovTSup, 104; Leiden: E. J. Brill, 2002).

27.   In earlier scholarship see, e.g., Heinrich Julius Holtzmann, *Lehrbuch der neutestamentlichen Theologie* (2 vols.; Freiburg im Breisgau and Leipzig: J. C. B. Mohr [Paul Siebeck], 1897): 'Es besteht sogar die Möglichkeit, dass Jak, der sich sonst so vielfach an

thought when giving this paper at the November 2005 Annual SBL meeting. Yet the configuration of the present argument, which emphasizes the role of 1 Corinthians and draws upon patristic interpretation of Paul to highlight interpretive problems created by the *corpus Paulinum*, may represent a unique constellation of arguments, so I offer it in that spirit, aware that it moves into well-developed territory. It should be said up front that all who investigate these problems deal with much the same data; I offer this proposal as yet another configuration of the pieces of the puzzle, one that to my eyes makes good sense of the evidence.

3. The Arguments and Evidence

My argument is built on four propositions that constitute the essential building blocks for my suggestion that we reconsider the 'Paulinism' of James.[28]

---

paulin. Formeln anschliesst, mit seiner Polemik nur den Pls gegen Pls (unter einer Voraussetzung wie die II Pt 3.16 vorliegende) vertheidigen wollte, was dann freilich in überaus unvorsichtiger und missverständlicher Weise bewerkstelligt worden wäre' (vol. 2, p. 337). More recently, closest to my general proposal for 'concentrating on James' reception of Paul' is the lively essay by Kari Syreeni which I unfortunately only read after the SBL session in 2005: 'James and the Pauline Legacy: Power Play in Corinth?' in *Fair Play: Diversity and Conflicts in Early Christianity* (Festschrift Heikki Räisänen; ed. Ismo Dunderberg, Christopher Tuckett and Kari Syreeni; NovTSup, 103; Leiden: E. J. Brill, 2002), pp. 397–437. Despite many trenchant observations, however, Syreeni's reconstruction still relies too much on a presumed Jewish Christian/Gentile Christian dichotomy, and its concomitant assertion of 'anti-Paulinism', which I am seeking to call into question here (I am also not convinced that we can tell it was addressed to Corinth!)

For the purposes of the present argument I am focusing, as has the history of interpretation I am seeking to engage, upon James alone in relation to Paulinism, but I have been aware as I proceeded that the literary connections between James and 1 Peter beg to be considered as well. In that connection I was delighted to learn at our SBL session of the dissertation (Aberdeen, 2005) by David Nienhuis, *Not By Paul Alone: The Formation of the Catholic Epistle Collection and the Christian Canon* (Waco, TX: Baylor University Press, forthcoming), which makes a similar reading of James as I do (seeing James as part of 'Paulinism'), but places it, as I agree is necessary, within a larger argument about the formation of the corpus of the Catholic Epistles. I look forward to seeing his argument and am happy to direct readers to it.

28.   Each of these four points enters a vast terrain on which there is a plethora of scholarship. In the confines of this essay I have had to focus on how I read the primary sources, rather than the history of scholarship on each point.

a. *The Epistle of James breathes the same air as Pauline Christianity,*
and this 'air' constitutes a Pauline literary culture

A key reason to doubt that James can simply be called 'anti-Pauline' is
that the epistle holds so much in common with Paul's letters. On this point
I find staunch allies in the recent proponents of option 2 – Richard
Bauckham and Luke Timothy Johnson – who have argued that James,
taken to be the historical 'James, the brother of the Lord', though he
wrote independently of Paul, was actually much closer to Paul than the
exegetical traditions have appreciated. 'Of all the writings in the New
Testament', Johnson writes, 'James has the most profound kinship with
the letters of Paul.'[29] I agree! But not for the same reason. Both authors
emphasize the theological similiarities between James and Paul in service
of a reconstruction of a harmonious early Christianity,[30] as against the
famous F. C. Baur and the Tübingen School's theory of deep conflict at
the heart of early Christianity between Paul and his opponents (James and
Peter). Rather prophetically (in light of the present essay), Mark
Goodacre, in his review of Bauckham's *James*, remarked (though I
think tongue-in-cheek): 'Indeed Bauckham is so good at smoothing over
the differences between Paul, James and other streams of early
Christianity that one begins to think that Bauckham would be capable
of proving that Paul himself could have written this epistle.'[31] To this quip
I ask in turn: if not Paul, how about a Paulinist? Is there not a nagging
problem with the concordant pictures Bauckham and Johnson have
produced: does the Letter of James – like Acts (esp. ch. 15), which they
also hold as a largely reliable historical source – testify to a unity between
the historical Paul and the historical James, or to an agreement *within the*
literary traditions of Gentile Christianity, that is, within Paulinism?

Indeed, even before we get to specifics of the theological compatibility
between Paul and James on soteriology, Christology or eschatology, the
most obvious similarity between the two that we should not take for
granted is the fact that James' literary rhetorical world presumes that the
letter form is the medium through which Christ-believers engage in
theological and pastoral reasoning.

In my view this especially shows indebtedness to Paul, the first Christian
letter writer who set the movement on a literary path. Paul's letters were
the first Christian literature, were widely circulated in some collected form

---

29. Johnson, *Brother of Jesus*, p. 20; see also Johnson, *The Letter of James*, p. 112 ('on
the basis both of Acts and Galatians, the Jerusalem church is seen as in fundamental
agreement with Paul, and James is seen as fundamentally an ally of Paul'); Bauckham, *James*,
pp. 135–40 ('James and Paul on Common Ground').

30. Hence Johnson, *Brother of Jesus*, p. 12, speaks of 'the thick texture of language that
James and Paul each share as part of the developing Christian *argot*'.

31. Mark Goodacre, 'Review of Richard Bauckham, *James*', *Reviews in Religion and*
Theology 7 (2000), pp. 52–54.

beginning within a decade or two of his death, and became the basis for
new epistolary compositions in his name (the deutero-Paulines and
Pastorals). The early composition and circulation of the Pauline letters is
the most secure and best attested fact about early Christian literature.[32]
Consequently, their influence on 'James' (as on so many other later first-
century compositions) is inherently more likely, and on an evidentiary
basis far more secure than the poorly attested (if vividly envisioned) genre
of 'Disapora' letters from Jerusalem,[33] thought to have been a direct
influence on the historical James the brother of the Lord who saw himself
as naturally the heir of the various authoritative Jerusalem letter writers of
the past. But the letter nowhere mentions Jerusalem, nor does it claim to

32.   In the case of James, in contrast, we are faced with a strikingly different literary
history: no early attestation (rather remarkable for an alleged circular letter!), and no epigoni
or pseudepigraphical authors taking up and continuing the literary line of letters thus
launched. Jamesian pseudepigrapha are largely apocalyptic works (the *Apocryphon of James*,
1 and *2 Apocalypse of James* known from the Nag Hammadi corpus, and the charming
legendary narrative, the *Protevangelium of James*).

33.   In the discussion following my paper this issue came up immediately, with reference
to the work of Richard Bauckham, who has appealed to a 'tradition of letters from Jerusalem
to the Diaspora' (*James*, pp. 19–20), and Karl-Wilhelm Niebuhr (who was present at the
session), who has taken James on this basis to be an 'apostolischer Diasporabrief' ('Der
Jakobusbrief im Licht frühjüdischer Diasporabriefe', *NTS* 44 [1998], pp. 420–43 [421]). But
the case is not strong, for several reasons. First, for the distinctive genre they both appeal to
the data base of Jewish letters assembled earlier by Irene Taatz, *Frühjüdische Briefe: die
paulinischen Briefe im Rahmen der offiziellen religiösen Briefe des Frühjudentums* (NTOA, 16;
Göttingen: Vandenhoeck & Ruprecht, 1991). But Taatz had connected this literature, not
with James, but with *Paul's letters*, which she considers 'die ältesten uns erreichbaren
schriftlichen Quellen des Urchristentums' and remarks on 'die Bedeutung des Apostels für
die Entstehung der frühchristlichen Briefliteratur' (p. 7; on this page she leaves the
relationship between James and Paul's letters an open question, however). Second, the
similarities among these 'parallels' (2 Maccabees 1–2, *The Letter of Jeremiah*, Syriac Baruch
78–86, *Paraleipomena Jeremiou* 6–7, a few references to letters in rabbinic literature and the
Elephantini papyri) and between them and James, in terms of form, structure, content, types
of argumentation or length are not nearly as impressive as those between the Letter of James
and the Pauline epistles. Third, there are problems with the attempt to establish a uniform
category from even these few examples. For instance, Bauckham concludes that James fits
the subcategory of diasporan 'letters of more general advice and paraenesis', of which no
authentic example exists, and the pseudepigraphal ones to which he appeals are either not to
the Diaspora (*The Letter of Jeremiah* addresses Jews in Jerusalem before they are exiled,
according to its narrative framing -- it has no epistolary forms), or could not chronologically
constitute a literary precedent for the historical James on their dating (2 *Baruch* 78–86 is post-
70 CE). That leaves only one letter in the category: James. Lastly, even if we were to grant the
existence of this genre, there is no exegetical basis in the text of James for the claims that 'it
communicates to the Diaspora the teaching of *the revered head* of *the mother church* in
Jerusalem' (Bauckham, *James*, p. 20, emphasis added, to highlight these three terms which do
not appear anywhere in the Letter of James). Likewise, Niebuhr's claim that this letter is an
'apostolischer Diasporabrief' founders on the fact that the author of this letter nowhere
claims to be an apostle or to write with such authority (hence it clearly depends on a *Pauline*

emanate from a 'mother church'. Rather, the authorial voice of the Letter of James is very reminiscent of Paul,[34] with his use of the same vocatives to construct a relationship with readers as recipients, which easily translates across generations by its open-ended and hermeneutically reusable ὑμεῖς and ἀδελφοί μου ἀγαπητοί. There are also favoured locutions, like μὴ πλανᾶσθε (Jas 1.16; 1 Cor. 15.33), and use of question-and-answer style.[35] As with Paul's letters, that from 'James' houses a combination of argument and exhortation composed by means of a fresh combination of appeals to scripture (LXX), experience and common sense intermingled (both echoing words elsewhere attributed to Jesus of Nazareth but rarely or not at all citing him as the responsible for those words). James, as with the Paulines, deftly employs theological shorthand expressions that require expansion from the existing knowledge base of the readers.[36] A key instance is the cryptic formula they hold in common, ὁ κύριος τῆς δόξης (Jas 2.1, with ἡμῶν Ἰησοῦς Χριστός intervening; 1 Cor. 2.8).[37] Others include his self-designation as δοῦλος κυρίου Ἰησοῦ Χριστοῦ (Jas 1.1;[38] Rom. 1.1; Phil. 1.1; cf. Gal. 1.10), the locution παρουσία τοῦ κυρίου (Jas 5.7; 1 Thess. 2.19; 3.13; 5.23; 1 Cor. 15.23),[39]

---

reading of the Letter of James!). And the theological themes to which Niebuhr appeals – unity of the people in relationship to the one god and future expectation – are surely to be found in the Pauline letters, so they do not well serve as the basis for a generic distinction that justifies the claim of independence for the Letter of James from Pauline literary traditions.

34.   With a major exception: the complete lack of reference to the sender's own religious experience as a basis for authority. As commentators have long noted, a strong argument against historical genuineness of authorship is the fact that the epistolary James draws not at all on his special relationship with his brother, either before or after his death (as Paul must do).

35.   Johnson, *Letter of James*, pp. 59–64, accounts for the similarity in diction generally by appeal to the shared diatribe style and common role of the two authors as 'moral teachers', but one certainly could not place Epictetus, for instance, or even Ben Sirach, in their company and find the same level of correspondence in both style, terminology and thematic concerns.

36.   Fuller discussion of this phenomenon in Margaret M. Mitchell, 'Rhetorical Shorthand in Pauline Argumentation: The Functions of "The Gospel" in the Corinthian Correspondence', in *Gospel in Paul: Studies on Corinthians, Galatians and Romans* (Festschrift Richard N. Longenecker; ed. L. A. Jervis and P. Richardson; Sheffield: Sheffield Academic Press, 1994), pp. 63–88.

37.   Which is not found elsewhere in the NT (there is, as is well known, much dispute about how the genitive construes), but see ὁ κύριος τῆς δόξης in another Paulinist document, *Barn.* 21.9.

38.   In compound also with θεοῦ, a self-designation, as commentators have observed, that is odd for 'James the brother of the Lord', if he is the presumed author.

39.   It should be noted that Paul's major shorthand term, εὐαγγέλιον, is, however, not found in James. That author prefers Paul's shorthand for that shorthand, λόγος (e.g., 1 Thess. 1.6; Gal. 6.6; the referents of λόγος in Jas 1.21-23 are widely disputed, perhaps precisely because it *is* shorthand), or λόγος ἀληθείας (Jas 1.18; cf. 2 Cor. 6.7; Eph. 1.13; Col. 1.5).

ὄνομα as an apparent reference to baptism in the name of Jesus (Jas 2.7; 1 Cor. 6.11),[40] ἐκκλησία (Jas 5.14; ubiquitously in Paul's letters from 1 Thess. 1.1 forward), and a constellation of shorthand terms like πίστις τοῦ κυρίου Ἰησοῦ Χριστοῦ, ἔργα and δικαιοσύνη, which serve to redefine the apparently self-evident denotation 'νόμος', either in whole or part (as well as the use of the love command Lev. 19.18).[41] The focal point here is not just the content of these terms and whether the author of James uses them entirely the same way as does Paul,[42] but the literary-theological poetics of shorthand locutions that readers schooled in the Pauline epistolary (including modern scholars!) are used to filling out from a presumed stock of shared assumptions.

The social-historical world constructed in James is also quite similar to that in Paul's letters, with the 'present' set within the template of apocalyptic eschatology, and unspecified (and hence hermeneutically reusable) 'afflictions' or 'trials', occasioning from the author's exhortations to the requisite virtues of wakefulness, strengthened heart[43] and patience. Both engage in discussion of Jewish law and its importance, but strangely for a first-century Jewish context do not mention Sabbath or temple cult.[44] Concern is expressed for 'holiness/sanctification', but it is metaphorical, not connected with cleansing rituals (Jas 1.27; 4.8; 1 Thess. 3.13, etc.). The local situation involves a congregational context (ἐκκλησία) with gatherings including rich and poor (Jas 2.1-7; 1 Cor. 11.17-22), and stereotypical community problems of backbiting, judging, bickering and factions diagnosed as a failure of sectarian boundaries against 'the wisdom of this world' (1 Cor. 1.20; 3.19; Gal. 5.15-21; Jas 3.15-16).

The theological/religious world of the Letter of James also bears much in common with the Pauline letters: monotheism is proclaimed and uncontested (Jas 2.19; 1 Cor. 8.6; cf. Gal. 2.20); 'God' is understood without argument to be the one God of the Scriptures (γραφαί) of Israel,

40.   Compare also other actions done ἐν τῷ ὀνόματι τοῦ κυρίου in Jas 5.10 and 14 and Rom. 15.9; 1 Cor. 5.4; Col. 3.17 (this is a Septuagintalism, however).

41.   Parallels are too numerous to cite, but a comparison of James 1–2 with Romans 2–3 and Galatians 2–6 makes this quite clear.

42.   Like William Brosend, I much enjoyed Sharon Dowd's neat phrase that 'James is using Paul's vocabulary, but not his dictionary' ('Faith that Works: James 2.14-26', *RevExp* 97 [2000], pp. 195–205 [202]). But it is problematic to assume that Paul's dictionary only included one gloss for each term! BDAG has three entries for πίστις and more than ten subcategories within them, and sprinkles Pauline usages liberally among them (and the pseudepigraphal Paulines follow suit).

43.   στηρίξατε τὰς καρδίας ὑμῶν (Jas 5.8); εἰς τὸ στηρίξαι ὑμῶν τὰς καρδίας (1 Thess. 3.13).

44.   The absence of reference to circumcision in James points also to its Paulinist background; as in the deutero-Paulines and Acts, the actual dispute over circumcision of Gentile converts stands in the past, now resolved.

who stands in mythological opposition to the σατανᾶς or διάβολος, with active belief in demons (Jas 2.19; 1 Cor. 10.20-21) and exhortations to petitionary prayer as effective. God is seen as judge (hence concern for ἁμαρτία) but also merciful; humans are enjoined not to engage in judgment here and now, with a strikingly similiar rhetorical barb (σὺ δὲ τίς εἶ ὁ κρίνων τὸν πλησίον; [Jas 4.12]; σὺ τίς εἶ ὁ κρίνων ἀλλότριον οἰκέτην; [Rom. 14.4]). The forms and paradoxes of paraenesis are shared as well: the recipients, addressed as 'you', alternately singular and plural, are admonished and encouraged not just to be hearers (ἀκροαταί) of the law, but doers (ποιηταί) (Jas 1.22-23; Rom. 2.13), even as the ethical impulse to do the good is theoretically already said to be within them (Jas 1.21; Gal. 5.18). Those who do not fulfil the law are called παραβάται (Gal. 2.18; Rom. 2.25, 27; Jas 2.11; 2.9).[45]

Above all, both the author of the Letter of James and Paul and his followers presume that theological advance and change should come from literary texts (letters) and discussion about their meaning;[46] texts beget other texts, which massage and reinterpret the meaning of key statements, words and concepts. The words of Scripture (LXX) are knitted into the arguments, but are not the main focus of exposition (as in a homily, for instance), which seems to be refining Christian traditions against misunderstanding. It is especially in this respect that we can see how much the textual programme of James bears affinities with documents of later Paulinism (ca. 70 to 120 CE). They share the following elements (in common distinction from the genuine Paulines):[47]

a. Pseudepigraphy as a customary vehicle for authoritative teaching for the present grounded in the *Christian* past, including as senders or recipients figures named in Paul's letters (Paul, Peter, James, Timothy, Titus, Barnabas, [Clement?]).[48]

b. Invocation of Paul by name, allusion or textual echo as authoritative teacher.[49]

c. Free incorporation of other materials, both traditional and original, with 'Pauline' teaching.[50]

---

45. The only places the term is used in the NT (with the exception of the unique D text logion inserted at Lk. 6.4).

46. See Gamble on 'the intense literary activity that characterized the Pauline theological tradition in the late first century' (*Books and Readers in the Early Church*, p. 198).

47. I am assuming here the seven Pauline *homologoumena*.

48. The almost total lack of attempt at verisimilitude in James corresponding to a named figure and context (outside of the prescript in 1.1) is closest to the latter two documents, and the Pauline pseudepigraphon Ephesians.

49. Interestingly, this parallels the way Paul invoked Jesus!

50. Because other pseudo-Paulines do this so liberally, it is not a decisive counter-argument to my proposal that not everything in the Letter of James is paralleled in the Pauline epistles (as is indeed the case). Drawing on the other Pauline pseudepigrapha as our

d.   Lack of reference to real disputes over circumcision.

e.   Lack or diminished mention of Paul's characteristic theme of the cross/crucifixion.[51]

f.   De-emphasis on the Christological title 'Son of God'.[52]

g.   Insistence on traditional forms of ethical behaviour (εὐσέβεια in Pastorals; care of the poor and orphans and widows in James).

h.   Emphasis on church offices (ἐπίσκοποι, πρεσβύτεροι) and on the concordant running of the οἶκος.[53]

i.   An attempt to insist upon the 'right interpretation' of Paul, both by re-presenting his authority in one particular manner, and by a two-pronged rhetorical strategy that can also be found in Paul's genuine letters: first, a rhetoric characterized by invective, excoriation, even cursing of the opposition for having misunderstood the 'real' Paul and the traditions he has left behind (e.g., 2 Thess. 2.1-15; 1 Tim. 1.18-20; 4.1-7; 6.20-21; 2 Tim. 1.13-18; 2.14-21; 3.1-9), and second, an irenic appeal to 'the ties that bind' and to a unified ecclesial vision with collegial apostolic roots that extend to the very beginning (Ephesians [esp. 2.14–3.19]; Acts). This involves both placing Paul harmoniously in the company of the other apostles (Eph. 2.20; cf. 3.8!) and fashioning Peter and James in a Pauline mode.[54]

b. *The Letter of James not only shows knowledge of Galatians and/or Romans, but also 1 Corinthians, and hence the author knew the Pauline letters as interpretively shaped by some form of the Pauline letter collection*

The pseudepigraphical Letter of James, 'slave of God and the Lord Jesus Christ', is also 'on the Pauline page'. As stated above, I regard the

---

model (perhaps with one exception, 2 Thessalonians, which so closely fits 1 Thessalonians), that is precisely what we should expect. The new letters do not just restate the past, but they address the present through interpretation of the prior texts and assimilation of new material to them.

51.   This is the case with the Pastorals, not the deutero-Paulines (Eph. 2.16; perhaps Col. 1.20; 2.14).

52.   Two exceptions in the deutero-Paulines are Col. 1.13 and Eph. 4.13.

53.   James does not have a full household code, but it does assume the role of elders in the church (οἱ πρεσβύτεροι τῆς ἐκκλησίας in 5.14), something the genuine Paulines do not, but the Pastorals do (1 Tim. 5.17, 19; 4.14; Tit. 1.5)

54.   With, *inter alia*, Ernst Haenchen, *The Acts of the Apostles: A Commentary* (Hermeneia; Philadelphia: Westminster, 1971), p. 469: '1. Peter's speech is a Lucan composition without value as a historical source; 2. James's scriptural proof cannot possibly derive from him, for it presupposes Hellenistic Gentile Christian interpretation of LXX...the whole scene of [Acts] 15.4-18 is an integral essay on the part of Luke to depict and at the same time justify the ultimate acceptance of the Gentile mission without circumcision.'

arguments for the author of James' knowledge of Galatians, on the basis of Jas 2.14-26, to be convincing. In brief, they are:

a) 'The thesis ἐκ πίστεως μόνον which James contradicts is nowhere met with in the whole literature of Judaism and of the earliest Christianity except only in Paul.'[55]

b) The implicit dichotomy of πίστις and ἔργα in relation to their effectiveness for δικαιοῦσθαι is a uniquely Pauline formulation.

c) The use of δικαιοῦσθαι and σῴζεσθαι as synonyms is characteristic of Pauline soteriological shorthand.

d) The same exemplum of Abraham, and same strategy found in history of Paul's own letters of picking different episodes from the Abraham cycle in Genesis 11–25 to make one's point.

e) The same Scripture quotation, Gen. 15.6, used to pick out the same key terms.

f) Not only the same vocabulary, but even the same parallel antithetical structure:[56]

ἵνα δικαιωθῶμεν ἐκ πίστεως Χριστοῦ καὶ οὐκ ἐξ ἔργων νόμου, ὅτι ἐξ ἔργων νόμου οὐ δικαιωθήσεται πᾶσα σάρξ. (Gal. 2.16)

ἐξ ἔργων δικαιοῦται ἄνθρωπος καὶ οὐκ ἐκ πίστεως μόνον. (Jas 2.24)

But the author of James also had 1 Corinthians in his *corpus Paulinum*,[57] and drew plentifully on it in composing his letter.[58] The most clear evidence of literary dependence is some characteristic patterns of diction in 1 Corinthians found also found in James. Note the following phrases, which keep the same word order in each instance, but differ solely with the adjective (a variation made by Paul himself, as you can see):

---

55. Joachim Jeremias, 'Paul and James', *ExpTim* 66 (1955), pp. 368–71 (368).

56. This is less so for Rom. 3.28, which is materially but not formally similar: λογιζόμεθα γὰρ δικαιοῦσθαι πίστει ἄνθρωπον χωρὶς ἔργων νόμου.

57. I am not the first to argue this. See Edgar J. Goodspeed, *Introduction to the New Testament* (Chicago: University of Chicago Press, 1937), pp. 291–92: 'He shows use of Romans, 1 Corinthians, and Galatians and probably used Ephesians and Philippians. He knows Hebrews, too'; Birger A. Pearson, *The Pneumatikos-Psychikos Terminology in 1 Corinthians. A Study in the Theology of the Corinthian Opponents and its Relation to Gnosticism* (SBLDS, 12; Missoula, MT: Society of Biblical Literature, 1973), p. 14: Syreeni, 'James and the Pauline Legacy', p. 400. Even earlier Mayor, *St. James*, pp. xci–xcix, catalogued a host of resemblances between James and 1 Corinthians as part of his argument for reverse influence ('while St. James has no reference to St. Paul, St. Paul on the contrary writes with constant reference to St. James' [p. xcii]). Differently, see Luedemann, *Opposition to Paul*, p. 145: 'there are no other passages [besides Rom. 4.2-3; 3.28; Gal. 2.16] from the Pauline letters reflected in James'. But what form of the *corpus* could possibly have mediated this patchwork knowledge of the letters?

58. This would explain the preponderance of reference to 1 Corinthians in Bauckham's argument for the commonalities between James and Paul (*James*, pp. 136–40).

Εἴ τις δοκεῖ θρησκὸς εἶναι. (Jas 1.26)
εἰ τις δοκεῖ σοφὸς εἶναι. (1 Cor. 3.18)
Εἰ δέ τις δοκεῖ φιλόνεικος εἶναι. (1 Cor. 11.16)
Εἴ τις δοκεῖ προφήτης εἶναι ἢ πνευματικός. (1 Cor. 14.37)

These four citations the only instances of this syntactical construction in the NT, are in these two letters, James and 1 Corinthians. The same is true of another pair of identical sentences:

Τί τὸ ὄφελος; (Jas 2.14)
τί τὸ ὄφελος; (Jas 2.16)
τί μοι τὸ ὄφελος; (1 Cor. 15.32)[59]

A last, most telling example is:

Μὴ πλανᾶσθε. (Jas 1.16)
Μὴ πλανᾶσθε. (1 Cor. 6.9)
Μὴ πλανᾶσθε. (1 Cor. 15.33)
Μὴ πλανᾶσθε. (Gal. 6.6)

This might seem to be conventional exhortatory vocabulary that could be shared by a host of authors in the ancient world (Christian and non-Christian).[60] However, Paul is actually the first attested user of the phrase in Greek literature and, apart from a single instance in Epictetus (*Diss.* 4.6.23), the phrase is found only in Christian texts.[61] What is most telling is that in usage the imperatival phrase is entirely linked to Paul. Virtually all Christian authors who use it down through late antiquity are quoting one of these Pauline sentences, with two exceptions – Ignatius, who is clearly imitating Paul,[62] and James. I take this as strong evidence that James is alluding to Paul (by quotation or imitation) here, as well. This is confirmed also by the fact that he even follows it up with the Pauline: ἀδελφοί μου ἀγαπητοί.[63]

Dependence on 1 Corinthians is also strikingly clear from places where a concatenation of phrases and content from a section or sections of 1 Corinthians are reprised in James.

---

59.   Observed by Syreeni, 'James and the Pauline Legacy', p. 403 (with n. 24).

60.   Without further evidence one would have to admit this for the parallel ἀλλ' ἐρεῖ τις in Jas 2.18, as in 1 Cor. 15.35, for instance.

61.   The one exception being, strictly speaking, the emperor Julian's quotation of 1 Cor. 6.9 in *contra Galilaeos* 209!

62.   Ignatius quotes 1 Cor. 6.9, beginning with Μὴ πλανᾶσθε in *Eph.* 16.1 and *Phld.* 3.3, so it seems quite clear that (as often) he is imitating Paul when he writes, Μὴ πλανᾶσθε ταῖς ἑτεροδοξίαις μηδὲ μυθεύμασιν τοῖς παλαιοῖς ἀνωφελέσιν οὖσιν in *Magn.* 8.1.

63.   1 Cor. 15.58 ἀδελφοί μου ἀγαπητοί (note exact same word order); also Phil. 4.1. Paul of course can use either ἀδελφοί or ἀγαπητοί alone, also (Rom. 12.19; 1 Cor. 10.14).

δόκιμος γενόμενος λήμψεται τὸν στέφανον τῆς ζωῆς ὃν ἐπηγγείλατο
τοῖς ἀγαπῶσιν αὐτόν. (Jas 1.12)
πᾶς δὲ ὁ ἀγωνιζόμενος πάντα ἐγκρατεύεται, ἐκεῖνοι μὲν οὖν ἵνα
φθαρτὸν στέφανον λάβωσιν, ἡμεῖς δὲ ἄφθαρτον ... ἀλλὰ ὑπωπιάζω
μου τὸ σῶμα καὶ δουλαγωγῶ, μή πως ἄλλοις κηρύξας αὐτὸς
ἀδόκιμος γένωμαι. (1 Cor. 9.25-27) cf. earlier: ἃ ἡτοίμασεν ὁ θεὸς τοῖς
ἀγαπῶσιν αὐτόν.

Here the James sentence grabs the full gist of Paul's argument in 1 Cor.
9.25-27, undoes the litotes of a favoured Pauline term[64] (from
μή...ἀδόκιμος to δόκιμος) and compresses the athletic imagery into
terse formulation, combining it also with the notion of apocalyptic divine
gifts found in the enigmatic 1 Cor. 2.9.

This method of use – by contextual recasting and recombination – of 1
Corinthians can also be found in the following:

οὐχ ὁ θεὸς ἐξελέξατο τοὺς πτωχοὺς τῷ κόσμῳ πλουσίους ἐν πίστει
καὶ κληρονόμους τῆς βασιλείας ἧς ἐπηγγείλατο τοῖς ἀγαπῶσιν
αὐτόν; (Jas 2.5)

ἀλλὰ τὰ μωρὰ τοῦ κόσμου ἐξελέξατο ὁ θεὸς ἵνα καταισχύνῃ τοὺς
σοφούς, καὶ τὰ ἀσθενῆ τοῦ κόσμου ἐξελέξατο ὁ θεὸς ἵνα καταισχύνῃ τὰ
ἰσχυρά, καὶ τὰ ἀγενῆ τοῦ κόσμου καὶ τὰ ἐξουθενημένα ἐξελέξατο ὁ
θεός, τὰ μὴ ὄντα, ἵνα τὰ ὄντα καταργήσῃ. (1 Cor. 1.27-28)
ἢ οὐκ οἴδατε ὅτι ἄδικοι θεοῦ βασιλείαν οὐ κληρονομήσουσιν; μὴ
πλανᾶσθε. (1 Cor. 6.9) ἃ ἡτοίμασεν ὁ θεὸς τοῖς ἀγαπῶσιν αὐτόν. (1
Cor. 2.9)

A final example of this combinatory hermeneutic throws into relief a
major element in how the author of James understood 1 Corinthians:

οὐκ ἔστιν αὕτη ἡ σοφία ἄνωθεν κατερχομένη, ἀλλὰ ἐπίγειος, ψυχική,
δαιμονιώδης. ὅπου γὰρ ζῆλος καὶ ἐριθεία, ἐκεῖ ἀκαταστασία καὶ πᾶν
φαῦλον πρᾶγμα. (1 Jas. 3.15-16):
ψυχικὸς δὲ ἄνθρωπος οὐ δέχεται τὰ τοῦ πνεύματος τοῦ θεοῦ, μωρία
γὰρ αὐτῷ ἐστιν, καὶ οὐ δύναται γνῶναι... ἔτι γὰρ σαρκικοί ἐστε.
ὅπου γὰρ ἐν ὑμῖν ζῆλος καὶ ἔρις, οὐχὶ σαρκικοί ἐστε καὶ κατὰ
ἄνθρωπον περιπατεῖτε; (1 Cor. 2.14-3.3)
οὐ γάρ ἐστιν ἀκαταστασίας ὁ θεὸς ἀλλὰ εἰρήνης. (1 Cor. 14.33)

In particular, the author who adopts the name 'James' found the unity
topoi and terminology Paul had used in 1 Corinthians[65] particularly
congenial to his purposes. Shared lexical terms used to refer to

---

64. Both terms are found only in Pauline and pseudo-Pauline texts elsewhere in the NT.
65. Arguments for this reading may be found in Mitchell, *Paul and the Rhetoric of
Reconciliation.*

factionalism, *which in several cases significantly are found mostly or exclusively in 1 Corinthians*[66] *and James in the NT*, include:

    a. ἀκαταστασία/ἀκατάστατος (1 Cor. 14.33; Jas 1.8; 3.16).[67]
    b. ζῆλος conjoined with ἔρις/ἐριθεία (1 Cor. 3.3; Jas 3.14, 16).[68]
    c. ζηλοῦσθαι (1 Cor. 13.4; cf. 12.31; 14.1, 39; Jas 4.2).
    d. ψυχικός (1 Cor. 2.14; 15.44, 46; Jas 3.15).[69]
    e. μέλος (1 Cor. 6.15; 12.12, 14, 18, 19, 20, 22, 25, 26, 27; Jas 3.5, 6; 4.1).
    f. (κατα)καυχᾶσθαι (1 Cor. 1.29, 31; 3.21; 4.7; 13.3; Jas 1.9; 2.13; 3.14; 4.16).[70]
    g. κενή, -ός (1 Cor. 15.14 – of πίστις; Jas 2.20 of a man with idle πίστις).

This understanding of 1 Corinthians as an argument for concord in the ἐκκλησία which draws upon popular Greek political *topoi* extends also to the author of the Letter of James' appropriation of some of those *topoi* – tellingly, in their Christianized Pauline form – in his letter:

    a. Body and members, used both for individuals and the corporate entity, one member or other singled out for its role in relation to the health of the whole (1 Cor. 6.15-20; 12.12-13; Jas 3.5-6; 4.1).
    b. Factional strife as wisdom of 'this world', contrasted with spiritual wisdom, an unbridgeable dichotomy between which the hearer must choose allegiance (1 Cor. 1.18–4.21; Jas 3.13–4.12).
    c. Chiding for bad boasts (1 Cor. 5.6; Jas 4.16, etc.).
    d. Remedy of keeping your eye on the eschatological prize (9.24-27; Jas 1.12; 3.1; 5.1-8).
    e. Diagnosis that judging in the present leads to strife, and needs to be tempered by orientation to the threat of eschatological judgment to come (1 Cor. 4.1-5; Jas 4.11-12).

This body of evidence – patterns of diction, verbal linkages,[71] *topoi* and contextualized usage of the argument of 1 Corinthians – seems to me very

---

66.   In a few cases also in another Pauline letter (see notes 68 and 70).

67.   With one exception (Lk. 21.9), these terms are found in the NT only in James and Paul (also 2 Cor. 6.5; 12.20).

68.   Paul likes the pair, and also sets ἔρις and ἐριθεία in play together; see also 2 Cor. 12.20; Gal. 5.20.

69.   This word is only found here and in Jude 19 in the NT. Pearson (*Pneumatikos-Psychikos Terminology*, p. 14) posited James' dependence on 1 Corinthians for the term (discussion in Mitchell, *Paul and the Rhetoric of Reconciliation*, p. 212, n. 137).

70.   As is very well known, the language of boasting is a special predilection of Paul, who includes 56 instances collectively of the four cognate terms καυχᾶσθαι/κατακαυχᾶσθαι/καύχημα/καύχησις in the seven genuine letters. The only other NT writers to use it are the deutero-Pauline authors in Eph. 2.9; 2 Thess. 1.4; Heb. 3.6 and the author of James (fully five instances, employing three different cognate terms).

71.   To these we should also add the only uses of the term κριτήριον in the NT, in reference to court cases dividing the church community (1 Cor. 6.2, 4; Jas 2.6).

strong evidence that the author of James knew 1 Corinthians,[72] as well as Galatians.

c. *If the author of the Letter of James knew a collection of Paul's letters including at least 1 Corinthians and Galatians,[73] and incorporated elements of both in his letter, he may have been addressing some of the tensions between the two letters that later Pauline interpreters sensed so acutely*

Galatians and 1 Corinthians represent in some ways quite different, even conflicting Pauline voices, the former an adamant argument for the sole truth of his gospel in the face of other missionaries urging compulsory adherence to 'the law', and the latter an active plea for conciliation in the face of divisiveness, regarded as a 'worldly' and 'fleshly' pursuit not befitting the ἐκκλησία. It is here that fourth-century Pauline commentators help us to see that the earliest collection of the *corpus Paulinum*, even as it served to render 'occasional' and audience-specific writings available to a universalizing audience, would have revealed ways in which Paul was inconsistent and in various respects left a problematic legacy. It is clear that Galatians in particular was a problem, both for its combative tone and the evidence it gave of conflict between Paul and James and Cephas/ Peter. John Chrysostom, for instance, found Paul's words to Peter at Antioch so problematic that he devoted a special homily to them, and he addressed the problem of Pauline θυμός from the outset of his continuous commentary on Galatians.[74] The following excerpts from the occasional homily on Gal. 2.11-14 reveal the difficulty John saw in reading Galatians and 1 Corinthians side by side:

> So then, does it not disturb each person who hears this, that Paul stood up against Peter, that the pillars of the church are colliding and striking against one another [Ἄρα οὖν οὐ θορυβεῖ ἕκαστον τῶν ἀκουόντων τοῦτο, ὅτι Παῦλος ἀντέστη τῷ Πέτρῳ, ὅτι οἱ στῦλοι τῆς Ἐκκλησίας συγκρούονται καὶ ἀλλήλοις προσπίπτουσι]? ... Perhaps you praised Paul for his outspokenness, because he did not fear the station of the person in question, because for the sake of the gospel he did not blush before those present. But even if this is a praise of Paul, it redounds to

---

72. I would posit that this case is as strong as or stronger than that Johnson (who denies the use of Pauline letters by the author of James) seeks to make for the use of James by the author of *1 Clement* (Johnson, *Brother of Jesus*, pp. 52-56, 91-96).

73. There are good reasons to think that the author had a collection that contained also at least Romans, but I cannot go into that here. For the purposes of this argument it is enough to say that the tensions between Galatians and 1 Corinthians in the *corpus* are most striking, even as Romans may have acted (I think it did act) as a buffer between the two, and may have been an influence on this author (as on others in the history of Pauline interpretation) in seeking a middle path.

74. Πολλοῦ τὸ προοίμιον γέμει θυμοῦ καὶ μεγάλου φρονήματος (John Chrysostom, *comm. in Gal.* 1.1 [*PG* vol. 61, col. 611]).

our shame. Why, if Paul acted rightly? Because then Peter did badly, if Paul was not acting rightly. What gain then is it to me when either one of the yoked pair is hamstrung [Τί οὖν ἐμοὶ τὸ ὄφελος, ὅταν τῆς ξυνωρίδος θάτερος ἵππος χωλεύῃ]? . . .

Did you praise Paul? Hear now how what is said is a cause of accusation against Paul, if we do not hunt down the hidden sense in the words. What do you say, Paul? Did you rebuke Peter 'when you saw that he did not act rightly toward the truth of the gospel'? Well done. Then for what reason did you do it 'to his face'? For what reason 'before them all'? Was it not necessary to make the reproof without a witness present? Why is it that you set the trial in public and caused many to be witnesses of the accusation? Further, who would not say that you are doing this from enmity and envy and contentiousness? *Were not you the one who said, 'I have been to the weak as weak'* (1 Cor. 9.22) [καὶ τίς οὐκ ἂν εἴποι, ὅτι ἐξ ἀπεχθείας τοῦτο ποιεῖς, καὶ φθόνου, καὶ φιλονεικίας; οὐ σὺ ἦσθα ὁ λέγων,' Ἐγενόμην τοῖς ἀσθενέσιν ὡς ἀσθενής;] What does it mean 'to the weak as weak'? 'Accommodating and wrapping up their wounds', he says, 'and not allowing them to fall into shamelessness'. Then, if you were so full of care and philanthropy for the disciples, were you a misanthrope concerning your fellow apostle? . . . And what could be more fervent than Paul, who day by day died for the sake of Christ (1 Cor. 15.31)? But now our homily is not about courage (for what does that have to do with the case at hand?), but *whether Paul was in a state of enmity toward the apostle*, or whether this fight was a matter of some vainglory or contentiousness [ἀλλ' εἰ ἀπεχθῶς πρὸς τὸν ἀπόστολον διέκειτο, ἢ εἰ κενοδοξίας τινὸς καὶ φιλονεικίας ἦν αὕτη ἡ μάχη]. But not even this can one say. No way! For Paul was not only the slave of Peter, the highest of those saints, but even of all the apostles collectively, and though he outstripped all of them in his labours, yet nevertheless he used to consider himself to be least: *'For,' he said, 'I am the least of the apostles, who am not worthy to be called an apostle'* (1 Cor. 15.9). And not only of the apostles, but even of all the saints collectively. For 'to me', he said, 'the least of all the saints, this grace was given' (Eph. 3.8).[75]

A second example, from Pelagius, brings us immediately to the theme of faith and works and the direct juxtaposition of 1 Corinthians and Romans:

Some people abuse this passage [Rom. 3.28 = Gal. 2.16] to annihilate works of justice, affirming that faith alone is able to suffice [for one baptized], *although the same apostle said in another place, 'And if I have all faith, so that I even move mountains, but I do not have love, I receive no benefit'* [1 Cor. 13.2]. . . *But if these statements* [i.e., Rom.

---

75. John Chrysostom, *In faciem ei restiti*, selections from paragraphs 3 and 7 (*PG* vol. 51, cols. 372–74, 378), my translation.

3.28 and 1 Cor. 13.2 (and Rom. 13.10)] *appear to be contradictory to the sense of the former*, 'apart from what works [of the law]' is the apostle believed to have said a human being is justified by faith? Surely [the works] of circumcision and sabbath and others like those, but not works of justice, *about which blessed James said*, 'faith without works is dead' [Jas 2.26].[76]

In Pelagius' view, 'the blessed James' serves as a mediating force between Paul and himself, that is, between the Paul of Galatians/Romans and that of 1 Corinthians, particularly on the issue of faith. For him 1 Cor. 13.2 is no less 'Pauline' in its depiction of faith than Rom. 3.28/Gal. 2.16. Pelagius, like Augustine (with whom he is in agreement on this point!), was a faithful reader of Paul, seeking to interpret the epistolary apostle toward the issues of his day. Was he reading James against the grain, or replicating the very purpose this Letter of James sought to enact? Were these late-fourth-century writers (to whom we can add Augustine, with whom this essay began) the first to notice these tensions inside the *corpus Paulinum*, and attempt to mediate them textually? The answer to that question is clearly no, and it leads me to my final proposition.

d. *James is no more 'anti-Pauline' than other early authors whose Pauline pedigree is impeccable, and utterly unquestioned*

Calling the Letter of James 'anti-Pauline' assumes that in the eyes of its author Paul and his followers were opponents who stood outside of his orbit. But many of the earliest Paulinists – the writer of *1 Clement*, Ignatius of Antioch, Polycarp of Smyrna, the author of Acts – were, like that author, seeking to reconcile the epistolary Paul with himself and with the 'pillars' he contentiously (and, for later interpreters, rather embarrassingly) named in Gal. 2.6-9, 11-14. The author of the Letter of James was neither the first nor the last Paulinist to use Paul's political rhetoric of concord in 1 Corinthians to soften more extreme interpretations of the apostle and his theological legacy.[77] James is in many ways closest in this

---

76.   *Abutuntur quidam hoc loco* [Rom 3.28 = Gal. 2.16] *ad destructionem operum iustitiae, solam fidem [baptizato] posse sufficere adfirmantes, cum idem alibi dicat apostolus:* 'et si habuero omnem fidem, ita ut montes transferam, caritatem autem non habeam, nihil mihi prodest' [1 Cor. 13.2] ... *quod si haec eorum sensui uidentur esse contraria, sine quibus operibus [legis] apostolus iustificari hominem per fidem dixisse credendus est? scilicet circumcisionis uel sabbati et ceterorum huius[ce]modi, non absque iustitiae operibus, de quibus beatus Iacobus dicit:* 'fides sine operibus mortua est' [Jas 2.26] (Pelagius, *expositio in Romanos* 3.28), 34 (text Alexander Souter, *Pelagius' Expositions of Thirteen Epistles of St. Paul* [2 vols.; Cambridge: Cambridge University Press, 1926], my translation). I thank Prof. Mark Reasoner for drawing my attention to this passage in connection to the present argument.

77.   I would include the author of Ephesians here, as well.

regard to *1 Clement*[78] – a document which overtly acknowledges the author's knowledge of 1 Corinthians (47.1-3).[79] *1 Clement* can also be seen to temper the potentially divisive effects of Galatians by recourse to Paul's own rhetoric of reconciliation of 1 Corinthians. In the process we see the same combinatory hermeneutic observed in 'James' use of 1 Corinthians, and in so doing observe how Paul's statements about δικαιοσύνη in Gal. 2.16 are softened along lines very similar to what we see in Jas 2.14-26. Here I can give just a few illustrations.

The author opens the letter with concern, in Paul's own terms, with the newest generation of Corinthian factionalists: Ἐκ τούτου ζῆλος καὶ φθόνος, καὶ ἔρις καὶ στάσις, διωγμὸς καὶ ἀκαταστασία, πόλεμος καὶ αἰχμαλωσία (*1 Clem.* 3.2). In ch. 5 the author seeks to link Peter and Paul together *as pillars* (rather than reserving the term for the Jerusalem leaders, as Paul had in Gal. 2.9), and as victims commonly of poisonous rivalry at the hands of others (rather than opposing one another 'face to face' [Gal. 2.11]): Διὰ ζῆλον καὶ φθόνον οἱ μέγιστοι καὶ δικαιότατοι στῦλοι ἐδιώχθησαν καὶ ἕως θανάτου ἤθλησαν (*1 Clem.* 5.2). Paul for this author is associated with δικαιοσύνη, but not in opposition to faith (κῆρυξ γενόμενος ἔν τε τῇ ἀνατολῇ καὶ ἐν τῇ δύσει, τὸ γενναῖον τῆς πίστεως αὐτοῦ κλέος ἔλαβεν, δικαιοσύνην διδάξας ὅλον τὸν κόσμον, καὶ ἐπὶ τὸ τέρμα τῆς δύσεως ἐλθὼν καὶ μαρτυρήσας ἐπὶ τῶν ἡγουμένων, οὕτως ἀπηλλάγη τοῦ κόσμου καὶ εἰς τὸν ἅγιον τόπον ἀνελήμφθη ὑπομονῆς γενόμενος μέγιστος ὑπογραμμός [5.6-7]).

Similarly, the Pauline *exemplum* of Abraham, together with the Scriptural tag of Gen. 15.6, is moderated from a 'faith only' stance by reference to his famous acts: Ἐπίστευσεν δὲ Ἀβραὰμ τῷ θεῷ, καὶ ἐλογίσθη αὐτῷ εἰς δικαιοσύνην. Διὰ πίστιν καὶ φιλοξενίαν ἐδόθη αὐτῷ υἱὸς ἐν γήρᾳ, καὶ δι' ὑπακοῆς προσήνεγκεν αὐτὸν θυσίαν τῷ θεῷ πρὸς ἕν τῶν ὀρέων ὧν ἔδειξεν αὐτῷ (*1 Clem.* 10.6-7). The same is true of Rahab, of course: Διὰ πίστιν καὶ φιλοξενίαν ἐσώθη Ραὰβ ἡ πόρνη. [12.1]), who is a complementary *exemplum* with Abraham also in James 2. This is consistent with the summary comment about the patriarch in *1 Clem.* 31.2: Τίνος χάριν ηὐλογήθη ὁ πατὴρ ἡμῶν Ἀβραάμ, οὐχὶ δικαιοσύνην καὶ ἀλήθειαν διὰ πίστεως ποιήσας.

The combinatory Pauline hermeneutic we have discussed in James is (as is widely recognized) easily evident in passage of *1 Clement* such as: Μὴ

---

78. Luedemann, *Opposition to Paul*, pp. 147–48 rather astoundingly seeks to call *1 Clement* and James 'documents of an un-Pauline Christianity'. But the basis for this distinction is his own unique categories which govern his judgments ('one must make a distinction between what the author attempted and what he really presents' [p. 288, n. 42]).

79. But not the Letter of James! Johnson (*Brother of Jesus*, pp. 91–96) argues that the author of *1 Clement* knew the Letter of James, but it is just as possible, if not more likely, that the author of James knew *1 Clement* (unfortunately I do not have enough time to pursue the crucial δίψυχος question here!), and learned some of his conciliatory hermeneutic from it.

καυχάσθω ὁ σοφὸς ἐν τῇ σοφίᾳ αὐτοῦ μηδὲ ὁ ἰσχυρὸς ἐν τῇ ἰσχύϊ αὐτοῦ μηδὲ ὁ πλούσιος ἐν τῷ πλούτῳ αὐτοῦ, ἀλλ' ὁ καυχώμενος ἐν κυρίῳ καυχάσθω, τοῦ ἐκζητεῖν αὐτὸν καὶ ποιεῖν κρίμα καὶ δικαιοσύνην (13.1), or Κολληθῶμεν οὖν ἐκείνοις, οἷς ἡ χάρις ἀπὸ τοῦ θεοῦ δέδοται· ἐνδυσώμεθα τὴν ὁμόνοιαν ταπεινοφρονοῦντες, ἐγκρατευόμενοι, ἀπὸ παντὸς ψιθυρισμοῦ καὶ καταλαλιᾶς πόρρω ἑαυτοὺς ποιοῦντες, ἔργοις δικαιούμενοι καὶ μὴ λόγοις (30.3). The softening of Gal. 2.16 – by employment of unity *topoi* in or inspired by 1 Corinthians – in a passage like *1 Clement* 32–34 is unmistakable. Like the writer of the Pastoral Epistles,[80] the author of *1 Clement* affirms Paul's emphasis on the signal role of faith in justification (οὐ δι' ἑαυτῶν δικαιούμεθα οὐδὲ διὰ τῆς ἡμετέρας σοφίας ἢ συνέσεως ἢ εὐσεβείας ἢ ἔργων ὧν κατειργασάμεθα ἐν ὁσιότητι καρδίας, ἀλλὰ διὰ τῆς πίστεως, δι' ἧς πάντας τοὺς ἀπ' αἰῶνος ὁ παντοκράτωρ θεὸς ἐδικαίωσεν [32.4]), even as he issues in the next breath the exhortation: 'let us work the work of justification with our whole heart!' (ἐξ ὅλης τῆς ἰσχύος ἡμῶν ἐργασώμεθα ἔργον δικαιοσύνης).[81]

The same is true for the Letter of Polycarp to the Philippians, which is also explicit in referring to Paul's letters as authoritative and citing them both selectively and interpretively. Polycarp repeats the Eph. 2.8 recasting of the antithesis Gal. 2.16: in 1.3, ὅτι χάριτί ἐστε σεσωσμένοι, οὐκ ἐξ ἔργων, but then can posit that resurrection is conditional upon deeds (ὁ δὲ ἐγείρας αὐτὸν ἐκ νεκρῶν καὶ ἡμᾶς ἐγερεῖ, ἐὰν ποιῶμεν αὐτοῦ τὸ θέλημα καὶ πορευώμεθα ἐν ταῖς ἐντολαῖς αὐτοῦ καὶ ἀγαπῶμεν, ἃ ἠγάπησεν [2.2]). Praising Paul's letters, and even emulating his use of the triad of faith, hope and love, Polycarp, who names the topic of his own letter as δικαιοσύνη (Ταῦτα, ἀδελφοί, οὐκ ἐμαυτῷ ἐπιτρέψας γράφω ὑμῖν περὶ τῆς δικαιοσύνης [3.1]), urges attendance on neighbour-love (as did Paul in Gal. 5.14), and says that the person who remains in those three things 'has fulfilled the commandment of justification' (πεπλήρωκεν ἐντολὴν δικαιοσύνης [3.3]).

If the Letter of James shares this harmonizing Paulinist hermeneutic, then why has the 'anti-Pauline' charge even been levelled? Luther's disparagement of the epistle ('we should throw the epistle of James out of this school!')[82] has of course played an enormous role in the history of research since early modernity, but also the prosopopoeia with τις in Jas 2.14, 16, 18 has temptingly been applied *to Paul* (rather than *another Pauline reader*, as in the Pastorals). But ironically one can regard that τις

---

80. e.g., 1 Tim. 2.10; 3.1; 5.10, 25; 6.18; 2 Tim. 2.21; 3.17; 4.14; cf. 1.9!; Tit. 1.16; 2.7, 14; 3.1, 5, 8, 14.

81. ἀλλὰ σπεύσωμεν μετὰ ἐκτενείας καὶ προθυμίας πᾶν ἔργον ἀγαθὸν ἐπιτελεῖν (1 Clem. 33.1); Ἴδωμεν, ὅτι ἐν ἔργοις ἀγαθοῖς πάντες ἐκοσμήθησαν οἱ δίκαιοι, καὶ αὐτὸς δὲ ὁ κύριος ἔργοις ἀγαθοῖς ἑαυτὸν κοσμήσας ἐχάρη (1 Clem. 33.7).

82. '*Epistolam Iacobi eiciemus ex hac schola, denn sie soll nichts. Nullam syllabam habet de Christo*' (Martin Luther, 'Tischreden' no. 5443 [1542], vol. 5, p. 157). I cite this impassioned injunction from Luther because it is less well-known than the famous 'epistle of straw' epithet.

as itself a Pauline inheritance, for the apostle himself used that rhetorical question form (τις) to raise and dismiss a possible false interpretation of his words by one of his own readers in 1 Cor. 15.35.

4. *Conclusion*

I have argued that scholars cannot merely sidestep the question of the relationship of the Letter of James to Paul, as recent voices have sought to, but would do well to reorient the question in two ways from the older approaches: (1) away from overly rigid assumptions about what is truly Paul or misunderstood Paul, and (2) toward investigation of James' Paulinism in relation to the history of the *corpus Paulinum* and its earliest interpreters. If it can be shown that the author of the Letter of James knew, not just Galatians and/or Romans, but also 1 Corinthians, then we should take seriously the impact of the hermeneutical tensions inherent in even the early forms of the collection of Paul's letters on this act of Pauline interpretation. Seen in this way the author of James, like the author of *1 Clement* and Polycarp, saw the rhetoric of reconciliation in Paul's 1 Corinthians to be a resource for resolving the tensions caused by its proximity to Galatians, which we know from later interpretation to have left a problematic Pauline legacy. At first glance this might sound like a return to the older Baur theory of 'early catholicism' reconciling Gentile and Jewish Christianity, but it is not, for the reconciliation I posit here is entirely within Gentile Christianity, that is, within the Paulinist literary traditions. The historical James, 'the brother of the Lord', may well have represented something *we* might choose to call and recover as 'Jewish Christianity', but his own authentic voice has not been preserved, probably because he was not an author (and why should he have been?)

So why a letter from 'James a slave of God and the Lord Jesus Christ' to address pastoral questions among later Gentile Christians, and resolve tensions evident within the *corpus Paulinum*? The answer can reasonably be found in the scandal that results from the authority ascribed to Galatians in the earliest collection of the Pauline epistles in the late first century: like 1 Peter (with which many see a direct literary relationship), the Letter of James is a conscious attempt to include all parties at the notorious 'Antioch incident' as actually (despite Gal. 2.10-14) on the same page (cf. Acts 15). The authorial prescript uses a Pauline self-designation (cf. Rom. 1.1; Phil. 1.1; Gal. 1.10; Tit. 1.1; cf. Jude 1) to introduce a Pauline 'tool' (the epistle as vehicle of teaching) in which the named author, James, has no definable self-characterization thereafter, but presents a theological formulation that reconciles Paul with Paul and, implicitly, Paul with the 'pillars'. It is significant in this respect that our two focal texts, Galatians and 1 Corinthians, are the only Pauline letters that mention 'James' (1 Cor. 15.7; cf. 9.5; Gal. 1.19; 2.9, 12).

An Assessment of the Rhetoric and Rhetorical Analysis of the Letter of James

Duane F. Watson

Interpreters of the Epistle of James have frequently remarked that it lacks literary and thematic structure. Martin Dibelius boldly asserted of James that, '*the entire document lacks continuity in thought*. There is not only a lack of continuity in thought between individual sayings and other smaller units, but also between larger treatises.'[1] This lack of continuity is usually attributed to the predominant role of paraenesis in the epistle; the paraenesis being understood as exhortation arranged like pearls on a string with no intended order.[2] This understanding was concretized and popularized by Dibelius in his commentary on James that has wielded enormous influence to this day.[3] Dibelius claimed that James shared important characteristics with paraenesis: 'pervasive eclecticism' and 'lack of continuity'.[4] Stanley Stowers is correct to state that, 'James consists of a series of seemingly disjointed hortatory *topoi* without any apparent unifying model or models.'[5] There is rhetorical structure, but a unifying rhetorical model has not been found.

However, there is an emerging consensus that James has considerable rhetorical structure originating within the Jewish and Graeco-Roman rhetorical traditions. Wilhelm Wuellner's investigation of the rhetoric of the Epistle of James published in 1978 was a major impetus to the modern

---

1. Martin Dibelius, *James: Commentary on the Epistle of James* (ed. H. Koester; rev. H. Greeven; trans. M. Williams; Hermeneia; Philadelphia: Fortress, 1976), p. 1.

2. Stanley K. Stowers, *Letter Writing in Greek Antiquity* (LEC, 5; Philadelphia: Westminster, 1986), p. 97. For assessment of the structure of the Epistle of James, see Peter H. Davids, *The Epistle of James: A Commentary on the Greek Text* (NIGTC; Grand Rapids: Eerdmans, 1982), pp. 22–28; Luke Timothy Johnson, *The Letter of James* (AB, 37A; New York: Doubleday, 1995), pp. 11–16; Ralph P. Martin, *James* (WBC, 48; Waco, TX: Word, 1988), pp. xcviii–civ; Ernst Baasland, 'Literarische Form, Thematik und geschichtliche Einordnung des Jakobusbriefes', *ANRW* 2.25.5, pp. 3646–84 (3648–61).

3. Dibelius, *James*, pp. 5–7.

4. Dibelius, *James*, p. 5.

5. Stowers, *Letter Writing*, p. 97.

study of the rhetoric of this epistle.[6] Current rhetorical analysis of James has discovered much about its invention, arrangement, style and overall rhetorical strategy. This discovery began primarily as a description of the rhetoric, but now includes an effort to determine the function of the rhetoric as well. As rhetorical criticism of James matures, so does our grasp of its rhetorical and historical contexts, as well as its social, cultural and ideological textures.

It is the objective of this essay to assess the rhetorical criticism of the Epistle of James to date. This essay will identify current issues in the rhetorical criticism of this epistle.[7] The rhetorical criticism of James is part of several current issues in the broader work of rhetorical criticism of the NT. Such issues include the appropriate role of ancient and modern rhetoric in rhetorical analysis of the NT, the rhetorical role of paraenesis and features of the diatribe in a literary work, the role of rhetoric in epistolary theory and ancient letters, the extent of the rhetorical training of the biblical authors, new developments in intertextuality and socio-rhetorical criticism and the classification of NT letters within ancient rhetorical traditions. To the current study I would like to add my own proposal which I think takes many of these issues into consideration.

1. *The Selection of Ancient Rhetoric or Modern Rhetoric or Both as a Basis for Rhetorical Analysis*

Rhetorical critics analysing James have the choice of using Graeco-Roman rhetoric, modern rhetoric or a combination of the two. They are also at liberty to be interdisciplinary and combine rhetorical criticism with other disciplines, such as social-scientific studies. Using Graeco-Roman rhetoric places James in its oral and written culture and analyses it by the conventions of invention, arrangement and style of its day. Using modern rhetoric places the letter within a broader understanding of rhetoric conceptualized in contemporary terms. This conceptualization contains the improvements in rhetorical study that have occurred since the Graeco-Roman era.

To date a large proportion of rhetorical criticism of James has used Graeco-Roman rhetorical convention that was basic to education, utilized in speeches and epistles and systematized in rhetorical handbooks. Such criticism has particularly relied on the methodology of George Kennedy

---

6. Wilhelm Wuellner, 'Der Jakobusbrief im Licht der Rhetorik und Textpragmatik', *LB* 43 (1978), pp. 5–66.

7. For a discussion of the rhetorical criticism of the Epistle of James and the Catholic Epistles as a whole, see Duane F. Watson, 'Rhetorical Criticism of Hebrews and the Catholic Epistles Since 1978', *CRBS* 5 (1997), pp. 175–207.

that utilizes Graeco-Roman rhetoric.[8] Many interpreters legitimately find
rhetorical criticism of the NT using Graeco-Roman rhetoric to be
limited.[9] They argue that modern rhetoric addresses theoretical, practical
and philosophical problems posed by speech that Graeco-Roman
rhetorical theory does not address. Modern rhetoric is the reconceptual-
ization of Graeco-Roman rhetoric, such as the New Rhetoric and much
more.[10] Modern rhetoric is often used in combination with other related
methodologies to create unique interdisciplinary studies. Using Graeco-
Roman and modern rhetoric to analyse James has proven very fruitful.

a. *The Role of Graeco-Roman Rhetoric*

J. H. Ropes gave this assessment of the relation of James to Graeco-
Roman rhetoric: 'As in the diatribes, there is a general controlling motive
in the discussion, but no firm and logically disposed structure giving a
strict unity to the whole and no trace of the conventional arrangement
recommended by the elegant rhetoricians.'[11] However, recent rhetorical
criticism of the Epistle of James using Graeco-Roman rhetoric seriously
challenges the latter part of this assessment. There are 'traces of
conventional arrangement recommended by the elegant rhetoricians'
found in this epistle as we will now demonstrate.

Using Kennedy's method of rhetorical criticism, Van der Westhuizen
analyses Jas 2.14-26.[12] He classifies this section as deliberative rhetoric
because it seeks to persuade the audience to take action (add faith to
works), its main argumentation is based on examples (that of Abraham
and Rahab) and it emphasizes the advantage of taking the course of
action prescribed by the author (salvation and justification).[13] He
identifies the basis or stasis of the argument as fact because this section
seeks to answer the question: 'What kind of faith is real'? (However, as he
defines it, this question concerns the nature of something which is
indicative of the stasis of quality.)

8. George A. Kennedy, *New Testament Interpretation through Rhetorical Criticism*
(Chapel Hill: University of North Carolina Press, 1984).

9. For this critique and its assessment, see Duane F. Watson and A. J. Hauser, *Rhetorical
Criticism of the Bible: A Comprehensive Bibliography with Notes on History and Method* (BIS,
4; Leiden: E. J. Brill, 1994), pp. 109–12; Duane F. Watson, 'Rhetorical Criticism of the
Pauline Epistles Since 1975', *CRBS* 3 (1995), pp. 219–48 (220–22).

10. Chaïm Perelman and Lucie Olbrechts-Tyteca, *The New Rhetoric: A Treatise on
Argumentation* (trans. J. Wilkinson and P. Weaver; Notre Dame: University of Notre Dame
Press, 1969).

11. James H. Ropes, *A Critical and Exegetical Commentary on the Epistle of St. James*
(ICC; Edinburgh: T&T Clark, 1916), p. 14.

12. J. D. N. Van der Westhuizen, 'Stylistic Techniques and Their Functions in James
2.14-26', *Neot* 25 (1991), pp. 89–107.

13. Van der Westhuizen, 'Stylistic Techniques', pp. 91–92.

Van der Westhuizen discusses the invention, arrangement and style of this pericope in depth. The pericope employs logos, ethos and pathos – the three proofs of invention. Particularly noteworthy are external proofs from Scripture (2.21, 25) and internal or artistic proofs. The latter include inductive and deductive proofs. Inductive proofs are from examples drawn from everyday life (2.15-16), Jewish tradition (2.21-25) and nature (2.26). Deductive proof is from an enthymeme (2.26).[14] He suggests that the pericope is a form of *synkrisis* that compares faith without works to faith with works.

Van der Westhuizen describes the arrangement of 2.14-26 as *proem* (v. 14), proposition (vv. 14, 17), possible *narratio* (vv. 15-16), proof (vv. 18-25) and epilogue (v. 26).[15] He demonstrates that the pericope employs a host of stylistic techniques common to Jewish tradition and Graeco-Roman literature of the period. These include metonymy, hyperbaton, *inclusio*, epanadiplosis, duadiplosis, erotesis, irony, homoeoteleuton, personification, antimetathesis, apostrophe, parallelism, paronomasia, polysyndeton, euphemism, prosopographia, simile and epexegesis. He emphasizes that the style of this section clarifies and amplifies the argumentation and helps the author address the rhetorical situation.[16] This study clearly demonstrates that Graeco-Roman rhetorical elements of invention, arrangement and style are found in James.

While a fine analysis, especially of style, Van der Westhuizen's study too rigidly applies Kennedy's method and the conventions of Graeco-Roman rhetoric to James. In accord with Graeco-Roman rhetorical invention, we do not expect to find the elements of rhetorical arrangement for an entire speech in miniature in a single section. However, certain portions of a speech may have analogous outlines and functions because arrangement is about beginning, middle and closing in the overall speech and in smaller sections.

In two articles I argue that all of James 2.1–3.12 is deliberative rhetoric aimed at advising the audience to take certain courses of action and dissuade it from others.[17] James 2 seeks to dissuade the audience from showing partiality and claiming to have faith when the absence of works shows otherwise. James 3.1-12 seeks to dissuade the audience from aspiring to the teaching office without considering the uncontrollable and destructive nature of the tongue. Dibelius noted that 'Jas 2.1–3.12, the core of the writing, is composed of three expositions, each having

---

14. Van der Westhuizen, 'Stylistic Techniques', pp. 92–94.
15. Van der Westhuizen, 'Stylistic Techniques', pp. 94–95.
16. Van der Westhuizen, 'Stylistic Techniques', pp. 95–105.
17. Duane F. Watson, 'James 2 in Light of Greco-Roman Schemes of Argumentation', *NTS* 39 (1993), pp. 94–121; Duane F. Watson, 'The Rhetoric of James 3.1-12 and a Classical Pattern of Argumentation', *NovT* 35 (1993), pp. 48–64.

characteristics of a treatise.'[18] He argued that this section was the expansion of paraenetic sayings in diatribe form. My discussion refines his observations in light of Graeco-Roman rhetorical convention.

The argumentation and *topoi* in these sections of James are typical of deliberative rhetoric. Argumentation is based on example and comparison of example. The *topoi* used concern what is advantageous, honourable and necessary – and their opposites. In 2.1-26, the reception of the rich man and the poor man by the church is an example of partiality (2.1-13), while Abraham and Rahab are examples of faith accompanied by works (2.14-16). James 3.1-12 uses the comparison of the bits–horses and rudders–ships with the tongue–body (vv. 3-5) and the tamed animals with the untamable tongue (vv. 7-8), as well as the comparison of the spring, fig tree and grapevines with the duplicity of the tongue (vv. 11-12). In ch. 2, to show partiality is dishonourable (vv. 6-7) and to be a transgressor of the whole law (vv. 9-10). To quit being partial and supplement faith with works is to do well (vv. 8. 19), profit (vv. 14, 16) and experience mercy rather than judgment (v. 13). In 3.1-11 it is not advantageous and expedient that many become teachers because of the dual nature of the tongue. The stasis or basis of the argument in all of 2.1–3.11 is quality. In 2.1-26 the argument is concerned with the nature of partiality and faith and in 3.1-11 it is concerned with the nature of the tongue as it relates to teaching.[19]

These three sections in James 2.1–3.12 use the Graeco-Roman pattern of elaboration for themes and complete arguments: 2.1-13; 2.14-26; and 3.1-12.[20] The elaboration of themes is outlined in the *Rhetorica ad Herennium* (4.43.56–44.58) and the elaboration of the complete argument is outlined in the *Rhetorica ad Alexandrum* (1.1422a.25-27), *Rhetorica ad Herennium* (2.18.28–2.29.46; 3.9.16), Hermogenes 'Elaboration of Arguments',[21] and Hermogenes *Progymnasmata* in the discussion of the elaboration exercise for the chreia.[22]

In these three sections of James, the author advises his audience that

18. Dibelius, *James*, p. 1.

19. Watson, 'James 2', pp. 100–102; Watson, 'James 3.1-12', pp. 53–54.

20. For discussion of this pattern of amplification of themes and complete arguments, see Burton L. Mack, *Anecdotes and Arguments: The Chreia in Antiquity and Early Christianity* (Occasional Papers of the Institute for Antiquity and Christianity, 10; Claremont: Claremont Graduate School, 1987), pp. 15–28; Burton L. Mack, *Rhetoric and the New Testament* (GBS; Minneapolis: Fortress, 1990), pp. 41–47; Burton L. Mack and Vernon K. Robbins, *Patterns of Persuasion in the Gospels* (Sonoma, CA: Polebridge, 1989), pp. 31–67.

21. H. Rabe (ed). *Hermogenis Opera* (Rhetores Graeci, 6; Leipzig: Teubner, 1913), pp. 148–50.

22. Rabe, *Hermogenis Opera*, pp. 1–27. English translation by C. S. Baldwin, *Medieval Rhetoric and Poetic (to 1400)* (Gloucester, MA: Peter Smith, 1959), pp. 23–38; Burton L. Mack and Edward N. O'Neil, 'The Chreia Discussion of Hermogenes of Tarsus', in *The Chreia in Ancient Rhetoric*, vol. 1 *The Progymnasmata* (ed. R. F. Hock and E. N. O'Neil;

partiality is inconsistent with faith (2.1-13), faith without works does not profit (2.14-26) and not many should become teachers (3.1-12). The pattern used to elaborate each of these propositions into complete arguments is: *propositio* (proposition), *ratio* (reason for the *propositio*), *confirmatio* (proof of the *ratio* by comparison, example and amplification), *exornatio* (embellishment of the *confirmatio*) and *complexio* (conclusion drawing the argument together). Paraenetic and diatribal features are incorporated into this pattern of argumentation as major components of the amplification of the argument. This pattern can be broadly outlined as follows for 2.1-13: *propositio* (v. 1), *ratio* (vv. 2-4), *confirmatio* (vv. 5-7), *exornatio* (vv. 8-11) and *complexio* (vv. 12-13); for 2.14-26: *propositio* (v. 14), *ratio* (vv. 15-16), *confirmatio* (vv. 17-19), *exornatio* (vv. 20-25) and *complexio* (v. 26); and for 3.1-12: *propositio* (v. 1a), *ratio* (v. 1b), *confirmatio* (v. 2), *exornatio* (vv. 3-10a) and *complexio* (vv. 10b-12).[23]

Turning to studies of the rhetoric of the entire Epistle of James, one early study is that of E. Baasland.[24] He classifies James as deliberative rhetoric. It is a protreptic, wisdom speech in letter form. He gives the outline of *exordium* (1.2-18) with a *transitus* (1.16-18), *propositio* (1.19-27), *confirmatio* (2.1–3.12), *confutatio* (3.13–5.6) and *peroratio* (5.7-20). The numerous figures of style clarify and amplify the argumentation. In his later commentary he modified his rhetorical outline of James as *exordium* (1.2-15), *propositio* (1.16-22) with amplification (1.23-27), *argumentatio* (2.1–3.12), second *propositio* (3.13-18) with amplification (4.1-6), *argumentatio* (4.7–5.6) and *peroratio* (5.7-20).[25]

In his article, Thurén challenges Dibelius' assessment that James does not address an actual situation or develop themes because it is loosely fitting ethical instruction of paraenesis not aimed at any particular situation.[26] He points out that since Dibelius it has been shown that paraenesis can be addressed to an actual situation in a rhetorically effective manner. The literary Koine Greek of the author and the careful use of language, especially figures of speech in service of the argument, indicate that the author intends to persuade a particular audience. The author paid careful attention to the structure of the epistle as well as to its style – even if the structure is somewhat obscure to us.[27]

Thurén proposes to understand the nature of the epistle less through its

---

SBLTT, 27; Atlanta: Scholars Press, 1986), pp. 153–71; George A. Kennedy, *Progymnasmata: Greek Textbooks of Prose Composition and Rhetoric* (Writings from the Greco-Roman World, 10; Atlanta: Scholars Press, 2003), pp. 73–88.

23. For a more detailed outline, see Watson, 'James 2', p. 118 and *idem*, 'James 3.1-12', p. 64.

24. Baasland, 'Literarische Form', pp. 3649–61.

25. E. Baasland, *Jakobsbrevet* (KNT, 16; Uppsala: EFS, 1992), pp. 177–78.

26. Lauri Thurén, 'Risky Rhetoric in James?', *NovT* 37 (1995), pp. 262–84.

27. Thurén, 'Risky Rhetoric', pp. 262–65.

contents per se and more from trying to understand its persuasive goal. He classifies the epistle as epideictic rhetoric because it reinforces values to which the audience already adheres. He classifies the stasis of the epistle as quality because the credibility of the issues at hand (e.g. joy in trial) is the question. He analyses the rhetoric of the entire epistle according to Graeco-Roman categories, paying particular attention to the functional or pragmatic level. The *exordium* (1.1-18) introduces the two central themes of perseverance in trials in the practical areas of wisdom/speech and money/action. The *propositio* (1.19-27) is to accept and live by the word. The *argumentatio* (2.1-5.6) develops the two themes of the *exordium* in three parts: 2.1-26 on money/action, 3.1-4.12 on wisdom/speech and 4.13-5.6 supplying a climax dealing with both themes focusing on the rich man. The *peroratio* (5.7-20) consists of *recapitulatio* or reiteration of themes (perseverance, speech) and *conquestio* or final exhortation (5.12-20).[28]

Thurén explains the obscurity of the structure and message on the surface level of the epistle as the use of *insinuatio* or subtlety in rhetorical approach to avoid being too obvious to a rhetorically sophisticated audience.[29] However, it is more likely that the Epistle of James does not conform in its overall structure to Graeco-Roman standards of arrangement. James is less complex structurally than Thurén suggests, except for the use of the Graeco-Roman pattern of elaboration for themes and the complete argument in 2.1–3.12.

To date, the use of Graeco-Roman rhetoric to analyse James has discovered many Graeco-Roman elements of invention, arrangement and style. Matters of style in James are not subject to much debate because stylistic matters are well defined in antiquity and readily detectable in the text. However, how to describe the invention, and the arrangement of the letter that facilitates that invention, has eluded consensus from a standard rhetorical analysis.

b. *The Role of Modern Rhetoric and Interdisciplinary Studies*

W. Wuellner analyses James using the New Rhetoric and semiotic and communications theory.[30] He argues that James is a pragmatic and his goal is not teaching, but recruiting. He outlines James as epistolary prescript (1.1), *exordium* (1.2-4), *narratio* (1.5-11), *propositio* (1.12), *argumentatio* in five units (1.13–5.6) and *peroratio* (5.7-20) consisting of a *recapitulatio* (5.7-8) and a *peroratio* proper (5.9-20).

This role of style in the Epistle of James is emphasized in the

28. Thurén, 'Risky Rhetoric', pp. 268–81.
29. Thurén, 'Risky Rhetoric', pp. 282–84.
30. Wuellner, 'Jakobusbrief'.

dissertation by Geiger.[31] He provides an exhaustive study of the stylistic figures of James as reconfigured in more modern terms: resemblance (comparison, representation and implication), change (substitution, alliteration and transposition), amplification (repetition, expansion and description) and condensation (omission and discontinuation). He examines how these figures function in the argumentation. In a confused conclusion he states that the author was 'intentionally and skillfully' using figures of speech that were impressive to his readers and communicate ideas appropriate to the subject, but this usage does not imply that his goal was 'artful rhetoric'.[32] Studies published since this 1981 dissertation are much less reluctant to see artful rhetoric in James or any other NT book – and rightfully so.

Building upon the rhetorical outline of Wuellner, Elliott uses both rhetorical and social-scientific studies to discover a thematic cohesion in the Epistle of James.[33] The introduction (1.1-12) contains an epistolary address and salutation (1.1-2), a statement of the main theme – the wholeness of both the individual and the community and the relationship of both to God (and by implication the opposite of division and fragmentation and alienation from God) (1.3-4) – and related contrasts (1.5-12). The main body of the epistle consists of exhortation in seven subsections contrasting negative indictments of division with positive recommendations for integrity and wholeness (1.13–5.12). Throughout the argumentation of the main body of the epistle, the author develops the main theme of division and wholeness with a series of contrasts including: doubt and vacillation versus trust and faith; separation versus integration of hearing and doing; faith and action; partiality versus impartiality; duplicity versus sincerity; uncontrolled versus controlled speech; war and discord versus harmony and peace; friendship with society and the devil versus friendship with God; arrogant boasting versus humility; instability versus steadfastness; and pollution versus purity. The conclusion reiterates the themes of the introduction (5.13-20). The epistle encourages the recipients to work to restore holiness and wholeness in the community rather than division and the devilish on the correlated personal, social and cosmic levels. It encourages the community to re-establish the distinctive Christian ethos of a holy community over against the unholy society at large.

Using the work of the anthropologist Mary Douglas, Elliott demon-

---

31. L. Geiger, 'Figures of Speech in the Epistle of James: A Rhetorical and Exegetical Analysis' (unpublished doctoral dissertation; Southwestern Baptist Theological Seminary, 1981).

32. Geiger, 'Figures of Speech', p. 203.

33. John H. Elliott, 'The Epistle of James in Rhetorical and Social Scientific Perspective: Holiness-Wholeness and Patterns of Replication', *BTB* 23 (1993), pp. 71–81.

strates that, in social-scientific perspective, societies use purity/pollution schemes as a classification system to define order and reinforce codes of belonging and behaviour. Underlying these schemes is a desire to maintain the wholeness of the individual, society and both of these in relation to the design of the cosmos. These schemes played a role in Second Temple Judaism and early Christianity. The author of James addresses the issue of division and wholeness on the three interrelated levels of the personal, the social and the cosmological. The cosmological dimension in which God's holy purposes appear validates the exhortation to form a society informed by divine wisdom on the personal and communal levels, rather than a society informed by devilish wisdom. Elliott identifies key *topoi* in James and places them within an argumentative strategy built on contrasts derived from the personal, communal and cosmological dimensions. While not strictly rhetorical, this study demonstrates the value of interdisciplinary study in which rhetorical elements (e.g., *topoi* and strategy) and their purpose are conceptualized from another discipline.

2. *The Rhetorical Role of Paraenesis and the Diatribe*

Two other features of James that are central to a discussion of its rhetoric are paraenesis and the diatribe. The former provides *topoi* and the content of moral exhortation and the latter provides a rhetorical mode of argumentation.

a. *The Role of Paraenesis*
Paraenesis is moral exhortation that is generally accepted as true by an audience and is not subject to refutation. It seeks to motivate the audience to a certain course of action acceptable to a community, often by proffering examples of those persons exhibiting the virtues being espoused and by calling the audience to similar honourable action.

As previously mentioned, interpreters often assume that James lacks structure and is perhaps even chaotic. The paraenetic content of the epistle is often identified as the culprit for this lack of structure. Dibelius was very influential in popularizing this understanding. He identified James as belonging to the paraenesis genre.[34] As paraenesis, James is a 'stringing together of admonitions of general ethical content'.[35] James is not

---

34. Dibelius, *James*, pp. 2–11. For a refinement of paraenesis as a genre, see J. G. Gammie, 'Paraenetic Literature: Toward the Morphology of a Secondary Genre', in *Paraenesis: Act and Form* (ed. L. G. Perdue and J. G. Gammie; Semeia, 50; Atlanta: Scholars Press, 1990), pp. 41-77.

35. Dibelius, *James*, p. 3.

assumed to have careful structure or to reveal a particular social situation.
It presents traditional moral exhortation without a rhetorical plan.
Exhortation does not give insight into the social and historical situation
underlying the text. Dibelius says of James: 'The author nowhere states
that he is writing to the readers because he has heard this or that about
them. The author's excitement about the elaboration of pressing dangers
are never so great as to allow us to view those concerns as the actual
occasion for his "letter".'[36]

Dibelius was correct that James contains paraenesis. As Malherbe has
described it, paraenesis has the following characteristics: (1) it is
unoriginal and traditional, (2) it can be applied to many life situations,
(3) it is addressed to those familiar with the paraenesis and only need to be
reminded of it and exhorted to act according to its wisdom; and (4) it uses
examples of those who embody the virtues and call others to emulate
them.[37] James has these features. The author uses traditional material
drawn from the words of Jesus, the OT, Jewish wisdom (see the section on
intertextuality below). The exhortation of James is widely applicable to
daily life which is why it retains its popularity to this day. James exhorts
his audience concerning matters they already know. The topics of
hearing–forgetting and knowing–doing are central to James, especially in
1.19-27 and 4.13-17. James holds up others for emulation including
Abraham and Rahab for hospitality (2.14-26), the Hebrew prophets and
Job for patience under affliction (5.7-11) and Elijah for the power of the
prayer of a righteous man (5.13-20).[38]

While Dibelius may have been correct in associating James with
paraenesis, he was wrong to assume that the presence of paraenesis means
that James lacks rhetorical structure or strategy. Paraenesis often assumed
an important role in structuring rhetorically sophisticated texts, including
letters. Pseudo-Libanius even has a letter style designated ἐπιστολή or
'paraenetic letter'.[39] He describes this letter style this way: 'The paraenetic
style is that in which we exhort someone by urging him to pursue
something or to avoid something. Paraenesis is divided into two parts,
encouragement and dissuasion.'[40] By nature, persuasion and dissuasion
require rhetorical structure and style and it would be no less the case when
paraenesis is incorporated into a persuasive strategy.

Far from contributing to a lack of structure, paraenesis is part of a

---

36. Dibelius, *James*, p. 2.
37. Abraham J. Malherbe, 'Hellenistic Moralists and the New Testament', *ANRW*
2.26.1, pp. 267–333 (278–93).
38. Leo G. Perdue, 'Paraenesis and the Epistle of James', *ZNW* 72 (1981), pp. 241–56
(242–46).
39. Pseudo-Libanius, 'Epistolary Types', in *Ancient Epistolary Theorists* (ed. A. J.
Malherbe; SBLSBS, 19; Atlanta: Scholars Press, 1988), pp. 66–81 (68–69).
40. Pseudo-Libanius, 'Epistolary Types', p. 69.

structured, sophisticated use of rhetoric in the Epistle of James.[41] A good example is 3.1-12 where moral exhortation pertaining to the tongue is used within the development of the argument that not all should become teachers. Paraenetic elements are used as components of the argument's *propositio* (e.g., not many should become teachers, v. 1a), *ratio* (e.g., because teachers will be judged with greater strictness, v. 1b) and *confirmatio* (e.g., blessings and cursing should not come from the same mouth, v. 10).[42]

However, even with the central role of paraenesis in the rhetorical strategy of James, the epistle does not exhibit the formal features of paraenetic works. For example, James does not contain traditional exhortation to character that upholds a model for imitation, with maxims on specific attitudes and behaviours arranged antithetically that define that character.[43] The paraenesis in the Epistle of James is not a dominant, organizing feature, but is subsumed to the needs of broader argumentation and rhetorical strategy.

While Dibelius was correct to associate James with paraenesis, he was wrong to assume that the presence of paraenesis – with its general nature applicable to many situations – meant that James does not give us insight into the situation that it is addressing. Dibelius was discussing individual exhortations in paraenetic texts and not paraenetic texts themselves. With its use in rhetorical strategies, paraenesis can be indicative of social and historical backgrounds. The author's choice of using a paraenetic letter indicates the nature of the relationship between the two. The paraenetic letter is used in contexts in which there is a positive relationship between the author and the audience. The relationship can take a form analogous to the parent and child or to friendship. The author is also generally the moral superior of the audience, someone older and wiser. This positive relationship is assumed as the author feels free to give advice to the audience, expecting a positive response.[44]

Rhetoricians were always concerned to use and mould material that would be pertinent and useful in addressing their audiences. This would be no less applicable to paraenesis.[45] Even though paraenesis is general and applicable to a wide variety of situations, the selection of paraenesis for argumentation is guided by the needs of the audience. 'Even when the material is almost purely traditional, the author has selected and edited it

41. For an extensive discussion of James as wisdom and paraenesis, see Luke L. Cheung, *The Genre, Composition and Hermeneutics of the Epistle of James* (Paternoster Biblical and Theological Monographs; Carlisle: Paternoster, 2003).

42. Watson, 'James 3.1-12', pp. 54–64.

43. Malherbe, 'Hellenistic Moralists', pp. 278–93; Johnson, *James*, pp. 18–20.

44. Stowers, *Letter Writing*, pp. 94–96.

45. Johnson, *James*, pp. 18–19.

with a particular situation in mind.'[46] Thus we can assume that the topics of the paraenesis in James relate to the situation at hand, even if only in an analogous way. As part of a larger rhetorical strategy, paraenesis is indicative of the values a community already holds and issues that are a present concern of the author and the community addressed. Paraenesis gives us insight into the community and its situation at the time of the writing. The community of James was likely struggling with partiality, faith without works and problems with teachers – to name a few issues – because the paraenesis chosen by the author pertains to these issues.

b. *The Role of the Diatribe*

David E. Aune defines a diatribe as 'a modern literary term describing an informal rhetorical mode of argumentation principally characterized by a lively dialogical style including the use of imaginary discussion partners (often abruptly addressed), to whom are attributed hypothetical objections and false conclusions'.[47] Interpreters have noticed that several characteristics of the diatribe are characteristic of the rhetorical argumentation of James, especially elements in the more structured middle section of 2.1–3.12 and 4.13–5.6.[48] The following elements of the diatribe are also found in James:[49] introducing an imaginary interlocutor in the third person as 'someone will say' (2.18); a turn from speaking to the audience to introduce a dialogue with imaginary interlocutors in the second person, simulating direct address (2.18-23; 4.13; 5.1); objections and false conclusions from the imaginary interlocutor (2.18a, 19); a series

---

46. Stowers, *Letter Writing*, p. 95.

47. David E. Aune, *The Westminster Dictionary of New Testament and Early Christian Literature and Rhetoric* (Louisville: Westminster John Knox, 2003), p. 127.

48. Ropes, *James*, pp. 10–18; Dibelius, *James*, pp. 1–2, 38, 124–25; H. Songer, 'The Literary Character of the Book of James', *RevExp* 66 (1969), pp. 379–89 (385); Stanley K. Stowers, 'The Diatribe', in *Greco-Roman Literature and the New Testament* (ed. D. E. Aune; SBLSBS, 21; Atlanta: Scholars, 1988), pp. 71–83 (82); D. E. Aune, *The New Testament in Its Literary Environment* (LEC, 8; Philadelphia: Westminster, 1987), pp. 200, 202; Baasland, 'Literarische Form', pp. 3649–54; Watson, 'James 2', pp. 118–20. Cf. the assessment that diatribe plays a very limited role in James: A. Wifstrand, 'Stylistic Problems in the Epistles of James and Paul', *ST* 1 (1947), pp. 170–82 (177–78); James B. Adamson, *James: The Man and His Message* (Grand Rapids: Eerdmans, 1989), pp. 103–104; Davids, *James*, pp. 12, 23.

49. Rudolf Bultmann, *Der Stil der paulinischen Predigt und die kynisch-stoische Diatribe* (FRLANT, 13; Göttingen: Vandenhoeck & Ruprecht, 1910), pp. 10–64; Paul Wendland, *Die hellenistische–römische Kultur in ihren Beziehungen zu Judentum und Christentum* (HNT, 1: Tübingen: J. C. B. Mohr [Paul Siebeck], 2nd edn, 1912); H. Thyen, *Der Stil der jüdisch-hellenistischen Homilie* (Göttingen: Vandenhoeck & Ruprecht, 1955), pp. 40–63; Stanley K. Stowers, *The Diatribe and Paul's Letter to the Romans* (SBLDS, 57; Chico, CA: Scholars Press, 1981), pp. 79–174; Stanley K. Stowers, 'The Diatribe', pp. 74–76; Aune, *The New Testament in Its Literary Environment*, pp. 200–202; Klaus Berger, 'Hellenistische Gattungen in Neuen Testament', *ANRW* 2.25.2, pp. 1031–432, 1831–85 (1124–32).

of rhetorical questions in rapid succession (2.4, 5, 6, 7, 14, 16, 20; 3.11, 12); a series of questions and answers to the interlocutor (2.20-23; 3.11-12a; 4.14), some of which are designed to force him or her to reject their content (3.11-12; cf. 2.20); censure of the audience for its behaviour (2.2-6, 8-13, 14-17, 18-20); illustration of vices (2.2-4, 15-16); censorious rhetorical questions which characterize the interlocutor's vice, including a harsh term of address like 'fool' (2.20, ὦ ἄνθρωπε κεγέ); maxims and quotations of poets and philosophers (2.8, 10, 11, 23); examples (2.1-7; 21-26; 3.3-5); comparisons (2.26; 3.3-5a, 5b-6, 11-12; 4.14; 5.2-3); antitheses (2.2-4, 8-9, 15-16; 21-23, 25; 3.2-5a, 9; 4.14); irony and sarcasm (2.18-20); personification (2.13, 17, 26; 3.5-6, 8; 5.3-4); special moral and philosophical topics like word versus deed (2.1-26); and stock formulas like τί ὄφελος (2.14, 16), δεῖζόν μοι (2.18), θέλεις δὲ γνῶναι (2.20), βλέπεις (2.22), ὁρᾶτε (2.24), διὸ λέγει with a quotation (4.6), ἰδού (3.4, 5; 5.4) and ἄγε (4.13, 5.1).[50]

When utilized in literary works, the elements of the diatribe were used freely to meet the needs of the rhetorical situation being addressed. James demonstrates how adaptable features of the diatribe are to rhetorical argumentative schemes. The author has conscripted prominent features of the diatribe to serve within the pattern for the elaboration of a theme or entire argument, particularly to amplify the argument (2.1–3.12),[51] as well as rebuke the assumptions of his opposition (4.13–5.6). Elements of the diatribe are used to present paraenesis in effective ways. For example, in 2.5 a rhetorical question is used to present a saying of Jesus on the nature of the poor. In 2.21 and 2.26 the examples of Abraham and Rahab that are to be emulated are presented by rhetorical questions. Personification of judgment and faith is used in paraenesis in 2.13 and 2.17.

3. *The Relationship Between Epistolary and Rhetorical Theory*

There has been considerable debate about the relationship between rhetoric and the epistle in antiquity and in the NT. Should we expect to find rhetorical invention, arrangement and style in epistles?[52] Today there is greater acknowledgement of rhetoric's role in NT epistles. We have reevaluated Adolf Deissmann's false distinction between literary epistles

---

50. Watson, 'James 2', pp. 118–20. Ropes, *James*, p. 13.

51. Watson, 'James 2', pp. 102–16. The role of the diatribe in rhetorical amplification is discussed by George L. Kustas, *Diatribe in Ancient Rhetorical Theory* (Center for Hermeneutical Studies in Hellenistic and Modern Culture; Protocol Series of the Colloquies of the Center, 22; Berkeley: Center for Hermeneutical Studies, 1976), pp. 6–15.

52. For an overview of this debate, see Watson and Hauser, *Rhetorical Criticism of the Bible*, pp. 120–24; Watson, 'Rhetorical Criticism of the Pauline Epistles Since 1975', pp. 222–24.

(rhetorical) and non-literary, documentary letters (non-rhetorical). He classified the NT as letters falling into the latter category.[53] In a brief discussion of James he says: 'the Epistle of James is nevertheless a product of popular literature'.[54] However, the former category of literary epistles is more appropriate to the letters of the NT.They fit Aune's definition of a literary letter: 'Literary letters are those which were preserved and transmitted through literary channels and were valued either as epistolary models, as examples of literary artistry, or as vignettes into earlier lives and manners.'[55]

The letter type, form and rhetorical features of James clearly indicate considerable rhetorical skill and justify its classification as a literary letter. Regarding type, as noted above, James is a paraenetic letter with the rhetorical purpose to persuade and dissuade its audience to adopt a course of action and emulate the behaviour of others held up as examples. Wachob argues that James conforms to the encyclical form of the literary epistle used for administrative and religious purposes and more specifically, a Jewish encyclical letter. The epistle's use of maxims and exhortation move it into the domain of public address (Demetrius, *Eloc.* 231b-232), like letter essays and philosophical letters in which rhetoric abounds.[56]

Regarding form, Francis's formal analysis of the opening of Hellenistic letters with introduction and repetition of topics developed later indicates that James is a literary epistle.[57] He notes that the opening of James and 1 John are similar to Hellenistic public and private epistles, both those having and not having situational immediacy. In these epistles, the opening states and restates topics developed later in the epistle and provides some structure for it. This is true of James and 1 John. The introduction of these epistles state and restate topics that are developed in the remainder of the epistle.[58] James 1.1-27 is composed of two sections that repeat three key topics in the same order: 1.2-11 and 1.12-27. These topics are testing/steadfastness (1.2-4, 12-15), wisdom–words/reproaching (1.5-8, 19-21) and rich–poor/doers (1.9-11, 22-25). These topics provide structure to the letter, for the topics are developed in reversed order in the

---

53. Adolf Deissmann, *Light From the Ancient East* (trans. L. Strachan; London: Hodder & Stoughton, 1927), pp. 233–45.

54. Deissmann, *Light from the Ancient East*, p. 243.

55. Aune, *The New Testament in Its Literary Environment*, p. 165.

56. Wesley H. Wachob, *The Voice of Jesus in the Social Rhetoric of James* (SNTSMS, 106; Cambridge and New York: Cambridge University Press, 2000), pp. 6–8.

57. Peter H. Davids, 'The Epistle of James in Modern Discussion', in *ANRW* 2.25.5: pp. 3621–45 (3627–28).

58. Fred O. Francis, 'The Form and Function of the Opening and Closing Paragraphs of James and 1 John', *ZNW* 61 (1970), pp. 110–26.

body of the letter (2.1–5.12).[59] The closing of James (5.13-21) recapitulates the topics of strife (v. 9) and steadfastness (vv. 10-11).[60]

Regarding rhetorical features, James as a literary epistle is confirmed by its rhetoric. By the first century BCE, rhetorical education had incorporated instruction on letters and had exerted a strong influence on epistolary composition among the educated.[61] There is virtually no debate that Jewish and Graeco-Roman rhetoric play a role in the epistle. The role of rhetoric is not assumed to be merely stylistic, but involved at the level of argumentation and overall strategy. James is highly rhetorical and intended to be heard by the audience addressed.

4. *The Rhetorical Training of the Author*

In the Hellenistic world, rhetoric was central to secondary education and public oratory. The rhetorical sophistication of many of the epistles of the NT, especially those of Paul, has led several scholars to assert that these authors are doing more than just imitating written and spoken communication witnessed in public life where rhetorical practice abounded. They are utilizing a studied application of rhetorical conventions that may stem from rhetorical training. For example, Aune can state of Hebrews: 'The author obviously enjoyed the benefits of a Hellenistic rhetorical education through the tertiary level.'[62] The correspondence between the *exordium* and the *peroratio* of James leads Thurén to claim that the author of James is a 'conscious orator'.[63] I have tried to demonstrate that the author of James used the Graeco-Roman pattern of elaboration for themes and complete arguments as taught in secondary school within the *progymnasmata* or rhetorical exercises.[64] This use is perhaps the strongest indication that the author of James had received rhetorical education.

More specifically, the mix of rhetorical forms in James – a mix including Jewish and Graeco-Roman forms – may indicate that the author received rhetorical training within a Jewish context with strong Hellenistic influence. For example, paraenesis in 1.1-27 is given an argumentative format that introduces and develops topics, but does not quite break out of the mode of wisdom of successive introduction of topics to become a

59. Francis, 'Form and Function', pp. 118–21.
60. Francis, 'Form and Function', pp. 124–26.
61. Aune, *The New Testament in Its Literary Environment*, p. 160.
62. Aune, *The New Testament in Its Literary Environment*, p. 212.
63. Thurén, 'Risky Rhetoric', p. 275.
64. Watson, 'James 2' and 'James 3.1-12'; followed with modification and elaboration by Wachob, *The Voice of Jesus*, pp. 59–113.

structured *exordium*. Then the author turns around and develops three complete arguments in 2.1–3.12 like a Graeco-Roman trained orator.

5. Intertextuality

Intertextuality is an emerging discipline that is a natural companion of rhetorical analysis. Intertextuality is the identification of oral and written sources from outside the text that a text has used, how these sources have been moulded by the text and how these sources currently function in the rhetorical strategy of the new work in which they have been incorporated. Intertextuality examines the power or ethos that a new text draws from these other authoritative sources which it has alluded to, referenced or quoted.

James utilizes the OT and the Jesus tradition as two sources, incorporating them mainly through allusion rather than quotation. James explicitly quotes the OT three times, referring to the OT as a γραθή ('writing'): 2.8 (Lev. 19.18); 2.23 (Gen. 15.6); and 4.5-6 (Prov. 3.34). These are found in contexts of controversy and give additional authority to the arguments.[65] There are also other allusions to the Scriptures spread throughout the epistle and these near quotations seem to be drawn from the Septuagint and used in more combative sections.[66] These sources are used in the new context of James to meet the demands of the rhetorical situation the community is facing.

Wachob has provided an intertextual study of Jas 2.1–3.12 that many have defined as the heart of the epistle.[67] James also utilizes the Jesus tradition as known from the Sermon on the Mount (Matthew 5–7) and the Sermon on the Plain (Lk. 6.17-49). More specifically, James draws from a pre-Matthaean version of the Sermon on the Mount moulded from a version of Q different from the version of Q used by Luke in composing the Sermon on the Plain. This usage of the Jesus tradition is completely by allusion. The author never quotes the Jesus tradition directly. This allows the author to speak with the authoritative words of Jesus throughout the epistle, adding ethos or authority to his argumentation.

More specifically, Wachob argues that Jas 2.5 is central to the epistle: 'Listen, my beloved brothers and sisters. Has not God chosen the poor in the world to be rich in faith and to be heirs of the kingdom that he has

---

65. John Painter, 'The Power of Words: Rhetoric in James and Paul', in *The Missions of James, Peter and Paul: Tensions in Early Christianity* (ed. B. Chilton and C. A. Evans; NovTSup, 115; Leiden: E. J. Brill, 2005), pp. 236–73 (254).

66. Wiard Popkes, 'James and Scripture: An Exercise in Intertextuality', *NTS* 45 (1999), pp. 213-29.

67. Wachob, *The Voice of Jesus*, pp. 114–53. See Painter, 'The Power of Words', pp. 253–60, 268–73 which relies heavily upon Wachob's work.

promised to those who love him?' (NRSV). James 2.5 addresses the social issue of conflict between the rich and poor which is a central issue in the community (1.9-11; 2.1-13, 15-16; 4.13–5.6). This emphasis is indicative of the large problem of the social disparity in the Mediterranean world at this time, with so few controlling so much of the wealth. James 2.5 is akin to the words of Jesus found in Mt. 5.3 (Lk. 6.20; *Gos. Thom. 54*; Polycarp, *Phil.* 2.3). This usage of the Jesus tradition allows James to work within a subculture of Judaism which the Sermon on the Mount represents as well as being countercultural on the matter of rich and poor as far as the dominant society is concerned. In 2.5 and the surrounding argumentation of 2.1-13, the intertextual connections between what James says and the Jesus tradition allows him to speak with the authority of Jesus to persuade the audience to love and to deny partiality.

In a later and more specific essay, Wachob explores the intertexture of apocalyptic discourse in James.[68] He examines topics at home in apocalyptic literature and found in James as well, including trials of faith, justice, the *parousia* of the Lord, judgment, the rich and poor and the kingdom of God. These topics are central to the deliberative rhetorical strategy of the epistle which is trying to persuade an audience to take a particular course of action. By emphasizing that the Torah is fulfilled in the love command according to the teaching of Jesus, James is countercultural within Judaism. It is a Christian version of Jewish culture. From this countercultural perspective, James uses apocalyptic topics to support his argument and appeal to his community to live as Jesus lived. The eschaton should influence present behaviour. The community should live as Christ did in light of the future consummation. In relation to the larger Graeco-Roman world, apocalyptic intertexture provides a counter-cultural stance.

6. *Socio-Rhetorical Analysis*

A recent development in the study of James is socio-rhetorical criticism as developed by Vernon K. Robbins. This interpretive analytic creates dialogue between general rhetorical analysis and interrelated disciplines like social-scientific and intertextual studies – to name a few.[69] This is an interdisciplinary analysis that investigates the inner texture, intertexture,

---

68. Wesley H. Wachob, 'The Apocalyptic Intertexture of the Epistle of James', in *The Intertexture of Apocalyptic Discourse* (ed. D. F. Watson; SBLSS, 14; Atlanta: Scholars Press, 2002), pp. 165–85

69. Vernon K. Robbins, *Exploring the Texture of Texts: A Guide to Socio-Rhetorical Interpretation* (Valley Forge, PA: Trinity Press International, 1996); *idem*, *The Tapestry of Early Christian Discourse: Rhetoric, Society and Ideology* (London and New York: Routledge, 1996).

social and cultural texture and ideological texture of texts. An important study using socio-rhetorical analysis on the Epistle of James is the aforementioned study of Wachob, a student of Robbins.[70] He examines the rhetorical scheme in 2.1-13 and its appropriation of a saying of Jesus in 2.5 to address the social issue of the conflict between the rich and poor. Wachob argues that 2.1-13 is deliberative rhetoric that is subcultural within Jewish society and countercultural within Graeco-Roman society. In his study of inner texture he discovers the use of the elaboration of a theme or argument of the *progymnasmata* in 2.1-13: theme (2.1), argument from comparison (2.2-4), argument from example with its opposite and social example (2.5-7), argument from judgment based on written law (2.8-11) and conclusion (2.12-13).[71] His study of intertexture shows that 2.5 is a performance of the Jesus saying in Mt. 5.3 (Q). The social and cultural texture of 2.1-13 indicates that 2.5 establishes that God's kingdom belongs to the poor and determines the identity and behaviour of the community. The ideological texture of 2.5 brings the beliefs and values of the communiuty to bear in order to persuade it that partiality is incompatible with the Christian faith. It establishes a particular community self-understanding (the pious poor of Jewish piety) and boundaries of acceptable behaviour (giving to those in need).

This brief summary by no means does justice to the importance of Wachob's study, but does illustrate that when we discuss the rhetoric of James, it is no longer in isolation, but in dialogue with a host of other disciplines. The result is a fuller understanding of the dynamics between author and audience, the rhetorical strategy and its components and the social, cultural and ideological features of the text that are intrinsic to the rhetorical composition, force and reception of any text.

7. *The Placement Within Ancient Rhetorical Traditions*

Another issue is the placement of James within ancient rhetorical traditions. Does it belong within the Jewish or Graeco-Roman rhetorical tradition? Does this question contain a false distinction since Graeco-Roman rhetoric had influenced Jewish rhetoric by the first century of the Common Era? Many Graeco-Roman rhetorical conventions had been incorporated in some form by Jewish rhetorical practice and education during the Hellenistic period. Also, many Jewish and Graeco-Roman

---

70.   Wachob, *The Voice of Jesus*. Also see Wesley H. Wachob, 'The Epistle of James and the Book of Psalms: A Socio-Rhetorical Perspective of Intertexture, Culture and Ideology in Religious Discourse', in *Fabrics of Discourse* (Festschrift Vernon K. Robbins; ed. D. B. Gowler, L. G. Bloomquist and D. F. Watson; Harrisburg: Trinity Press International, 2003), pp. 264–80.

71.   Cf. Watson, 'James 2'; Watson, 'James 3.1-12'.

rhetorical conventions were shaped independently by the needs of a predominantly oral culture. Most people were illiterate and rhetorical forms developed to facilitate hearing and memorization. This included the multitude of figures of speech and thought and repetitive structural forms.

James has elements of Jewish and Graeco-Roman rhetoric. The introduction of topics in its introduction (1.2-21) and reiteration in its conclusion (5.14-18) as noted above, is common in oral cultures to help the audience follow and remember what is being said. Comparison of examples for moral imitation is common to both cultures. The wisdom in 1.2-27 and 3.13–5.20 is characteristic of Jewish rhetorical tradition. The use of a pattern of elaboration for themes and complete arguments in 2.1–3.12 is Graeco-Roman in origin and is a full development of what 1.2-27 and 3.13–5.20 anticipate that the author is capable of. Overall James does not conform to Graeco-Roman rhetorical convention in its structure and strategy. No scheme of *exordium, narratio, probatio* and *peroratio* has been found. However, 1.2-27 introduces *topoi* like an *exordium* and 5.14-18 reiterates *topoi* like a *peroratio*.

These questions of the place of James within ancient rhetorical traditions cannot be fully answered until further research rectifies the lack of a broad-based study of Jewish rhetoric in the Hellenistic period. A thorough study needs to be made of what is distinctly Jewish rhetoric, what elements of Jewish rhetoric are influenced or borrowed from Graeco-Roman rhetoric and what elements are shared with Graeco-Roman rhetoric by virtue of the needs of an oral society.

8. *The Rhetoric of James: A Proposal*

We have reviewed the current literature and thought on the rhetoric of James. We recognize that James is highly rhetorical and many of its rhetorical features have been studied with benefit. However, its overall rhetorical strategy escapes our grasp. Or is the strategy so obvious that we are overlooking it? I think this is the case.

In comparison with works in the Jewish wisdom tradition to which James is akin, we see that much of the wisdom in James is shared with this tradition. However, the presentation of wisdom is quite different. When we look at Jewish wisdom like Proverbs and the later Sirach from the early second century BCE in Jerusalem, wisdom is presented as authoritative statements or aphorisms from a wisdom teacher. The wisdom teacher is authoritative and so is the wisdom he is imparting. There is also the assumption that the community will listen and wants to implement this wisdom in its life. There is no need to prove anything. Wisdom is presented without logical proof or topical development. Absent are such logical connectives as 'for' and 'because' that help form enthymemes.

Absent too are elaborate examples of those persons that exhibit the vices being railed or virtues being rallied. One notable difference important for our discussion is that, whereas Proverbs is a string of short wisdom sayings or aphorisms, Sirach is composed of units of wisdom that are 10 to 23 lines long and develop the topic at hand more fully.

The Wisdom of Solomon from the first century BCE contains the longer units that develop the wisdom topics in a fashion akin to the earlier Sirach. However, the presentation of wisdom has logical connectives of 'for' and 'because'. The Wisdom of Solomon explains the facets of the wisdom topics and the importance of following them. It attempts to persuade the community addressed to follow wisdom. The opening provides a good example: 'Love righteousness, you rulers of the earth, think of the Lord in goodness and seek him with sincerity of heart; *because* he is found by those who do not put him to the test and manifests himself to those who do not distrust him' (1.1-2 NRSV, italics mine).

The wisdom in James is also presented in the longer units like those in Sirach and the Wisdom of Solomon. James also has logical proof derived from the development of topics and arguments that rely upon enthymemes, examples and comparison of examples which is characteristic of the Wisdom of Solomon. James is the product of a Jewish context in which Hellenistic rhetoric had influenced the wisdom tradition and the construction and arrangement of argumentation – just like the Wisdom of Solomon that is suspected to originate in the Jewish community in Alexandria. The author of James uses logical proof to present wisdom. It is not that his community does not hold him or his wisdom as authoritative, but their desire to live by this wisdom is questionable and the very reason he is writing. The wisdom in James comes with logical development because there is a need to persuade the audience of the merits of adhering to the wisdom being presented. Examples of this kind of reasoning are found in James from the start. Consider trials as joy *because* the testing of faith produces endurance and in turn let the endurance have full effect *so that* you may be mature (1.2-4). Ask in faith *for* the doubter can expect nothing (1.5-8). And so forth. This logical development of arguments is very much influenced by Graeco-Roman rhetoric as seen in our discussion above, especially on Jas 2.1–3.12.

This early Christian author constructs a text with introduction of topics, followed by the development and reiteration of those topics in Hellenistic fashion. However, reliance on the Jewish wisdom tradition guides the arrangement. The author goes from topic to topic in the fashion of the wisdom tradition much like the Wisdom of Solomon does. Although he develops wisdom topics in Graeco-Roman argumentative fashion, he does not move further to organize the epistle with explicit elements of arrangement that spell out topics, to develop them and then to reiterate them in the explicit way that Graeco-Roman rhetoric typically does. I think that this dynamic is the key to understanding the structure and the rhetoric of James. It is a Jewish-Christian wisdom work influenced by Hellenistic rhetoric, but is arranged overall in the topic-to-topic fashion of Jewish wisdom texts. The Wisdom of Solomon provides a similar work for comparison of topical development and arrangement in sequential topics from a Hellenized Jewish context.

My proposal is partially supported by Cheung. He makes a careful study of the close relationship between paraenesis and wisdom which are two genres playing a role in James. Subcategories of paraenesis are moral exhortation (Hellenistic paraenesis) and instructions (wisdom paraenesis). These subcategories overlap, but are distinguishable by origin. Moral exhortation looks to Greece and instruction looks to Egypt. Cheung writes: 'On stylistic grounds, it seems that James modeled itself more on wisdom instruction such as Ben Sira than on Hellenistic paraenesis. In terms of source of influence, there is no doubt that Jewish wisdom instructions (often modeled after Egyptian instructions) have a dominant influence of James.'[72] Cheung is correct to point out the dominance of wisdom instruction in James, but the better model for James would be the Wisdom of Solomon, not Ben Sira. The Hellenistic rhetorical influence in James is akin to that found in the Wisdom of Solomon which allows wisdom instruction to be freely moulded rhetorically to meet the needs of the audience.

9. *Conclusion*

We have made a radical turn in James studies by abandoning the assumptions of Dibelius that James lacks structure because it is paraenesis and Deissmann that James is a non-literary letter. There is a strong movement to find, not only individual arguments from logos, ethos and pathos, but larger patterns of argumentation and rhetorical strategies in James. There is a greater awareness of the interrelationship between literary forms and genres and their rhetorical features. There is also a movement from the identification and description of rhetorical elements in James to an attempt to explain how James functions for the author and the community addressed.

From the study of the rhetoric of James conducted so far, we can dismiss the assessment of Dibelius that James lacks discernible structure. Clearly there is rhetorical structure in the epistle. This includes portions that develop topics and complete arguments (2.1–3.12) and the overall development of topics. This development of topics and arguments exhibits

---

72. Cheung, *The Genre, Composition and Hermeneutics*, 40.

a careful use of paraenesis, elements of the diatribe and stylistic figures for moral exhortation.

However, overall James does not conform to Graeco-Roman standards of invention and arrangement. Attempts to outline the epistle from *exordium* to *peroratio* are unconvincing. The mix of Jewish, Graeco-Roman and early Christian rhetorical traditions is partly responsible. The epistle has a rhetorical strategy, even though there is disagreement about how to describe this elusive strategy.

Rhetorical analysis, using both ancient and modern rhetoric and related interdisciplinary studies show that topical development is a major concern of the epistle. However, the topical development is structured more like wisdom literature with topic following topic than it is Graeco-Roman oratory with a central thesis, list of topics that will develop the thesis, development of topics and reiteration of topics.

Rhetorical analysis assists us in unveiling the cultural, social and ideological background of the author and audience of James. The rhetoric employed gives us insight into the assumptions and values of the author and his community. The assumptions and values underlying the stated and unstated premises of argumentation are assumed by the author to be shared by the community. Community assumptions and values undergird the praise and denunciation, honour and shame language in the text. With these values and assumptions the author establishes and reorders boundaries for community behaviour. The use of traditional wisdom topics in James indicates a community steeped in the wisdom tradition of Judaism and the shared values undergirding that wisdom, but the reconfiguring of that tradition enables the author to realign the shared values according to a more Christian emphasis.

The rhetorical strategy of a text also helps discover the perception of the author and community in relation to culture, whether as members of the dominant culture, a subculture, a counterculture, etc. Focusing on the function of rhetoric opens NT texts to their Mediterranean culture in new ways.[73] The rhetorical strategy of James informs us how an early Christian leader used rhetoric to help the community with self-definition and the inculcation of its distinctive values using a mix of rhetoric that defies clean classification and structure. The author comes from a Jewish background influenced by Hellenistic rhetoric. To address his audience he uses the epistolary genre and a mix of rhetorical elements to produce this early attempt at a Christian rhetoric. If James is dated to the 50s CE as I believe it should be, then we see an early Christian leader trying to give voice to the gospel with lots of tools at hand, but no conventional blueprint as to how to proceed.

---

73. Good examples include Elliott, 'The Epistle of James in Rhetoric and Social Scientific Perspective' and Wachob, *The Voice of Jesus* discussed above.

THE EMULATION OF THE JESUS TRADITION IN THE LETTER OF JAMES

John S. Kloppenborg

Commentators on the Letter of James frequently observe the close conceptual parallels between James and the Jesus tradition, in particular the sayings usually ascribed to Q. There is disagreement over just how many 'parallels' exist; a survey of commentators up to the late 1980s indicated that on average, interpreters find about eighteen echoes of the Jesus tradition in James.[1]

In an earlier essay, I surveyed the models for conceptualizing the relationship of James to the Jesus tradition.[2] These include some who deny any relation outright; others argue that the similarities between James and the Jesus tradition are due to the fact that both employ stereotypical paraenetic *topoi*; a few have argued that James knew and used Matthew; some explain the contacts with the Jesus tradition by the theory that the author was Jesus' brother and had assimilated Jesus' manner of speech; the majority hold that the similarities are due to James' use of oral Jesus tradition; and a few have argued that James knew Q.[3]

Patrick Hartin has put the case for James' dependence on Q (or

---

1.   This claim is based on the work of Dean B. Deppe, 'The Sayings of Jesus in the Epistle of James' (D. Th. diss., Free University of Amsterdam; Ann Arbor: Bookcrafters, 1989), pp. 231–50, who surveyed sixty authors from Thiele (1833) to Davids (1985). Deppe's table (pp. 233–37) shows that almost every verse of James has been connected with the Jesus tradition by some interpreter. The 27 most commonly cited parallels are: 1.2 (Q 6.22-23a), 4 (Mt. 5.48), 5 (Q 11.9), 6 (Mt. 21.21; Mk 11.23), 10-11 (Q 12.28), 17 (Q 11.13), 19b-20 (Mt. 5.22a), 22-25 (Q 6.47-49); 2.5 (Q 6.20b), 8 (Mt. 22.39; Mk 12.31; Lk. 10.27), 13 (Mt. 5.7; Lk. 6.36); 3.12 (Q 6.44), 18 (Mt. 5.9; Lk. 6.43); 4.2-3 (Q 11.9), 4a (Mt. 12.39a; 16.4a; Mk 8.38), 4b (Q 16.13), 9 (Lk. 6.21, 25b), 10 (Q 14.11; 18.14b), 11-12 (Q 6.37), 13-14 (Mt. 6.34; Lk. 12.16-21); 5.1 (Lk. 6.24, 25b), 2-3 (Q 12.33b), 9b (Mt. 24.33b), 10-11a (Q 6.22-23b), 12 (Mt. 5.33-37), 17 (Lk. 4.25), 19-20 (Q 17.3).

2.   John S. Kloppenborg, 'The Reception of the Jesus Tradition in James', in *The Catholic Epistles and the Tradition* (ed. J. Schlosser; BETL, 176; Leuven: Peeters, 2004), pp. 91–139.

3.   B. H. Streeter, *The Primitive Church: Studied with Special Reference to the Origins of Christian Ministry* (London: Macmillan, 1929), p. 193 was the first to think that James 'had read Q in the recension known to Luke'.

Matthew's version of Q) most compellingly[4]: of 26 possible parallels between James and the Synoptics he identified, 21 appear in the Sermon on the Mount (see Table 1, pp. 143–48). Since James does not betray knowledge of the specific elements of Matthaean redaction, it is unlikely that the letter is directly dependent upon Matthew.

The parallels between James and the sermon might of course mean either that James and Q 6.20-49 drew on common oral tradition, or that James knew Q. In order to make the latter possibility the more likely, Hartin argued that additional knowledge of Q is betrayed by Jas 1.5-8; 4.3 (Q 11.9-13); 5.2-3 (Q 12.33-34), 19-20 (Q 17.3); 2.10 (Q 16.17); 4.4 (Q 16.13) and 4.10 (Q 14.11). James in fact displays knowledge of sayings from many of Q's major sub-divisions: the sayings on prayer (Q 11.2-4, 9-13), on anxieties (12.22-31, 33-34), on discipleship (Q 17.1-6), and the block of miscellaneous sayings in Q 13.23–16.18.[5] Of course, 5.12 is the clearest point of contact with 'M' tradition (Mt. 5.33-37) and indicates that James also knew tradition within the Matthaean orbit.

Hence, Hartin puts the choice thus:

> Only two possible explanations can be given of these similarities. Either both James and Q are dependent upon a common tradition which is reflected in these examples; or James is dependent directly on the Q tradition. The argument of this investigation supports the direct dependence of James on Q. The main reason for opting for this second possibility arises from the closeness of the language used. While no one example is capable of proving the point conclusively, all these examples taken together provide an argument from convergence. If one were to opt for the first possibility whereby James and Q are independent of each other, yet dependent upon a common tradition, one would in fact have to postulate a common tradition very similar to Q.[6]

---

4.   Patrick J. Hartin, *James and the 'Q' Sayings of Jesus* (JSNTSup, 47; Sheffield: Sheffield Academic Press, 1991), chs 5–6; Patrick J. Hartin, 'James and the Q Sermon on the Mount/ Plain', in *Society of Biblical Literature 1989 Seminar Papers* (ed. David J. Lull; SBLSP, 28; Atlanta: Scholars Press, 1989), pp. 440–57.

5.   Hartin adopts the division of Q proposed by Athanasius Polag, *Fragmenta Q: Textheft zur Logienquelle* (Neukirchen-Vluyn: Neukirchener Verlag, 1979), pp. 23–26. Alternative divisions of Q proposed by Wolfgang Schenk, *Synopse zur Redequelle der Evangelien: Q-Synopse und Rekonstruktion in deutscher Übersetzung* (Düsseldorf: Patmos Verlag, 1981), pp. 5–9 or John S. Kloppenborg, *The Formation of Q: Trajectories in Ancient Wisdom Collections* (Studies in Antiquity and Christianity; Philadelphia: Fortress, 1987), p. 92 would not alter the substance of Hartin's point.

6.   Hartin, *James and the Q Sayings*, p. 186. Hartin employs the work of Richard J. Bauckham, 'The Study of Gospel Traditions Outside the Canonical Gospels: Problems and Prospects', in *The Jesus Tradition Outside the Gospels* (ed. David Wenham; Gospel Perspectives, 5; Sheffield: JSOT Press, 1985), pp. 369–419, who argues (a) that Q was

I have attempted to buttress Hartin's appeal to the principle of parsimony in explanations with two further observations which may be summarized briefly.

First, when Jas 1.2 and 5.10 refer to the *suffering* of the prophets in order to undergird an exhortation to rejoice in the midst of testing, James is echoing an argument that is due to the *redaction* of Q. The 'persecution beatitude' is found in five different versions: Q 6.22-23; *Gos. Thom.* 68, 69a; 1 Pet. 3.14; 4.13-14. Only one, however, invokes the analogy of the persecution of the prophets, οὕτως γὰρ [[διώξωσιν]] τοὺς προφήτας τοὺς πρὸ ὑμῶν. The phrase is superfluous, since the motive clause for 'rejoice' is already supplied by ὅτι ὁ μισθὸς ὑμῶν πολὺς ἐν τῷ οὐρανῷ. That Q 6.23c is redactional has been long recognized[7] and it is usually thought that the presence of this motif in Q 6.22-23 is due to the redactional activities of the compilers of Q, who wished to underscore the connection of the Q group with the prophets, understood through the lens of Deuteronomistic theology.[8] Hence, when James echoes this argument, he appears to be leaning on a connection already made in Q.

Second, it is widely held that a relationship exists between Jas 1.5, εἰ δέ τις ὑμῶν λείπεται σοφίας, αἰτείτω παρὰ τοῦ διδόντος θεοῦ πᾶσιν ἁπλῶς καὶ μὴ ὀνειδίζοντος, καὶ δοθήσεται αὐτῷ, and Q 11.9, αἰτεῖτε καὶ δοθήσεται ὑμῖν, ζητεῖτε καὶ εὑρήσετε· κρούετε, καὶ ἀνοιγήσεται ὑμῖν. The 'seek/find' saying is widely attested in the Jesus tradition, appearing in Q 11.9-10; Jas 1.5; *POxy* IV 654,6-9 (*Gos. Thom.* 2), *Gos. Thom.* 92, 94; *Gos. Heb.* 4a.b; *Dial. Sav.* 9-12, 20d; Jn 14.13-14; 15.7, 16b; 16.23-24, 26 – twelve occurrences. Most of these performances have to do with the seeking of wisdom or life – appropriate, of course, given the association in wisdom literature between the verbs ζητεῖν and εὑρίσκειν and wisdom or life.[9] In the Sayings Gospel Q, however, the 'seek–find' saying has been transformed and related to the practice of prayer and is employed to explicate the Lord's Prayer (Q 11.2-4). The aphorism is then buttressed by the illustrations in Q 11.11-13, unattested in any of the other occurrences of the admonition. As Piper observes, Q's interest in the admonition is neither in 'seeking/finding' nor in 'knocking/opening', but only in 'asking

---

compiled from originally independent blocks and (b) that in order to show any writer's dependence on Q one would have to show that it contained 'allusions to a wide range of Q material' (p. 379).

7. For a discussion, see John S. Kloppenborg, 'Blessing and Marginality: The "Persecution Beatitude" in Q, Thomas and Early Christianity', *Forum* 2.3 (1986), pp. 36–56 (44–49).

8. See John S. Kloppenborg, *Excavating Q: The History and Setting of the Sayings Gospel* (Minneapolis: Fortress; Edinburgh: T&T Clark, 2000), pp. 118–22, 149–50.

9. E.g., σοφία: Job 28.12-13, 20; 32.13; Prov. 1.28; 2.4; 3.13; 8.17; 14.6; Qoh. 7.25; Sir. 4.11; 6.18; 18.28; 25.10; 51.20, 26; Wis. 6.12; ἐπίγνωσις θεοῦ: Prov. 2.5; 8.9; φρόνησις: Sir. 25.9; χάρις: Prov. 3.3; 12.3; ζωή: Prov. 21.21; ἀνάπαυσις: Sir. 28.16; παιδεία: Sir. 51.13, 16.

and receiving'.[10] Thus, Piper argues, an admonition that did not originally have *specifically* to do with prayer has been given a setting where αἰτεῖν now means 'to pray'.

Of the twelve occurrences of the admonition, only Q, Jas 1.5 and three occurrences in John include the verb αἰτεῖν and apply it to prayer. James' particular use of the the admonition betrays acquaintance with the particulars of Q's usage. For Q elaborates the 'seek/find' admonition with an illustration (11.9-11) that appeals to the super-generous character of God. James echoes this in his phrase, παρὰ τοῦ διδόντος θεοῦ πᾶσιν ἁπλῶς. That is, James' application of the admonition to the practice of prayer seems to derive from Q's secondary elaboration of the aphorism. Of course it cannot be shown that James depends on the *final* form of Q, since the unit in Q 11.2-4, 9-13 is not usually thought to derive from Q's final redaction.[11] Nevertheless, Q's application of the seek/find saying to prayer is clearly the result of redactional arrangement in Q at some stage.

Not all of Hartin's candidates for parallels of Q and James are equally persuasive. There are, nevertheless, a sufficient number of likely contacts (1.2, 5, 12; 2.5; 4.2c-3, 4, 9, 10; 5.1, 2-3, 9, 10 and perhaps 5.19-20 [see Table 2, pp. 148–50]), drawn from various parts of Q, to sustain his thesis, as a full analysis could show.[12] The fact that James applies the seek/find saying to prayer, and that it reflects Q's penchant for correlating persecution with those of the prophets (6.23c; 11.49-51; 13.34-35) makes best sense if James is aware not merely of 'Q tradition' but of the document itself, to be sure in a somewhat elaborated, pre-Matthaean form.

10. Ronald A. Piper, 'Matthew 7,7-11 par. Lk 11,9-13: Evidence of Design and Argument in the Collection of Jesus' Sayings', in *Logia: Les Paroles de Jésus – The Sayings of Jesus* (Festschrift Joseph Coppens; ed. Joël Delobel; BETL, 59; Leuven: Peeters, 1982), pp. 411-18 (412).

11. For a survey of redactional approaches to Q, see John S. Kloppenborg, 'The Sayings Gospel Q: Literary and Stratigraphic Problems', in *Symbols and Strata: Essays on the Sayings Gospel Q* (ed. Risto Uro; Publications of the Finnish Exegetical Society, 65; Helsinki: Finnish Exegetical Society; Göttingen: Vandenhoeck & Ruprecht, 1996), pp. 1–66 (appendix B). Of the eight approaches surveyed, only Sato included Q 11.2-4, 9-13 among the 'late unsystematic additions' and even he recognized that 11.2-4, 9-13 was an earlier cluster of sayings incorporated into Q.

12. After surveying many of the over 180 possible allusions to the Jesus tradition, Deppe ('Sayings of Jesus', pp. 219–21) lists eight that he thinks are likely (1.5; 2.5; 4.2c-3, 9, 10; 5.1, 2-3a, 12); six have parallels in content: 1.6, 12, 17, 22-25; 3.12; 5.10-11a; nine have parallels in terminology: 1.21; 2.15; 4.4a, 8, 12, 17; 5.9a, 9b, 17; and twelve have more general parallels: 1.2, 4, 12, 19b-20; 2.10, 13, 14; 3.18; 4.4, 11-12; 5.6, 14.

1. Recitatio, *Paraphrase, Emulation and Attribution*

If it is granted that James echoes the Jesus tradition, two aspects of his use of the Jesus tradition remain puzzling. First, James never expressly appeals to the authority of Jesus, despite the fact that at six points he cites the authority of the Tanak.[13] Not only is Jesus not called on as an authority but the name 'Jesus' appears only twice in the letter (1.1; 2.1) and in its second occurrence it is found in a syntactically awkward formulation.[14] Second, none of the sayings that have been identified as potential parallels with the Jesus tradition, with the exception of the prohibition of oaths (5.12), bears an especially strong *verbal* similarity to its parallel.

Commentators have been rather unhelpful in dealing with either puzzle, being content merely to establish the thesis that James knew and used the Jesus tradition (or that he did not). Only two models have been advanced to account for James' actual use of the Jesus tradition, the first psychological and the second based on inferences from scribal practices.

Zahn explained the lack of verbal convergence with the elaborate speculation that although James had never been under Jesus' direct tutelage, nonetheless:

> There were not a few of these sayings which he had heard from Jesus' own lips, though often with doubt and disapproval. After he became a believer, what he learned from others and what he had heard himself fused together in his thought, and the impression of the personality of Jesus, under the influence of which he had been ever since his childhood, made the tradition so vital that it developed in him a Christian character which in the early Church made him seem all but superior to the apostles themselves.[15]

Mayor's account was not essentially different. He conjectured a process of Jesus' words 'sinking into the heart of the hearer [James], who reproduces them in his own manner'.[16]

---

13. Jas 2.8 = Lev. 19.18b; Jas 2.11a = Exod. 20.13 and Deut. 5.17; Jas 2.11b = Exod. 20.15; Deut. 5.18; Jas 2.23 = Gen. 15.6; Jas 4.5 alluding to Gen. 6.1-7; Jas 4.6 = Prov. 3.34.

14. Although there is no manuscript support for the omission of Ἰησοῦ Χριστοῦ at 2.1, a significant number of scholars have suspected it as a secondary insertion. See Dale C. Allison, 'The Fiction of James and its *Sitz im Leben*', *RB* 118 (2001), pp. 529–70 (541–43), for the most recent discussion and documentation of arguments since L. Massebieau "Épître de Jacques est-elle l'oeuvre d'un chrétien?', *RHR* 31–32 [1985]: 249–83) and Friedrich Spitta ('Der Brief des Jacobus', in *Zur Geschichte und Litteratur des Urchristentums* [Göttingen: Vandenhoeck & Ruprecht, 1896] 2.1-239, esp. 158–77).

15. Theodor Zahn, *Introduction to the New Testament* (Edinburgh: T&T Clark, 1909), vol. 1, p. 114.

16. Joseph B. Mayor, *The Epistle of St. James: The Greek Text with Introduction, Notes and Comments* (London: Macmillan, 1892; 3rd edn, 1913), p. lxii.

These explanations are of course wedded to the hypothesis of Jacobean authorship with all of its attendant problems. But they lack scientific control. Since we know nothing about the psychological dynamics within ancient Mediterranean families in general or Jesus' family in particular, or its age distribution, size and intergenerational aspects, or the psychosocial dynamics of first-century Nazareth, any speculations about whether James' linguistic and conceptual patterns might have been conformed to those of Jesus are merely wishful thinking. Neither Zahn nor Mayor attempted to construct a model for understanding linguistic and conceptual patterning in ancient Mediterranean families; instead, they presuppose an anachronistic and ethnocentric model of family exchange drawn from nineteenth-century European families, of younger brothers under the tutelage of older brothers.

Richard Bauckham proposed a much more controlled and serious model.[17] Bauckham also holds that James the brother of Jesus is the authority behind the letter and seeks a model for understanding the relationship between Jesus and his brother James. This he finds in Sirach, who composed a wisdom book in his own name (rather than attributing his work pseudonymously to some predecessor such as Solomon). Of course, Sirach did not compose his book *ex nihilo*, but employs predecessor texts. But in doing so, Sirach emulates rather than quotes those texts. Sirach's procedure is elevated to the level of self-conscious practice in Sir. 39.1-3, 6.

> 1 On the other hand he who devotes himself
> to the study of the law of the Most High
> will seek out the wisdom of all the ancients,
> and will be concerned with prophecies;
> 2 he will preserve the discourse of notable men
> and penetrate the subtleties of parables;
> 3 he will seek out the hidden meanings of proverbs
> and be at home with the obscurities of parables....
> 6 If the great Lord is willing
> he will be filled with the spirit of understanding;
> he will pour forth words of wisdom
> and give thanks to the Lord in prayer. (RSV)

Sirach here describes an intellectual process that is not simply a matter of replication or quotation of traditional sayings, but what I have elsewhere called 'sapiential research' – the effort of weighing, probing and evaluating traditional sayings – that leads to assimilation of the ethos of

---

17. Richard J. Bauckham, *James: Wisdom of James, Disciple of Jesus the Sage* (New Testament Readings; London and New York: Routledge, 1999), pp. 75, 81–83.

wisdom and, then, its emulation and reproduction by the speaker.[18] Thus, I am in essential agreement with Bauckham, who argues that James does not 'quote' Jesus' sayings, but instead reformulates them.

> He does not repeat [the wisdom of Jesus]; he is inspired by it. He creates his own wise sayings, inspired by several sayings, sometimes encapsulating the themes of many sayings, sometimes based on points of contact between Jesus' sayings and other Jewish wisdom. The creativity and artistry of these sayings are missed when they are treated as allusions to sayings of Jesus.[19]

The combination of references to predecessor texts and the creative reformulation of those texts can be seen vividly in Bauckham's examples of Sirach's transformation of earlier texts:[20]

18. See Kloppenborg, *Formation*, pp. 284–86, 302–306. See also Daniel J. Harrington, 'The Wisdom of the Scribe According to Ben Sira', in *Ideal Figures in Ancient Judaism* (ed. George W. E. Nickelsburg and John J. Collins; Chico, CA: Scholars Press, 1980), pp. 181–88.

19. Bauckham, *James*, pp. 82–83. Bauckham treats Sirach as a *novum* insofar as he is 'the first and almost the only Jewish sage in Antiquity to put his own wisdom in writing under his own name' (pp. 74–75) and concludes that 'Ben Sira and James are the only two ancient Jewish sages who collected their own wisdom in written works attributed to themselves'. Provided that one stresses 'Jewish' these statements might be correct. But once one sees sapiential literature in its broader context, the phenomenon to which Bauckham points is not unsual. It is true that the essentially conservative nature of sapiential works meant that attribution to ancient sages was often convenient. E.g., the instruction of Amenote son of Hapu (Ptolemaic period) is attributed to a scribe of Amenophis III (Ulrich Wilcken, 'Zur ägyptisch-hellenistischen Litteratur', in *Aegyptiaca* [Festschrift Georg Ebers; Leipzig: Wilhelm Engelmann, 1897], pp. 142–52). But in the Hellenistic period, we also have several collections attributed to otherwise unknown persons and no reason to doubt, for example, that the instruction of the Counsels of Piety of Sansnos (Etienne Bernand, *Inscriptions métriques de l'Egypte gréco-romaine: Recherches sur la poésie épigrammatique des Grecs en Egypte* [Annales littéraires de l'Université de Besançon; Centre de recherches anciennes, 98; Paris: Société d'édition 'Les Belles-lettres', 1969], p. 165) or the instruction of *P3-wr-dl* (Aksel Volten, 'Die moralischen Lehren des demotischen Pap. Louvre 2414', in *Studi in memoria di Ippolito Rosellini nel primo centenario della morte [4 guigno 1843]* [Pisa: V. Lischi, 1955], vol. 2, pp. 271–80) are not in the name of their actual authors.

20. Bauckham, *James*, p. 77.

καὶ ἀγαπήσεις κύριον τὸν θεόν
σου ἐξ ὅλης τῆς καρδίας σου καὶ ἐξ
ὅλης τῆς ψυχῆς σου καὶ ἐξ ὅλης
τῆς δυνάμεώς σου.

ἐν ὅλῃ ψυχῇ σου εὐλαβοῦ τὸν
κύριον καὶ τοὺς ἱερεῖς αὐτοῦ
θαύμαζε.
ἐν ὅλῃ δυνάμει ἀγάπησον τὸν
ποιήσαντά σε καὶ τοὺς
λειτουργοὺς αὐτοῦ μὴ
ἐγκαταλίπῃς.

You shall love the Lord your God
with all your heart and with all
your soul and with all your power.
(Deut. 6.5)

With all your soul fear the Lord
and revere his priests. And with all
your power love your maker and
do not neglect his ministers. (Sir.
7.29-30)

The verbatim agreements of Sirach with Deut. 6.5 are quite limited: Sirach preserves the phrases: ἐξ ὅλης τῆς ψυχῆς σου (ἐν ὅλῃ ψυχῇ σου) and ἐξ ὅλης τῆς δυνάμεώς σου (ἐν ὅλῃ δυνάμει) but introduces two new verbs (εὐλαβάνειν, θαυμάζειν), substitutes τὸν ποιήσαντά σε for the LXX's κύριον τὸν θεόν σου, and introduces the connection between 'loving God' and respect for the priesthood. With this, the admonition from the Torah is redirected to the concrete situation of second-century BCE Judah and its priestly aristocracy.

> Equipped with the analogy of scribal procedure as seen in Sirach, Bauckham argues that James is not quoting or alluding to the saying[s] of Jesus, but, in the manner of a wisdom sage, he is re-expressing the insight he has learned from Jesus' teaching... Just as Ben Sira, even when he repeats the thought of Proverbs, deliberately refrains from repeating the words, so James creates an aphorism of his own, indebted to but no mere reproduction of the words of Jesus.[21]

This model of verbal transmission and transformation is superior to the psychological model of Zahn and Mayor, since it is grounded not in pious fancy but in a model that was self-consciously undertaken and explicitly described by an ancient author. Moreover, since we have access to Sirach's sources, we are in a position to deduce some of the actual techniques of verbal transformation that he used. In other words, Bauckham proposes an empirically grounded model, and one that can be tested. It is a model with explanatory force.

Though Bauckham himself adheres to the notion of Jacobean authorship, it should be observed that the model he proposes does not logically require any assumptions about authorship. It would work just as well in accounting for the shape of James' text if James were dependent on oral tradition or an early written collection of Jesus' sayings. Both sources

---

21. Bauckham, *James*, p. 91.

could equally serve as examples for emulation, just as Deuteronomy and Proverbs did for Sirach. And although Sirach writes in his own name, the same process of emulation of older sayings might just as easily be found in a pseudepigraphon, as is the case with Ps-Phocylides' paraphrase of the Decalogue in lines 3–8 or the paraphrase of Lev. 19.15 in line 10:

μὴ ῥιψῃς πενίην ἀδίκως, μὴ κρίνε πρόσωπον	οὐ ποιήσετε ἄδικον ἐν κρίσει, οὐ λήψη πρόσωπον πτωχοῦ οὐδὲ θαυμάσεις πρόσωπον δυνάστου, ἐν δικαιοσύνη κρινεῖς τὸν πλησίον σου.
Cast the poor not down unjustly, judge not partially. (Ps-Phocylides, 10)	You shall commit no injustice in judgment, nor show partiality to the poor or defer to the great, but in righteousness shall you judge your neighbour. (Lev. 19.15)

Like Bauckham's example of Sir. 7.29-30, Ps-Phocylides paraphrases the predecessor text in a manner appropriate to his audience's situation. Rather than attributing the resulting paraphrase to Moses or representing it as his own, the author attributes the teaching to an ancient Greek teacher. Nonetheless it seems likely that a Jewish audience would recognize that Ps-Phocylides was paraphrasing the Torah. The key point is that like the audience of Sirach and Ps-Phocylides, the audience of James is likely to have recognized that the author was engaging in paraphrase of received wisdom and would not have been surprised that there was no attempt either at verbatim repetition or attribution to the actual source of the wisdom.

The model of verbal transmission and transformation that Bauckham proposes in order to account for the features of James' work is in fact much more widely attested than merely the world of Jewish scribes.[22] The basis of literate education in the Hellenistic and Roman eras was the copying, emulation, and imitation of predecessor texts, especially *gnomologia*, chria collections, Aesop's fables, and Homer.[23] While the most elementary forms of education involved the simple copying of exemplars, the preliminary stages of rhetorical education, as evidenced in

---

22. See Vernon K. Robbins, 'Progymnastic Rhetorical Composition and Pre-Gospel Traditions: A New Approach', in *The Synoptic Gospels: Source Criticism and New Literary Criticism* (ed. Camille Focant; BETL, 110; Leuven: Peeters, 1993), pp. 111–47.

23. Teresa Morgan, *Literate Education in the Hellenistic and Roman Worlds* (Cambridge Classical Studies; Cambridge and New York: Cambridge University Press, 1999), ch. 4; Raffaella Cribiore, *Writing, Teachers, and Students in Graeco-Roman Egypt* (American Studies in Papyrology, 36; Atlanta: Scholars Press, 1996).

the *Progymnasmata*, trained students to manipulate these materials in various ways through restatement (or paraphrase), supplying a rationale, and offering arguments from the contrary, analogies, examples, and other proofs. *Recitation* or *restatement* (ἀπαγγελεία), according to Aelius Theon, allowed for the reporting (or 'interpreting') of a saying or chria 'very clearly in the same words or in others as well' (αὐτοῖς ὀνόμασιν ἢ ἑτέροις σαφέστατα ἑρμηνεῦσαι).[24] The existence of large numbers of school notebooks, reproducing *gnomai* and containing rhetorical exercises, permits us to judge the scope of verbal transformation that was actually allowed in these exercises.[25]

In some cases the speech component of a *chria* might be reproduced unaltered, but the introduction modified, reframing to suit the rhetorical situation. Students learned to inflect *chriae* in all three grammatical numbers and five cases, and to state the *chriae* actively and passively.[26] A saying might also be reproduced verbatim, but its opening frame modified, as can be seen in a comparison of a *chria* recorded by Diogenes Laertius and in *P. Bouriant* I, a school exercise:

24.   Theon, *Progymnasmata* (L. Spengel [ed.], *Rhetores Graeci* [Leipzig: Teubner, 1853–56], vol. 2, p. 101; Ronald F. Hock and Edward N. O'Neil, *The Chreia in Ancient Rhetoric*, vol. 1 *The Progymnasmata* [SBLTT, 27; Atlanta: Scholars Press, 1986], pp. 94–95; George A. Kennedy, *Progymnasmata: Greek Textbooks of Prose Composition and Rhetoric* [Writings from the Greco-Roman World, 10; Atlanta: Society of Biblical Literature, 2003], p. 19). Compare also Quintilian 1.9.2-3: Students of rhetoric 'should learn to paraphrase Aesop's fables...in simple and restrained language and subsequently to set down the paraphrase in writing with the same simplicity of style; they should begin by analyzing each verse, then give its meaning in different language, and finally proceed to a freer paraphrase in which they will be permitted now to abridge and now to embellish the original, so far as this may be done without losing the poet's meaning... He should also set to write aphorisms (sententia), chriae, and delineations of character (ethologiae), of which the teacher will first give the general scheme, since such themes will be drawn from their reading. In all of these exercises the general idea is the same, but the form differs.' For a discussion of paraphrase, see Heinrich Lausberg, *Handbook of Literary Rhetoric: A Foundation for Literary Study* (trans. David E. Orton and R. Dean Anderson; Leiden and New York: E. J. Brill, 1998), §§1099–121.

25.   Janine Debut ('Les documents scolaires', *ZPE* 63 [1986], pp. 251–78) has compiled a list of school exercises on papyri and ostraka, supplemented and nuanced by Cribiore, *Writing, Teachers, and Students*, pp. 173–287 and Morgan, *Literate Education*, pp. 275–87.

26.   Theon, *Progymnasmata* (Spengel, *Rhetores Graeci*, vol. 2, pp. 101–102). Actual examples of the declension of a *chria* can be seen in Bodleian Greek, Inscription 3019; P. J. Parsons, 'A School-Book from the Sayce Collection', *ZPE* 6 (1970), pp. 133–49 (143–44); and Erich Gustav Ludwig Ziebarth, *Aus der antiken Schule: Sammlung griechischer Texte auf Papyrus, Holztafeln, Ostraka* (Kleine Texte für Vorlesungen und Ubungen, 65; Bonn: A. Marcus & E. Weber, 1910), nos. 37, 47.320-22.

Πρὸς τοὺς ἑρπύσαντας ἐπὶ τὴν
τράπεζαν μῦς, ἰδού, φησί, καὶ
Διογένης παρασίτους τρέφει.
When mice (μῦς) crept onto the
table, he addressed them, 'See, even
Diogenes keeps parasites.'
(Diogenes Laertius 6.40)

Ἰδὼν μυῖαν ἐπάνω τῆς τράπεζαν
αὐτοῦ εἶπεν· καὶ Διογένης
παρασίτους τρέφει.
Seeing a fly (μυῖα) on his table he
said, 'Even Diogenes keeps
parasites.' (*P. Bouriant* I.141-68)[27]

Two changes have been effected: the alteration of μῦς (mice) to μυῖα (a fly), and the standardization of the frame. The first is perhaps only a performantial variation; the second is formal. Both versions are what Theon calls a 'declarative chria that relates to a certain circumstance'.[28] But the writer of *P. Bouriant* standardized the introductory frame of the *chria* so that it corresponded to the other four *chriae* in this exercise book, each having the form, ἰδών + substantive + εἶπεν. In other exercise books the student has copied a string of chriae in responsive form (εἶδος ἀποκριτικὸν κατὰ πύσμα), with the form ἐρωτηθεὶς διὰ τί + ἔφη, followed by the saying.[29] Preliminary rhetorical training thus involved learning how to manipulate sayings to suit the grammatical construction in which they were to be used and to frame them as pronouncements, as responses to particular circumstances, as replies to questions, and so forth.

Advanced exercises involved more substantial paraphrase – shortening, lengthening, and substituting other vocabulary – and even introducing another conceptual framework.[30] Parsons notes an elaborate third-

27. Pierre Jouguet and P. Perdizet (eds), 'Le Papyrus Bouriant n. 1. Un cahier d'écolier grec d'Egypte', in *Kolotes und Menedemos* (ed. Wilhelm Crönert; Studien zur Paläographie und Papyruskunde, 6; Leipzig: E. Aveniarus, 1906; repr. Amsterdam: A. M. Hakkert, 1965), pp. 148–61 (153–54); Ronald F. Hock and Edward N. O'Neil (eds), *The Chreia and Ancient Rhetoric: Classroom Exercises* (Writings from the Greco-Roman World, 2; Atlanta: Society of Biblical Literature; Leiden: E. J. Brill, 2002), pp. 9–10.

28. Εἶδος ἀποφαντικὸν κατὰ περίστασιν: Theon, *Progymnasmata* (Spengel, *Rhetores Graeci*, vol. 2, p. 97); Kennedy, *Progymnasmata*, p. 16.

29. E.g., *P.Mich.* inv. 25 (Hock and O'Neil, *Chreia in Ancient Rhetoric*, pp. 13–19); *P.Mich.* inv. 41 (Hock and O'Neil, *Chreia in Ancient Rhetoric*, pp. 20–23); *P.Vindob.G.* 19766 (Hock and O'Neil, *Chreia in Ancient Rhetoric*, pp. 38–40); *P.Sorb.* inv. 2150 (Hock and O'Neil, *Chreia in Ancient Rhetoric*, pp. 41–44); *SB* I 5730 (Hock and O'Neil, *Chreia in Ancient Rhetoric*, pp. 45–49).

30. See above, n. 24. Theon supplies a typology of paraphrase: 'variation in syntax, by addition, by subtraction, and by substitution', and paraphrases combining several of these techniques plus combinations of these. 'Syntactical paraphrase: we keep the same words but transpose the parts, which offers numerous possibilities. By addition: we keep the original words and add to them; for example, Thucydides (1.142.1) said, "in war, opportunities are not abiding", while Demosthenes (4.37) paraphrased this, "opportunities for action do not await our sloth and evasions". By subtraction: speaking in an incomplete way, we drop many of the elements of the original. By substitution: we replace the original word with another; for

century CE prose paraphrase of the first 21 lines of the *Iliad*.[31] The student modified the texts in various ways, substituting Attic vocabulary for archaic words, omitting Homeric epithets and altering descriptions, for example changing 'and made themselves to be a spoil for dogs and all manner of birds' (*Il.* 1.4-5) to 'they abrogated the rule of burial for some' (lines 9–10). Morgan observes that the periphrast introduced the thoroughly unhomeric word 'hypothesis' (three times) to refer to his effort to give a rational explanation of the events which in Homer form a rather more tangled account.[32] Chryses' speech is recast in Athenian courtroom style and events are re-ordered to emphasize strict causality. Morgan observes philosophical influence and argues: 'it might indicate the extent to which the language and simplified concepts of philosophy seem to have been part of the ordinary frame of the educated mind, as seems to have been the case in the theory behind the teaching of grammar'.[33]

Hermogenes gives the example of the paraphrase of a γνωμή in his discussion of elaboration (ἐργασία).[34] The elaboration exercise begins with γνωμή which is then paraphrased:

Gnomē	Paraphrase
οὐ χρὴ παννύχιον εὕδειν βουληφόρον ἄνδρα.	δι' ὅλης νυκτὸς οὐ προσήκει ἄνδρα ἐν βουλαῖς ἐξεταζόμενον καθεύδειν.
A man who is a counsellor should not sleep throughout the night.	It is not fitting for a man, proven in councils, to sleep through the entire night.[35]

The *gnomē*, here taken from Homer, *Il.* 2.2.24, 61 and containing two uncommon words,[36] is rendered in good literary Attic by the paraphrase.

---

example, *pais* or *andrapodon* for *doulos*, or the proper word instead of a metaphor or a metaphor instead of the proper word, or several words instead of one or one instead of several' (Kennedy, *Progymnasmata*, p. 70). The translation is based on a restoration of lost Greek portions of Theon from Armenian fragments by Michel Patillon (ed.), *Aelius Théon, Progymnasmata: Texte établi et traduit par Michel Patillon avec l'assistance, pour l'Arménien, de Giancarlo Bolognesi* [Collection des universités de France; Paris: Editions 'Les belles lettres', 1997).

31. Parsons, 'School Book'; see also Morgan, *Literate Education*, pp. 205–208.

32. Morgan, *Literate Education*, p. 207.

33. Morgan, *Literate Education*, p. 207.

34. See another elaboration (of a maxim from Theognis, 175) in Aphthonius, *Progymnasmata* (Spengel, *Rhetores Graeci*, vol. 2, p. 27); Kennedy, *Progymnasmata*, p. 100.

35. Hermogenes, *Progymnasmata* (H. Rabe, *Hermogenis Opera* [Rhetores Graeci, 6; Leipzig: Teubner, 1913], p. 10); Kennedy, *Progymnasmata*, p. 78.

36. The Homeric βουληφόρος and παννύχιον were not common in the first and following centuries; they appear, respectively, in Apollonios' *Lex. Hom.* 52.30 (1st Cent. CE) and Julius Pollux's *Onom.* 1.64 (2nd Cent. CE).

The paraphrase is so extensive that only one word from the original, ἄνδρα, remains. Also worth noting is the fact that the Homeric source is not identified either in the initial citation of the *gnomē* or in the paraphrase; yet it is likely that Theon's audience would have recognized the source, since this Homeric verse was widely quoted in the first and second centuries CE in a *chria* concerning Alexander and Diogenes of Sinope.[37]

Examples of this sort could be multiplied almost indefinitely.[38] The key point is that verbatim repetition of predecessor texts was not always desirable, or even desirable at all, nor was it necessary to 'footnote' the predecessor text. Paraphrase, according to Quintilian and Theon, was not merely an explication of the original. 'Its duty', says Quintilian, 'is rather to rival and vie (*aemulatio*) with the original in the expression of the same thoughts' (10.5.5).

The rhetorical practice of paraphrase thus provides us with a model for understanding both the lack of verbatim agreement between a predecessor text and its re-performance, and the fact that the product of paraphrase might be represented as the work of the paraphrast rather than as a citation of some earlier text. In this sense, the predecessor text is not a 'source' but rather a 'resource' for rhetorical performance. The differences between the predecessor text and the paraphrase are not due to the vagaries of oral transmission but due instead to deliberate and studied techniques of verbal and conceptual transformation. And what we might call intellectual theft is what rhetoricians celebrated as *aemulatio* – the restating of predecessors' ideas in one's own words. It is relatively clear that Theon expected that his student audience would recognize the ultimate source of his paraphrases, especially when Homer was being paraphrased. Whether all audiences could be expected to recognize the predecessor texts is not clear, but it seems reasonable to assume that the rhetorician could count on some of his or her audience recognizing the predecessor text and thus appreciating the excellence of the formulation and its aptness in application, which was indeed the very goal of *aemulatio* for Theon and Quintilian.

2. *James and the Jesus Tradition*

James' use of paraphrase and *aemulatio* may now be illustrated by reference to a few sayings that I have identified above as most likely deriving from the Jesus tradition (Table 2, pp. 148–50). In an earlier essay I have already treated Jas 1.2, 12 || Q 6.22-23, Jas 1.5 || Q 11.9-10 and Jas

---

37. See Epictetus, *Diss.* 3.22.90; Theon, *Progymnasmata* (Spengel, *Rhetores Graeci*, vol. 2, p. 98). The verse is also quoted in Cornutus, *Nat. d.* 37.9.

38. See Kloppenborg, 'The Jesus Tradition in James', pp. 120–22.

2.5 ‖ Q 6.20b, and so will not repeat the analysis here.[39] In each of these cases there were reasonably strong verbal echoes of Q and so the case for knowledge, and emulation, of Q was relatively easy to make. In this essay I shall examine two further sayings where the verbal connection with Q is not so obvious but, as I hope to show, the emulation of Jesus sayings is just as clear. In each case it is necessary to show how the practice of *aemulatio*, the techniques of paraphrase and the rhetorical exigencies of the context in which the paraphrase occurs can account for details of the transformation that James has effected on the Jesus tradition.

a. *James 4.3-4 and Q 16.13*

Although Dibelius treated Jas 3.13–4.12 as a loosely connected miscellany,[40] Luke Johnson has argued persuasively that 3.13–4.10 is a single unit on the topic of envy (περὶ φθόνου).[41] Hartin adds that we have here an instance of a 'perfect argument', structured similarly to that found in Jas 2.1-13:[42] *propositio* (3.13); *ratio* (3.14); *confirmatio* (3.15-18); *exornatio* (4.1-6); *complexio* (4.7-10).[43] The proposition that James defends is that true wisdom reveals itself in a form of life characterized by meekness and humility (3.13). The *confirmatio* elaborates the factors (jealousy and ambition) that make this form of life impossible and consists of a comparison (*sygkrisis*) of the characteristics of 'the wisdom that is from above' and its opposite (3.15-18).

The *exornatio* continues this elaboration, but James here introduces language that implies that his addressees have divided loyalties. He addresses them as 'adulteresses' (4.4a) and as *dypsychoi* (4.8) and asserts that friendship with the world is antithetical to friendship with God. It is here that an allusion to Q 11.9-10 and a paraphrase of Q 16.13 occurs, framed now in the language of friendship. The allusion to Q 11.9-10, αἰτεῖτε καὶ δοθήσεται ὑμῖν…πᾶς γὰρ ὁ αἰτῶν λαμβάνει' had earlier appeared in Jas 1.5, where James both conveyed Q's extraordinary confidence in prayer but then added the qualification that 'asking' must be done without doubt or 'double-mindedness' if prayer is to be effective (1.6-8). In 4.2-3, however, Q 11.9-10 is again paraphrased, but its conclusion is reversed: οὐκ ἔχετε διὰ τὸ μὴ αἰτεῖσθαι ὑμᾶς' αἰτεῖτε καὶ οὐ

---

39. Kloppenborg, 'The Jesus Tradition in James', pp. 122–41.

40. Martin Dibelius, *James: A Commentary on the Epistle of James* (ed. H. Koester; rev. Heinrich Greeven; trans. Michael A. Williams; Hermeneia; Philadelphia: Fortress, 1976), p. 208 treated 3.13-17 and 4.16 as unified wholes, joined by an isolated saying (3.18) and continued by miscellaneous imperatives (4.7-12).

41. Luke Timothy Johnson, 'James 3.13–4.10 and the *Topos* ΠΕΡΙ ΦΘΟΝΟΥ', *NovT* 25 (1983), pp. 327–47.

42. On the argumentative structure of 2.1-13, see Duane F. Watson, 'James 2 in Light of Greco-Roman Schemes of Argumentation', *NTS* 39 (1993), pp. 94–121.

43. Patrick J. Hartin, *James* (SP, 14; Collegeville, MN: Liturgical Press, 2003), p. 207.

λαμβάνετε, διότι κακῶς αἰτεῖσθε, ἵνα ἐν ταῖς ἡδοναῖς ὑμῶν δαπανήσητε. As in 1.6-8 'asking' is effective only if it is not clouded by desire.

At this point the argument appears to change abruptly, to a saying about the impossibility of simultaneous friendship with God and with the world. It is here that there appears to be a transformation of Q's aphorism about servitude (δουλεύειν) into a *gnome* about friendship (φιλία). This provides an example of *aptum* in paraphrase: the reframing or rewording of a saying so that it now fits the discursive context – the idiom of the author and the social register of its addressees – in which it is to be used. Alicia Batten points out that James elsewhere develops the language of friendship, calling Abraham a 'friend of God' (2.23) on account of his actions, and stressing the virtues of single-mindedness and persistence in testing, both connected with friendship in Hellenistic ethics and in Hellenistic Judaism.[44]

But the appeal to friendship is especially apt and effective because it brought with it several popular philosophical maxims: that friends are 'one soul';[45] that friends hold things in common (κοινὰ τὰ τῶν φίλων), and that the wise live in community with the divine.[46] The combination of these maxims produced a famous syllogism: since friends share things in common and since the sage is a friend to God, the wise hold things in common with God. In the context of the urban culture of Diaspora Jews, the appeal to the trope of friendship was far more apt than an appeal to the language of servitude.

The appeal to this syllogism also makes sense of the positioning of 4.2c-3, which claims that the reason that the 'ask and you will receive' maxim has not been effective – that is, that real community with τὰ τοῦ θεοῦ has not been achieved – is due to fact that genuine friendship with God is not manifest. The chief culprits are envy (φθόνος, 4.5) and pride (ὑπερφανία, 4.6), which must be purged if God's superabundant gifts are to be given (μείζονα δὲ δίδωσιν χάριν, 4.6). Hence, James' argument in support of a

---

44. Alicia Batten, 'God in the Letter of James: Patron or Benefactor?' *NTS* 50 (2004), pp. 257-72 (265-66).

45. Euripides, *Orest.* 1045-6: ὦ φίλτατ᾽, ὦ ποθεινὸν ἥδιστόν τ᾽ ἔχων τῆς σῆς ἀδελφῆς ὄνομα καὶ ψυχὴν μίαν ('My dearest friend, you who have a name that sounds most loved and sweet to your sister, partner in one soul with her!').

46. The aphorism is very common, appearing in Euripides, *Orest.* 735 (συγκατασκάπτοις ἂν ἡμᾶς· κοινὰ γὰρ τὰ τῶν φίλων, 'You must destroy me also; for friends have all in common') and Menander, *Fragmenta* 9.1; 10.1, and especially in philosophical works: Plato, *Phaedr.* 279C; Alciphron, *Epistulae* 2.12.1.5-6; Plutarch, *Suav. viv.* 1102F (in discussing Diogenes of Sinope); Athenaeus, *Deipn.* 1.14.10. According to Diogenes Laertius, Diogenes of Sinope turned the aphorism into a syllogism: τῶν θεῶν ἐστι πάντα· φίλοι δὲ οἱ σοφοὶ τοῖς θεοῖς· κοινὰ δὲ τὰ τῶν φίλων· πάντ᾽ ἄρα ἐστὶ τῶν σοφῶν, 'to the gods belong all things; but the wise are friends to the gods; now since 'the things of friends are held in common', all things belong to the wise' (6.37.5-7; cf. 6.72.2-3).

humble and peaceable way of life appeals to self-interest: the addressees are still in want (ἐπιθυμεῖτε, καὶ οὐκ ἔχετε), contrary to their expectations that they will 'ask and receive'. These expectations will be met, but only provided that they manifest true friendship with God, which entails submission to God and, presumably, to one another. As proofs, James cites as scripture an unknown saying framed as a question, 'does the spirit that God caused to dwell in us yearn with envy?'[47] and then adapts Prov. 3.34, which brings him back to his defence of humility over pride.

Statement of Fact (Jas 4.2-3)
ἐπιθυμεῖτε, καὶ οὐκ ἔχετε· φονεύετε καὶ ζηλοῦτε, καὶ οὐ δύνασθε ἐπιτυχεῖν· μάχεσθε καὶ πολεμεῖτε. οὐκ ἔχετε διὰ τὸ μὴ αἰτεῖσθαι ὑμᾶς· αἰτεῖτε καὶ οὐ λαμβάνετε, διότι κακῶς αἰτεῖσθε, ἵνα ἐν ταῖς ἡδοναῖς ὑμῶν δαπανήσητε.

Gnomē (Q 11.9-10)
αἰτεῖτε καὶ δοθήσεται ὑμῖν... πᾶς γὰρ ὁ αἰτῶν λαμβάνει...

Gnomē (Q 16.13)
οὐδεὶς δύναται δυσὶ κυρίοις δουλεύειν· ἢ γὰρ τὸν ἕνα μισήσει καὶ τὸν ἕτερον ἀγαπήσει, ἢ ἑνὸς ἀνθέξεται καὶ τοῦ ἑτέρου καταφρονήσει. οὐ δύνασθε θεῷ δουλεύειν καὶ μαμωνᾷ.

Gnomē Paraphrased (4.4)
μοιχαλίδες, οὐκ οἴδατε ὅτι ἡ φιλία τοῦ κόσμου ἔχθρα τοῦ θεοῦ ἐστιν; ὃς ἐὰν οὖν βουληθῇ φίλος εἶναι τοῦ κόσμου, ἐχθρὸς τοῦ θεοῦ καθίσταται.

Elaboration (4.4-6)
ἢ δοκεῖτε ὅτι κενῶς ἡ γραφὴ λέγει, πρὸς φθόνον ἐπιποθεῖ τὸ πνεῦμα ὃ κατῴκισεν ἐν ἡμῖν; μείζονα δὲ δίδωσιν χάριν· διὸ λέγει, ὁ θεὸς ὑπερηφάνοις ἀντιτάσσεται, ταπεινοῖς δὲ δίδωσιν χάριν.

The paraphrase of Q 16.13 is key in James' argument, since it supplies the antithesis between God and worldly pursuits that is essential to his contention. For it is not merely that those who claim to be friends of God must ask in order to receive; they must also eschew worldly pursuits, since these essentially negate friendship with God. One cannot belong to both.

---

47. The NRSV renders this: 'God yearns jealously for the spirit that he has made to dwell in us', but as Luke Timothy Johnson (*The Letter of James* [AB, 37A; Garden City, NY: Doubleday, 1995], p. 281) and Hartin (*James*, p. 200) point out, ἐπιπόθειν is never used of God and φθόνος is always a vice in the LXX.

But James must also adjust Q's language of servitude to the language of friendship, both in order to invoke the maxim κοινὰ τὰ τῶν φίλων and to be true to his own idiom, according to which the righteous is the friend to God.

b. *James 5.1, 2-3 and Q 6.24; 12.33-34*

The sense of Jas 5.1-3 depends at least in part on how one understands the divisions of the letter. If Jas 4.13–5.6 is considered as a separate unit sandwiched between 4.11-12 and 5.7-11, both of which address ἀδελφοί, it could be treated as an apostrophe directed at merchants (4.13-17) and wealthy landowners (5.1-6).[48] In that case, the ostensible addressees might not be the faithful at all, but outsiders. This division treats 4.11-12 either as a short separate unit,[49] or as an appendix to 4.1-10.[50] Yet it is unlikely that *actual* outsiders are addressed. Moreover, Jas 4.13–5.6 is not entirely discontinuous with 3.13–4.10, but functions as a contrasting panel for the preceding section, which featured the contrast between friendship with God and friendship with the world (4.4) and declared that 'God opposes the arrogant' (4.6).[51] Konradt suggests that 4.13–5.6 be read on two levels, one intended for those in 3.13–4.10 who are called to repent, and the rich, upon whom judgment is pronounced.[52]

A better division of the letter, in my view, is that proposed by Johnson, who considers 4.11-12 to be the introduction to 4.13–5.6, on the topic of arrogance.[53] Although the ostensible focus of 4.11, slanderous speech (καταλαλεῖν), does not at first seem to cohere with the two subsequent condemnations of merchants and landowners, the key issue in 4.11-12, as

---

48.   Dibelius, *James*, pp. 230–40; Peter H. Davids, *James* (NIBC; Peabody, MA: Hendrickson, rev. edn, 1989), pp. 28, 171; Christoph Burchard, *Der Jakobusbrief* (HNT, 15/1; Tübingen: J. C. B. Mohr [Paul Siebeck], 2000), pp. x, 181–82; Wiard Popkes, *Der Brief des Jakobus* (THKNT, 14; Leipzig: Evangelische Verlags-Anstalt, 2001), pp. 284–313; Hartin, *James*, pp. 38, 217–40.

49.   Hartin, *James*, pp. 217–18.

50.   Davids, *James*, pp. 168–69; Burchard, *Jakobusbrief*, p. 178; Popkes, *Jakobus*, pp. 280–81. All of these authors consider 4.11-12 as a small unit by itself, but register discomfort with positing so small a unit, and so argue that its affinities are with the preceding section.

51.   Johnson, *James*, p. 306; Burchard, *Jakobusbrief*, p. 182.

52.   Matthias Konradt, *Christliche Existenz nach dem Jakobusbrief: Eine Studie zu seiner soteriologischen und ethischen Konzeption* (SUNT, 22; Göttingen: Vandenhoeck & Ruprecht, 1998), pp. 148–49: 'Durch die Verwendung des rhetorischen Mittels der Apostrophe baut Jakobus einen von den realen Adressaten unterschiedenen, aber doch in einer noch zu betstimmenden Weise mit diesen zusammenhängenden "uneigentlichen" Adressaten auf, so daß der Text auf zwei Bezugsebenen zugleich zu lesen ist.'

53.   Johnson, *James*, p. 292.

James' rationale makes clear, is arrogance[54] and it is this topic that joins 4.11-12 to 4.13-18.

If this is true, the entire unit (4.11–5.6) is addressed to the ἀδελφοί (4.11; cf. 4.17), like most of the other rhetorical units of James.[55] This might account for the change from the οὐαί of Q 6.24[56] to ἄγε νῦν (also in 4.13), an expression attested commonly in Homer and Aristophanes,[57] which is routinely followed by an imperative but which lacks the strongly negative sense of 'woe'. Hence, there is room to reconsider the common opinion of commentators, even those who consider 4.11–5.6 to be a single unit, that James has shifted from addressing community members to outsiders. On the contrary, the rationale provided by vv. 2-3 does not describe the miserable fate of the *wealthy* as James had earlier done in 1.10, where the wealthy person was said to be fated to pass away. Instead, the declaration has to do with the fate of the *wealth* in which the wealthy had put their trust. Moreover, the final rhetorical question, οὐκ ἀντιτάσσεται ὑμῖν; ('does [God] not oppose you?')[58] evidently picks up

54. Johnson (*James*, p. 293) is correct, I believe, to suggest that the logic of the statement 'whoever slanders a brother or judges his brother slanders the law and judges the law' presupposes Lev. 19.16 (οὐ πορεύσῃ δόλῳ ἐν τῷ ἔθνει σου, οὐκ ἐπισυστήσῃ ἐφ' αἷμα τοῦ πλησίον σου· ἐγώ εἰμι κύριος ὁ θεὸς ὑμῶν): 'To practice slander and judgment against a neighbor is...to assume not only an arrogant superiority toward an equal but also to assume an arrogant superiority toward the law that forbids such behavior.'

55. The vocative ἀδελφοί (μου) introduces units at 1.2 (1.2-27); 2.1 (2.1-13), 14 (2.14-26); 3.1 (3.1-12); 4.11 (4.11–5.6); 5.7 (5.7-11), 12 (5.12-18), 19 (5.19-20).

56. The International Q Project excluded Lk. 6.24-26 from Q, though with my dissent (James M. Robinson, Paul Hoffmann, and John S. Kloppenborg [eds], *The Critical Edition of Q: A Synopsis, Including the Gospels of Matthew and Luke, Mark and Thomas, with English, German and French Translations of Q and Thomas* [Hermeneia Supplements; Leuven: Peeters: Minneapolis: Fortress, 2000], pp. 54–55). For arguments in favour of the inclusion of Lk. 6.24-26 in Q, see John S. Kloppenborg, *Q Parallels: Synopsis, Critical Notes, & Concordance* (FFNT; Sonoma, CA: Polebridge, 1988), p. 26; Christopher M. Tuckett, 'The Beatitudes: A Source Critical Study', *NovT* 25 (1983), pp. 193–207 (199).

57. Homer (20 ×), *Il.* 5.226; 6.340, 354, 431; 15.258; 16.667; 19.108; *Od.* 1.271, 309; 3.17; 4.587; 8.241; 12.298; 14.393; 16.25; 17.190; 18.55; 19.357, 378; 23.20; Aristophanes (21 ×) *Ach.* 485; *Eq.* 1011; *Num.* 489; *Vesp.* 211, 202, 381; 1157, 1174, 1264; *Pax* 512, 1056; *Av.* 837, 1744; *Lys.* 1273; *Thes.* 213, 947; *Ran.* 382; *Eccl.* 149, 268; *Frag.* 590.1. Also Euripides, *Cycl.* 630; Xenophon, *Symp.* 4.20.1. Ἄγε by itself appears in Isa. 43.6 and Sir. 32.32, neither of them in a hostile sense.

58. The punctuation of 4.6b is controverted. Most read it as a statement with ὁ δίκαιος as the subject: Mayor, *St. James*, p. 160; Hans Windisch, *Die katholischen Briefe* (HNT, 4.2; Tübingen: J. C. B. Mohr [Paul Siebeck], 1911; 2nd edn, 1930), p. 30; Dibelius, *James*, p. 240; Franz Mussner, *Der Jakobusbrief* (HTKNT, 13/1; Freiburg: Herder, 3rd edn, 1975), p. 193; James B. Adamson, *The Epistle of James* (NICNT; Grand Rapids: Eerdmans, 1976), p. 188; Sophie Laws, *The Epistle of James* (BNTC; London: A & C Black, 1980), p. 207; Ralph P. Martin, *James* (WBC, 48; Waco, TX: Word Books, 1988), p. 181; Popkes, *Jakobus*, p. 312; Hartin, *James*, p. 231. Some take the sentence as a question, with ὁ δίκαιος as the subject ('does he not oppose you?'): James H. Ropes, *A Critical and Exegetical Commentary on the*

the same verb used in 4.6, where the appeal is to community members who are torn between pursuing 'love of the world' or 'love of God'.

The use of κλαίειν in 5.1 echoes Jas 4.9 (Q 6.25), as does the reappearance of ταλαιπωρία. The verb ὀλολύζειν, like ταλαιπωρεῖν earlier, occurs in the LXX in contexts having to do with disasters, real or anticipated.[59] The reuse of these lexemes and the recurrence of the spectre of coming disasters suggest that 5.1-6, like 4.7-10, functions as a call to the wealthy to adopt the meek posture recommended in 4.10 by declaring that the worldly basis of their confidence is empty and vain.

The 'disaster' itself is an elaboration of Q 12.33-34 which has been converted into the rationale for Jas 5.1. Since the focus of the imperative in 5.1 is on bewailing one's fate, James has taken over only the first (negative) half of Q's saying, converting its imperative mood into the indicative, and the tenses from the present to the perfect (σέσηπεν, σητόβρωτα γέγονεν, κατίωται). Nevertheless, Q's key lexemes, σής/ σήπειν, βρῶσις/βιβράσκω and θησαυρίζειν, and the central tropes of the transitory nature of wealth and its disfigurement, are preserved.[60]

In Q, the 'treasure' in view is undoubtedly the simplest forms of wealth present in towns and villages in agrarian societies – foodstuffs and clothing, which can be degraded through the activity of insects (σὴς καὶ βρῶσις)[61] or stolen in acts of housebreaking. In an example of rhetorical expansion and reframing, Q's 'treasures' have been parsed and elaborated: they include wealth (ὁ πλοῦτος ὑμῶν) – probably agricultural produce – which can rot (σήπειν); clothing (τὰ ἱμάτια ὑμῶν), which has become moth-eaten (σητοβριβάσκειν);[62] and precious metals (ὁ χρυσὸς ὑμῶν καὶ

Epistle of St. James (ICC; New York: Scribner's, 1916), p. 292; Peter H. Davids, *The Epistle of James: A Commentary on the Greek Text* (NIGTC; Grand Rapids: Eerdmans, 1982), p. 180; Burchard, *Jakobusbrief*, p. 195. Still others consider 'God' to be the subject (recalling 4.6): Luis Alonso Schökel, 'James 5.2 and 4.6', *Bib* 54 (1973), pp. 73–76; Pedrito U. Maynard-Reid, *Poverty and Wealth in James* (Maryknoll, NY: Orbis, 1987), p. 94; E. A. C. Pretorius, 'Drie nuwe verklaringsopsies in die Jakobusbrief (Jak 2.1; 4.5; 5.6)', *HvTSt* 44 (1988), pp. 650–64; Timothy Boyd Cargal, *Restoring the Diaspora: Discursive Structure and Purpose in the Epistle of James* (SBLDS, 144; Atlanta: Scholars Press, 1993), pp. 184–85; Johnson, *James*, p. 305.

59. Isa. 10.10; 13.6; 14.31; 15.2, 3; 16.7; 23.1, 6, 14; 24.11; 52.5; 65.14; Jer. 2.23; 31.20, 31; Ezek. 21.17; Hos. 7.14; Amos 8.3; Zech. 11.2.

60. Σήπειν occurs in the LXX at Job 16.7; 19.20; 33.21; 40.12; Ps. 37.6; Ezek. 17.9; Sir. 14.19; Ep. Jer. 1.71.

61. As BDAG (p. 185) rightly notes, there is no justification for rendering βρῶσις as 'rust'. Rather, what is in view are insects such as grasshoppers, as in Mal. 3.11.

62. Σητοβριβάσκω is rare, occurring only in Job 13.28 (ὥσπερ ἱμάτιον σητόβρωτον, 'like a moth-eaten garment') and Theophilus of Antioch, *Autol.* 2.36.65 (σητόβρωτα δέδορκε, πυκναῖς δ᾽ ἀράχναις δεδίασται, '[the gods] appear moth-eaten and are woven by thick cobwebs' = *Sib. Or.* frag. 3.26). See also Isa. 51.8: ὥσπερ γὰρ ἱμάτιον βρωθήσεται ὑπὸ χρόνου καὶ ὡς ἔρια βρωθήσεται ὑπὸ σητός, 'for as a garment will be eaten up by time,

ὁ ἄργυρος), which are disfigured through tarnish or 'rust'.[63] James' parsing focuses more attention on the degradation of clothing, a visible sign of status, and he has added a reference to precious metals – probably not coins but more likely, jewellery and ornaments. Thus he has shifted the 'social register' of wealth from the countryside to the city, where clothing and metals in the form of rings, pendants and earrings are the important markers of status and wealth.

James' argument against wealth, like his argument in 1.2-12, is based less on a notion of extrinsic punishment than it is on the intrinsically corrupting nature of wealth. His claim that 'it will eat your flesh like fire' (φάγεται τὰς σάρκας ὑμῶν ὡς πῦρ) is not unlike Plutarch's declaration in *Superst.* 164F–165A that a false valuing of riches 'consumes the soul'.[64] Nevertheless, an eschatological horizon is clearly visible, as it also is in 1.2-12. The final statement of the rationale, ἐθησαυρίσατε ἐν ἐσχάταις ἡμέραις, is probably intended ironically and refers to the store of now-corrupted wealth, which the wealthy hoped would serve them in their old age.[65] For James, however, ἐν ἐσχάταις ἡμέραις refers not to old age but, as ἐν ἡμέρᾳ σφαγῆς in 5.5 indicates, the coming judgment. James 5.1-3, like Q/Lk. 12.16-20, plays on the contrast between the beliefs and hopes of the wealthy, and God's view of wealth. Thus, we can understand James' paraphrase and elaboration of Q as follows:

---

and as wool is eaten by a moth'; Sir. 42.13: ἀπὸ γὰρ ἱματίων ἐκπορεύεται σὴς καὶ ἀπὸ γυναικὸς πονηρία γυναικός, 'for a moth goes out of clothing and from a woman comes a woman's wickedness'.

63. Κατιόομαι appears also in Sir. 12.10-11, μὴ πιστεύσῃς τῷ ἐχθρῷ σου εἰς τὸν αἰῶνα· ὡς γὰρ ὁ χαλκὸς ἰοῦται, οὕτως ἡ πονηρία αὐτοῦ· καὶ ἐὰν ταπεινωθῇ καὶ πορεύηται συγκεκυφώς, ἐπίστησον τὴν ψυχήν σου καὶ φύλαξαι ἀπ' αὐτοῦ καὶ ἔσῃ αὐτῷ ὡς ἐκμεμαχὼς ἔσοπτρον καὶ γνώσῃ ὅτι οὐκ εἰς τέλος κατίωσεν, 'Never trust your enemy, for like the rusting of copper, so is his wickedness. Even if he humbles himself and goes about cringing, watch yourself, and be on your guard against him; and you will be to him like one who has polished a mirror, and you will know that it was not hopelessly tarnished'. Gold and silver do not 'rust' – the usual meaning of κατιόομαι and its cognate ἰός. However, Diodorus Siculus 2.48.8 (καὶ πᾶς ὁ περὶ τὸν τόπον ἄργυρός τε καὶ χρυσὸς καὶ χαλκὸς ἀποβάλλει τὴν ἰδιότητα τοῦ χρώματος) and Strabo 16.2.42 (κατιόταται καὶ χαλκὸς καὶ ἄργυρος καὶ πᾶν τὸ στιλπνὸν μεχρὶ καὶ χρυσοῦ) both suggest that the atmosphere around Dead Sea was able even to cause these to tarnish.

64. Plutarch *Superst.* 164F–165A: ὑπολαμβάνει τις τὸν πλοῦτον ἀγαθὸν εἶναι μέγιστον· τοῦτο τὸ ψεῦδος ἰὸν ἔχει, νέμεται τὴν ψυχήν, ἐξίστησιν, οὐκ ἐᾷ καθεύδειν, οἴστρων ἐμπίπλησιν, ὠθεῖ κατὰ πετρῶν, ἄγχει, τὴν παρρησίαν ἀφαιρεῖται, 'Someone supposes that wealth is the greatest good; this is a poisonous lie. It feeds on his soul, distracts him, does not let him sleep, fills him with stinging desires, pushes him down precipices, chokes him, and robs him of him free speech.'

65. The motif of the vanity of storing up wealth is also attested in 2 Kgs 20.17; Bar. 3.17; Lk. 12.16-21.

Gnomē (Q 6.24)
πλὴν οὐαὶ ὑμῖν τοῖς πλουσίοις,
ὅτι ἀπέχετε τὴν παράκλησιν
ὑμῶν.

Gnomē Paraphrased (Jas 5.1)
ἄγε νῦν οἱ πλούσιοι, κλαύσατε
ὀλολύζοντες ἐπὶ ταῖς
ταλαιπωρίαις ὑμῶν ταῖς
ἐπερχομέναις.

Gnomē (Q 12.33-34)
μὴ θησαυρίζετε ὑμῖν θησαυροὺς
ἐπὶ τῆς γῆς, ὅπου σὴς καὶ
βρῶσις ἀφανίζει, καὶ ὅπου
κλέπται διορύσσουσιν καὶ
κλέπτουσιν·

θησαυρίζετε δὲ ὑμῖν θησαυρο... ἐν
οὐραν[ῷ], ὅπου οὔτε σὴς οὔτε
βρῶσις ἀφανίζει, καὶ ὅπου
κλέπται οὐ διορύσσουσιν οὐδὲ
κλέπτουσιν·

Gnomē as rationale (Jas 5.2-3)
ὁ πλοῦτος ὑμῶν σέσηπεν καὶ τὰ
ἱμάτια ὑμῶν σητόβρωτα
γέγονεν, ὁ χρυσὸς ὑμῶν καὶ ὁ
ἄργυρος κατίωται, καὶ ὁ ἰὸς
αὐτῶν εἰς μαρτύριον ὑμῖν ἔσται
καὶ φάγεται τὰς σάρκας ὑμῶν
ὡς πῦρ· ἐθησαυρίσατε ἐν
ἐσχάταις ἡμέραις.

3. *Conclusion*

This paper has been an experiment in deriving a selection of James' statements from Q, based on some of the principles of rhetorical emulation. The practice of *aemulatio* presupposes, on the one hand, that the audience will normally be able to identify the intertext that the author is paraphrasing, and thus will see how the author aligns himself or herself with the *ethos* of the original speaker. On the other, it assumes that the audience will appreciate the artistry of paraphrase and application of the old maxim to a new rhetorical situation.

Several features of rhetorical paraphrase can be seen at work in James' use of the Jesus tradition. In the earlier examination of Jas 1.2, 12 and 1.5, it was observed that James compressed the *gnomē*, but also added rationales, or selectively expanded portions of the *gnomē*.[66] The choice of compression or expansion has largely to do with the function that the allusion plays in James' larger argument – whether it belongs to the *probatio* or the *complexio* of an argument.

A second type of transformation has to do with the reframing of sayings so that they fit with the idiom of James' own argument. Thus, for

66. Kloppenborg, 'The Jesus Tradition in James'.

example, Q 12.33-34, which emphasizes the enduring nature of heavenly treasures, is reframed to stress the dangers of accumulating earthly wealth. Rather than describing the opposition between the world and God in terms of servitude, as Q 16.13 does, James adopts the trope of friendship, because it is consistent with his depiction elsewhere of the righteous as a 'friend of God' (2.23).

A third aspect of James' paraphrases is telling as far as the social register of its intended recipients is concerned. In James 1.12 he had described the reward of faithfulness not as a μισθός (Q 6.22-23) – a term that belongs to the realm of the waged agricultural day-labourer – but as a στέφανος, a term that come from the realm of civic and athletic honours. Appeal to the popular philosophical maxims, 'only the sage is a friend to God' and 'the sage shares τὰ πάντα with God', points to urban addressees with at least moderate education and aware of the discursive world of Hellenistic Judaism. James also employs the Homeric or Aristophanian ἄγε νῦν and parses Q's 'treasures' as the three most obvious items of movable wealth, agricultural produce, fine clothing, and silver and gold ornaments. Each of these features of James' paraphrases points to a social location of the letter's intended audience within the urban bourgeois rather than the less socially pretentious addressees of Q's rhetoric.

Each of these aspects of James' transformation of predecessor texts is intelligible given what we know elsewhere about the rhetorical practice of *aemulatio* – the paraphrase and re-presentation of commonly known texts in such a way that is apt to the argument at hand, 'beautiful' in its deployment, and at the same time subtly calls on the authority of the predecessor.

TABLE 1[67]

James	Sayings Gospel Q
A	*The Q Macarisms*
1 2.5 οὐχ ὁ θεὸς ἐξελέξατο τοὺς πτωχοὺς τῷ κόσμῳ πλουσίους ἐν πίστει καὶ κληρονόμους τῆς βασιλείας ἧς ἐπηγγείλατο τοῖς ἀγαπῶσιν αὐτόν;	Q 6.20b μακάριοι οἱ πτωχοί· ὅτι [[ὑμετέρα]] ἐστὶν ἡ βασιλεία τοῦ θεοῦ.
2 2.15-16 ἐὰν ἀδελφὸς ἢ ἀδελφὴ γυμνοὶ ὑπάρχωσιν καὶ λειπόμενοι τῆς ἐφημέρου τροφῆς, εἴπῃ δέ τις αὐτοῖς ἐξ ὑμῶν, ὑπάγετε ἐν εἰρήνῃ, θερμαίνεσθε καὶ χορτάζεσθε, μὴ δῶτε δὲ αὐτοῖς τὰ ἐπιτήδεια τοῦ σώματος, τί τὸ ὄφελος;	Q 6.21a μακάριοι *οἱ πεινῶντες*, ὅτι χορτασθήσ[[εσθε]].
3 4.9 ταλαιπωρήσατε καὶ πενθήσατε καὶ κλαύσατε· ὁ γέλως ὑμῶν εἰς πένθος μετατραπήτω καὶ ἡ χαρὰ εἰς κατήφειαν.	Q 6.21b μακάριοι οἱ [[πενθ]]ο[[ῦ]]ντες, ὅτι [[παρακληθήσεσθε]] Q [[6.25]] οὐαὶ ὑμῖν, οἱ ἐμπεπλησμένοι, ὅτι πεινάσετε. οὐαί, οἱ γελῶντες, ὅτι πενθήσετε καὶ κλαύσετε.
4 1.2 πᾶσαν χαρὰν ἡγήσασθε, ἀδελφοί μου, ὅταν πειρασμοῖς περιπέσητε ποικίλοις 5.10 ὑπόδειγμα λάβετε, ἀδελφοί, τῆς κακοπαθείας καὶ τῆς μακροθυμίας τοὺς προφήτας, οἳ ἐλάλησαν ἐν τῷ ὀνόματι κυρίου.	Q 6.22-23 μακάριοί ἐστε ὅταν ὀνειδίσωσιν ὑμᾶς καὶ [[διώξ]]ωσιν καὶ [[εἴπ]]ωσιν πᾶν πονηρὸν [[καθ']] ὑμῶν ἕνεκεν τοῦ υἱοῦ τοῦ ἀνθρώπου· χαίρετε καὶ [[ἀγαλλιᾶσθε]], ὅτι ὁ μισθὸς ὑμῶν πολὺς ἐν τῷ οὐρανῷ· οὕτως γὰρ [[ἐδίωξαν]] τοὺς προφήτας πρὸ ὑμῶν.

67. Hartin, *James and the Q Sayings of Jesus*. I have reorganized Hartin's discussion (pp. 148–64) in the interests of clarity. The Q text used is Robinson, Hoffmann and Kloppenborg (eds), *The Critical Edition of Q*, supplemented in the case of Q [[6.24, 25]] to indicate the possibility that the Lukan woes also derive from Q. Verbal agreements are marked in **bold**; agreements in sense are in *italics*.

	James	Sayings Gospel Q
5	5.1 ἄγε νῦν οἱ πλούσιοι, κλαύσατε ὀλολύζοντες ἐπὶ ταῖς ταλαιπωρίαις ὑμῶν ταῖς ἐπερχομέναις.	Q [[6.24]] πλὴν οὐαὶ ὑμῖν τοῖς πλουσίοις, ὅτι ἀπέχετε τὴν παράκλησιν ὑμῶν.
B		*(Pre)-Matthaean Elaborations of the Macarisms*
6	2.13 ἡ γὰρ κρίσις *ἀνέλεος* τῷ μὴ ποιήσαντι *ἔλεος·* κατακαυχᾶται *ἔλεος* κρίσεως. 5.11 πολύσπλαγχνός ἐστιν ὁ κύριος καὶ οἰκτίρμων	Mt. 5.7 μακάριοι οἱ *ἐλεήμονες,* ὅτι αὐτοὶ *ἐλεηθήσονται* Q 6.36 [[γίν]]εσθε οἰκτίρμονες ὡς ... ὁ πατὴρ ὑμῶν οἰκτίρμων ἐστίν.
7	4.8 ἐγγίσατε τῷ θεῷ, καὶ ἐγγιεῖ ὑμῖν. *καθαρίσατε* χεῖρας, ἁμαρτωλοί, καὶ ἁγνίσατε *καρδίας,* δίψυχοι.	Mt. 5.8 μακάριοι οἱ *καθαροὶ* τῇ *καρδίᾳ,* ὅτι αὐτοὶ τὸν θεὸν ὄψονται
8	3.18 καρπὸς δὲ δικαιοσύνης ἐν *εἰρήνῃ* σπείρεται τοῖς *ποιοῦσιν εἰρήνην*	Mt. 5.9 μακάριοι οἱ *εἰρηνοποιοί,* ὅτι αὐτοὶ υἱοὶ θεοῦ κληθήσονται.
C		*Other Portions of the Q Sermon*
9	2.11 ὁ γὰρ εἰπών, Μὴ μοιχεύσῃς, εἶπεν καί, Μὴ φονεύσῃς· 4.4 *μοιχαλίδες*	Mt. 5.27-30 ἠκούσατε ὅτι ἐρρέθη, οὐ μοιχεύσεις....
10	4.11 μὴ καταλαλεῖτε ἀλλήλων, ἀδελφοί· ὁ καταλαλῶν ἀδελφοῦ ἢ **κρίνων** τὸν ἀδελφὸν αὐτοῦ καταλαλεῖ νόμου καὶ κρίνει νόμον·	Q 6.37-38 μὴ **κρίνετε,** ... μὴ **κριθῆτε·** [[ἐν ᾧ γὰρ κρίματι κρίνετε κριθήσεσθε, καὶ ἐν]] ᾧ γὰρ μέτρῳ μετρεῖτε μετρηθήσεται ὑμῖν.
11	5.6 κατεδικάσατε, ἐφονεύσατε τὸν δίκαιον	Lk. 6.37 καὶ μὴ κρίνετε, καὶ οὐ μὴ κριθῆτε· καὶ μὴ **καταδικάζετε,** καὶ οὐ μὴ καταδικασθῆτε. ἀπολύετε, καὶ ἀπολυθήσεσθε· Cf. Q 6.37
12	5.9 μὴ στενάζετε, ἀδελφοί, κατ᾿ ἀλλήλων, ἵνα μὴ **κριθῆτε·**	Q 6.37-38 μὴ **κρίνετε,** ... μὴ **κριθῆτε·** [[ἐν ᾧ γὰρ κρίματι κρίνετε κριθήσεσθε, καὶ ἐν]] ᾧ γὰρ μέτρῳ μετρεῖτε μετρηθήσεται ὑμῖν.

	James	Sayings Gospel Q
13	3.12 μὴ δύναται, ἀδελφοί μου, συκῆ ἐλαίας ποιῆσαι ἢ ἄμπελος σῦκα; οὔτε ἁλυκὸν γλυκὺ ποιῆσαι ὕδωρ	Q 6.44b μήτι συλλέγουσιν ἐξ ἀκανθῶν σῦκα ἢ ἐκ τριβόλων σταφυλ[[άς;]]
14	1.22 γίνεσθε δὲ *ποιηταὶ λόγου* καὶ μὴ μόνον ἀκροαταὶ παραλογιζόμενοι ἑαυτούς.	Q 6.47-49 πᾶς ὁ ἀκούων μου τ( ) λόγ( ) καὶ *ποιῶν* αὐτούς...καὶ [[πᾶς]] ὁ ἀκούων [[μου τοὺς λόγους]] καὶ μὴ *ποιῶν* [[αὐτοὺς]]
D		*Other Portions of Q*
15	1.5 εἰ δέ τις ὑμῶν λείπεται σοφίας, αἰτείτω παρὰ τοῦ διδόντος θεοῦ πᾶσιν ἁπλῶς καὶ μὴ ὀνειδίζοντος, καὶ δοθήσεται αὐτῷ. 1.17 πᾶσα *δόσις* ἀγαθὴ καὶ πᾶν *δώρημα* τέλειον ἄνωθέν ἐστιν, καταβαῖνον ἀπὸ τοῦ πατρὸς τῶν φώτων 4.2c-3 οὐκ ἔχετε διὰ τὸ μὴ αἰτεῖσθαι ὑμᾶς· αἰτεῖτε καὶ οὐ λαμβάνετε, διότι κακῶς αἰτεῖσθε, ἵνα ἐν ταῖς ἡδοναῖς ὑμῶν δαπανήσητε.	Q 11.9-13 λέγω ὑμῖν, αἰτεῖτε καὶ δοθήσεται ὑμῖν, ζητεῖτε καὶ εὑρήσετε· κρούετε, καὶ ἀνοιγήσεται ὑμῖν...εἰ οὖν ὑμεῖς πονηροὶ ὄντες οἴδατε *δόματα* ἀγαθὰ διδόναι τοῖς τέκνοις ὑμῶν, πόσῳ μᾶλλον ὁ πατὴρ ἐξ οὐρανοῦ *δώσει* ἀγαθὰ τοῖς αἰτοῦσιν αὐτόν.
16	5.2-3 ὁ πλοῦτος ὑμῶν σέσηπεν καὶ τὰ ἱμάτια ὑμῶν σητόβρωτα γέγονεν, ὁ χρυσὸς ὑμῶν καὶ ὁ ἄργυρος κατίωται, καὶ ὁ ἰὸς αὐτῶν εἰς μαρτύριον ὑμῖν ἔσται καὶ φάγεται τὰς σάρκας ὑμῶν ὡς πῦρ· ἐθησαυρίσατε ἐν ἐσχάταις ἡμέραις.	Q 12.33 μὴ **θησαυρίζετε** ὑμῖν θησαυροὺς ἐπὶ τῆς γῆς, ὅπου σὴς καὶ βρῶσις ἀφανίζει, καὶ ὅπου κλέπται διορύσσουσιν καὶ κλέπτουσιν· **θησαυρίζετε** δὲ ὑμῖν θησαυρο.. ἐν οὐραν[[ῷ]], ὅπου οὔτε σὴς οὔτε βρῶσις ἀφανίζει, καὶ ὅπου κλέπται οὐ διορύσσουσιν οὐδὲ κλέπτουσιν·

	James	Sayings Gospel Q
17	5.19-20 ἀδελφοί μου, ἐάν τις ἐν ὑμῖν πλανηθῇ ἀπὸ τῆς ἀληθείας καὶ ἐπιστρέψῃ τις αὐτόν, γινωσκέτω ὅτι ὁ ἐπιστρέψας ἁμαρτωλὸν ἐκ πλάνης ὁδοῦ αὐτοῦ σώσει ψυχὴν αὐτοῦ ἐκ θανάτου καὶ καλύψει πλῆθος ἁμαρτιῶν.	Q 17.3 ἐὰν ἁμαρτήσῃ [[εἰς σὲ]] ὁ ἀδελφός σου ἐπιτίμησον αὐτῷ, καὶ ἐὰν [[μετανοήσῃ]], ἄφες αὐτῷ.
18	2.10 ὅστις γὰρ ὅλον τὸν **νόμον** τηρήσῃ, πταίσῃ δὲ ἐν ἑνί, γέγονεν πάντων ἔνοχος.	Q 16.17 [[εὐκοπώτερον δέ ἐστιν τὸν]] οὐρανο[[ν]] καὶ [[τὴν]] γῆ[[ν]] παρελθ[[εῖν ἢ ἰῶτα ἓν ἢ]] μία[[ν]] κεραία[[ν]] τοῦ **νόμου** [[πεσεῖν]]
19	4.4 οὐκ οἴδατε ὅτι ἡ φιλία τοῦ κόσμου ἔχθρα τοῦ θεοῦ ἐστιν; ὃς ἐὰν οὖν βουληθῇ φίλος εἶναι τοῦ κόσμου, ἐχθρὸς τοῦ θεοῦ καθίσταται.	Q 16.13 οὐδεὶς δύναται δυσὶ κυρίοις δουλεύειν· ἢ γὰρ τὸν ἕνα μισήσει καὶ τὸν ἕτερον ἀγαπήσει, ἢ ἑνὸς ἀνθέξεται καὶ τοῦ ἑτέρου καταφρονήσει. οὐ δύνασθε θεῷ δουλεύειν καὶ μαμωνᾷ.
20	4.10 ταπεινώθητε ἐνώπιον κυρίου, καὶ **ὑψώσει** ὑμᾶς	Q 14.11/18.14 πᾶς ὁ **ὑψῶν** ἑαυτὸν **ταπεινωθήσεται** καὶ ὁ **ταπεινῶν** ἑαυτὸν **ὑψωθήσεται**

James	Sayings Gospel Q
E	*Further Connections with Matthaean Tradition*
21	5.12 πρὸ πάντων δέ, ἀδελφοί μου, μὴ ὀμνύετε, μήτε τὸν οὐρανὸν μήτε τὴν γῆν μήτε ἄλλον τινὰ ὅρκον· ἤτω δὲ ὑμῶν τὸ ναὶ ναὶ καὶ τὸ οὒ οὔ, ἵνα μὴ ὑπὸ κρίσιν πέσητε.	Mt. 5.33-37 πάλιν ἠκούσατε ὅτι ἐρρέθη τοῖς ἀρχαίοις, Οὐκ ἐπιορκήσεις, ἀποδώσεις δὲ τῷ κυρίῳ τοὺς ὅρκους σου. ἐγὼ δὲ λέγω ὑμῖν μὴ ὀμόσαι ὅλως· μήτε ἐν τῷ οὐρανῷ, ὅτι θρόνος ἐστὶν τοῦ θεοῦ· μήτε ἐν τῇ γῇ, ὅτι ὑποπόδιόν ἐστιν τῶν ποδῶν αὐτοῦ· μήτε εἰς Ἱεροσόλυμα, ὅτι πόλις ἐστὶν τοῦ μεγάλου βασιλέως· μήτε ἐν τῇ κεφαλῇ σου ὀμόσῃς, ὅτι οὐ δύνασαι μίαν τρίχα λευκὴν ποιῆσαι ἢ μέλαιναν. ἔστω δὲ ὁ λόγος ὑμῶν ναὶ ναί, οὒ οὔ· τὸ δὲ περισσὸν τούτων ἐκ τοῦ πονηροῦ ἐστιν.
22	2.15-16 ἐὰν ἀδελφὸς ἢ ἀδελφὴ γυμνοὶ ὑπάρχωσιν καὶ λειπόμενοι τῆς ἐφημέρου τροφῆς, εἴπῃ δέ τις αὐτοῖς ἐξ ὑμῶν, ὑπάγετε ἐν εἰρήνῃ, θερμαίνεσθε καὶ χορτάζεσθε, μὴ δῶτε δὲ αὐτοῖς τὰ ἐπιτήδεια τοῦ σώματος, τί τὸ ὄφελος;	Mt. 25.34-35 τότε ἐρεῖ ὁ βασιλεὺς τοῖς ἐκ δεξιῶν αὐτοῦ, δεῦτε, οἱ εὐλογημένοι τοῦ πατρός μου, κληρονομήσατε τὴν ἡτοιμασμένην ὑμῖν βασιλείαν ἀπὸ καταβολῆς κόσμου· *ἐπείνασα* γὰρ καὶ ἐδώκατέ μοι φαγεῖν, ἐδίψησα καὶ ἐποτίσατέ με, ξένος ἤμην καὶ συνηγάγετέ με, Lk. 3.11 ἀποκριθεὶς δὲ ἔλεγεν αὐτοῖς, ὁ ἔχων δύο χιτῶνας μεταδότω τῷ μὴ ἔχοντι, καὶ ὁ ἔχων βρώματα ὁμοίως ποιείτω.

TABLE 2 James and the Jesus Tradition

	James	Sayings Gospel Q
1	1.2 πᾶσαν *χαρὰν* ἡγήσασθε, ἀδελφοί μου, ὅταν πειρασμοῖς περιπέσητε ποικίλοις. 12 *μακάριος* ἀνὴρ ὃς ὑπομένει πειρασμόν, ὅτι δόκιμος γενόμενος λήμψεται τὸν στέφανον τῆς ζωῆς, ὃν ἐπηγγείλατο τοῖς ἀγαπῶσιν αὐτόν. 5.10 ὑπόδειγμα λάβετε, ἀδελφοί, τῆς κακοπαθείας καὶ τῆς μακροθυμίας τοὺς *προφήτας*, οἳ ἐλάλησαν ἐν τῷ ὀνόματι κυρίου.	Q 6.22-23 *μακάριοί* ἐστε ὅταν ὀνειδίσωσιν ὑμᾶς καὶ [[διώξ]]ωσιν καὶ [[εἴπ]]ωσιν πᾶν πονηρὸν [[καθ᾽]] ὑμῶν ἕνεκεν τοῦ υἱοῦ τοῦ ἀνθρώπου· *χαίρετε* καὶ [[ἀγαλλιᾶσθε]], ὅτι ὁ μισθὸς ὑμῶν πολὺς ἐν τῷ οὐρανῷ· οὕτως γὰρ [[ἐδίωξαν]] τοὺς *προφήτας* πρὸ ὑμῶν.
2	1.5 εἰ δέ τις ὑμῶν λείπεται σοφίας, *αἰτείτω* παρὰ τοῦ *διδόντος* θεοῦ πᾶσιν ἁπλῶς καὶ μὴ ὀνειδίζοντος, καὶ *δοθήσεται* αὐτῷ. 17 πᾶσα *δόσις ἀγαθὴ* καὶ πᾶν δώρημα τέλειον ἄνωθέν ἐστιν, καταβαῖνον ἀπὸ τοῦ *πατρὸς* τῶν φώτων. 4.2c-3 οὐκ ἔχετε διὰ τὸ μὴ *αἰτεῖσθαι* ὑμᾶς· *αἰτεῖτε* καὶ οὐ *λαμβάνετε*, διότι κακῶς *αἰτεῖσθε*, ἵνα ἐν ταῖς ἡδοναῖς ὑμῶν δαπανήσητε. 1.12: See 1.2 1.17: See 1.5	Q 11.9 λέγω ὑμῖν, *αἰτεῖτε* καὶ *δοθήσεται* ὑμῖν, ζητεῖτε καὶ εὑρήσετε· κρούετε, καὶ ἀνοιγήσεται ὑμῖν... 13 εἰ οὖν ὑμεῖς πονηροὶ ὄντες οἴδατε *δόματα ἀγαθὰ* διδόναι τοῖς τέκνοις ὑμῶν, πόσῳ μᾶλλον ὁ *πατὴρ* ἐξ οὐρανοῦ δώσει *ἀγαθὰ* τοῖς *αἰτοῦσιν* αὐτόν.
3	2.5 οὐχ ὁ θεὸς ἐξελέξατο τοὺς *πτωχοὺς* τῷ κόσμῳ πλουσίους ἐν πίστει καὶ κληρονόμους τῆς *βασιλείας* ἧς ἐπηγγείλατο τοῖς ἀγαπῶσιν αὐτόν;	Q 6.20b *μακάριοι* οἱ *πτωχοί*· ὅτι [[ὑμετέρα]] ἐστὶν ἡ *βασιλεία* τοῦ θεοῦ.

James	Sayings Gospel Q
4.2c-3: See 1.5	
4 4.4 οὐκ οἴδατε ὅτι ἡ φιλία τοῦ κόσμου ἔχθρα τοῦ θεοῦ ἐστιν; ὃς ἐὰν οὖν βουληθῇ φίλος εἶναι τοῦ κόσμου, ἐχθρὸς τοῦ θεοῦ καθίσταται.	Q 16.13 οὐδεὶς δύναται δυσὶ κυρίοις δουλεύειν· ἢ γὰρ τὸν ἕνα μισήσει καὶ τὸν ἕτερον ἀγαπήσει, ἢ ἑνὸς ἀνθέξεται καὶ τοῦ ἑτέρου καταφρονήσει. οὐ δύνασθε θεῷ δουλεύειν καὶ μαμωνᾷ.
5 4.9 ταλαιπωρήσατε καὶ **πενθήσατε** καὶ **κλαύσατε·** ὁ γέλως ὑμῶν εἰς πένθος μετατραπήτω καὶ ἡ χαρὰ εἰς κατήφειαν.	Q 6.21b μακάριοι οἱ [[πενθ]]ο[[ῦ]]ντες, ὅτι [[παρακληθήσεσθε]] Q [[6.25]] οὐαὶ ὑμῖν, οἱ ἐμπεπλησμένοι, ὅτι πεινάσετε. οὐαί, οἱ γελῶντες, ὅτι **πενθήσετε** καὶ **κλαύσετε.**
6 4.10 **ταπεινώθητε** ἐνώπιον κυρίου, καὶ **ὑψώσει** ὑμᾶς	Q 14.11/18.14 πᾶς ὁ **ὑψῶν** ἑαυτὸν **ταπεινωθήσεται** καὶ ὁ **ταπεινῶν** ἑαυτὸν **ὑψωθήσεται**
7 5.1 ἄγε **νῦν** οἱ πλούσιοι, κλαύσατε ὀλολύζοντες ἐπὶ ταῖς ταλαιπωρίαις ὑμῶν ταῖς ἐπερχομέναις.	Q [[6.24]] πλὴν οὐαὶ ὑμῖν τοῖς πλουσίοις, ὅτι ἀπέχετε τὴν παράκλησιν ὑμῶν.
8 5.2-3 ὁ πλοῦτος ὑμῶν σέσηπεν καὶ τὰ ἱμάτια ὑμῶν σητόβρωτα γέγονεν, ὁ χρυσὸς ὑμῶν καὶ ὁ ἄργυρος κατίωται, καὶ ὁ ἰὸς αὐτῶν εἰς μαρτύριον ὑμῖν ἔσται καὶ φάγεται τὰς σάρκας ὑμῶν ὡς πῦρ· ἐθησαυρίσατε ἐν ἐσχάταις ἡμέραις.	Q 12.33 μὴ **θησαυρίζετε** ὑμῖν θησαυροὺς ἐπὶ τῆς γῆς, ὅπου σὴς καὶ βρῶσις ἀφανίζει, καὶ ὅπου κλέπται διορύσσουσιν καὶ κλέπτουσιν· **θησαυρίζετε** δὲ ὑμῖν θησαυρο... ἐν οὐραν[[ῷ]], ὅπου οὔτε σὴς οὔτε βρῶσις ἀφανίζει, καὶ ὅπου κλέπται οὐ διορύσσουσιν οὐδὲ κλέπτουσιν·.
9 5.9 μὴ στενάζετε, ἀδελφοί, κατ' ἀλλήλων, ἵνα μὴ **κριθῆτε·**	Q 6.37-38 μὴ **κρίνετε** ... μὴ **κριθῆτε·** [[ἐν ᾧ γὰρ κρίματι κρίνετε κριθήσεσθε, καὶ ἐν]] ᾧ γὰρ μέτρῳ μετρεῖτε μετρηθήσεται ὑμῖν.

	James	Sayings Gospel Q
	5.10: See 1.2	
10	5.19-20 ἀδελφοί μου, ἐάν τις ἐν ὑμῖν πλανηθῇ ἀπὸ τῆς ἀληθείας καὶ ἐπιστρέψῃ τις αὐτόν, 20 γινωσκέτω ὅτι ὁ ἐπιστρέψας ἁμαρτωλὸν ἐκ πλάνης ὁδοῦ αὐτοῦ σώσει ψυχὴν αὐτοῦ ἐκ θανάτου καὶ καλύψει πλῆθος ἁμαρτιῶν.	Q 17.3 ἐὰν ἁμαρτήσῃ [[εἰς σὲ]] ὁ ἀδελφός σου ἐπιτίμησον αὐτῷ, καὶ ἐὰν [[μετανοήσῃ]], ἄφες αὐτῷ.
		Matthew
11	5.12 πρὸ πάντων δέ, ἀδελφοί μου, μὴ ὀμνύετε, μήτε τὸν οὐρανὸν μήτε τὴν γῆν μήτε ἄλλον τινὰ ὅρκον· ἤτω δὲ ὑμῶν τὸ ναὶ ναὶ καὶ τὸ οὒ οὔ, ἵνα μὴ ὑπὸ κρίσιν πέσητε.	Mt. 5.33-37 πάλιν ἠκούσατε ὅτι ἐρρέθη τοῖς ἀρχαίοις, Οὐκ ἐπιορκήσεις, ἀποδώσεις δὲ τῷ κυρίῳ τοὺς ὅρκους σου. ἐγὼ δὲ λέγω ὑμῖν μὴ ὀμόσαι ὅλως· μήτε ἐν τῷ οὐρανῷ, ὅτι θρόνος ἐστὶν τοῦ θεοῦ· μήτε ἐν τῇ γῇ, ὅτι ὑποπόδιόν ἐστιν τῶν ποδῶν αὐτοῦ· μήτε εἰς Ἱεροσόλυμα, ὅτι πόλις ἐστὶν τοῦ μεγάλου βασιλέως· μήτε ἐν τῇ κεφαλῇ σου ὀμόσῃς, ὅτι οὐ δύνασαι μίαν τρίχα λευκὴν ποιῆσαι ἢ μέλαιναν. ἔστω δὲ ὁ λόγος ὑμῶν ναὶ ναί, οὒ οὔ· τὸ δὲ περισσὸν τούτων ἐκ τοῦ πονηροῦ ἐστιν.

THE LANGUAGES OF 'HOUSEHOLD' AND 'KINGDOM' IN THE LETTER OF JAMES: A SOCIO-RHETORICAL STUDY

Wesley H. Wachob

The purpose of this essay is to show how socio-rhetorical interpretation impacts on the study of the Epistle of James. A few introductory remarks about the so-called 'method' of socio-rhetorical criticism, what it is and what it seeks to do, are in order. The first thing to keep in mind is that socio-rhetorical criticism is not just another method in the interpretive repertoire. Because it presumes that no one method can exhaust the hermeneutical potential of a given text, it may be regarded as something of an anti-method. Because it is 'a multi-dimensional approach to texts guided by a multi-dimensional hermeneutic', it is more correctly under-stood as an 'interpretive analytic'.[1] Within the context of detailed exegesis, socio-rhetorical interpretation brings together in dialogical relation the resources of rhetoric, anthropology and sociology for analysing and interpreting texts.[2]

The term 'socio-rhetorical' is the coinage of Vernon K. Robbins and characterizes the interpretive process that he has developed, taught and practised for more than two decades.[3] In the introduction to his essay, 'Beginnings and Developments in Socio-Rhetorical Interpretation', he provides us with a brief overview of this multi-dimensional approach to texts:

---

1. Vernon K. Robbins, *The Tapestry of Early Christian Discourse: Rhetoric, Society and Ideology* (London and New York: Routledge, 1996), pp. 11–13.
2. See David B. Gowler, 'The Development of Socio-Rhetorical Criticism', in Vernon K. Robbins, *New Boundaries in Old Territory: Forms and Social Rhetoric in Mark* (ed. D. B. Gowler; Emory Studies in Early Christianity, 3; New York: Peter Lang, 1994), pp. 1–35; cf. Vernon K. Robbins, 'Introduction', in *Jesus the Teacher: A Socio-Rhetorical Interpretation of Mark* (Minneapolis: Fortress, rev. edn, 1992), pp. xix–xliv.
3. The very fine commentaries of Ben Witherington (e.g., *Conflict and Community in Corinth: A Socio-Rhetorical Commentary on 1 and 2 Corinthians* [Grand Rapids: Eerdmans; Carlisle: Paternoster; 1995] and *The Acts of the Apostles: A Socio-Rhetorical Commentary* [Grand Rapids: Eerdmans; Carlisle: Paternoster, 1998]) are not strictly socio-rhetorical commentaries. They remain in the mode of the historical-critical commentary and are more literary–theological in bent.

During the 1980s ancient *Progymnasmata* manuals guided the development of rhetorical strategies to interpret argumentation in first century
Christian and Greco-Roman literature. During the 1990s, investigation
of inner texture, intertexture, social and cultural texture, ideological
texture and sacred texture moved the approach into an interpretive
analytic. Currently, incorporation of conceptual blending and critical
spatiality theory is guiding interpretation of six rhetorolects in early
Christian discourse: wisdom, prophetic, miracle, precreation, priestly
and apocalyptic.[4]

At present, Robbins has given us two foundational studies that define and
demonstrate socio-rhetorical analysis in almost workbook fashion:
*Exploring the Textures of Texts: A Guide to Socio-Rhetorical
Interpretation* and *The Tapestry of Early Christian Discourse: Rhetoric,
Society and Ideology*.[5]

Socio-rhetorical interpretation is a dynamic, evolving analytics, one
that intentionally invites new methods and perspectives to become part of
the critical, interpretive dialogue.[6] Moreover, with its 'interdisciplinary
and intercultural base and focus', it is predisposed 'to move beyond
biblical studies into other disciplines and traditions' and has already done
so.[7] Because it uses 'a transmodern philosophical position of relationism
to interrelate ancient, modern and post-modern systems of thought with
one another. . . [we] can expect an even greater extension of this approach
into other fields in the coming years'.[8]

In brief, socio-rhetorical interpretation presupposes that all language is
a social possession. Language is also a tacit social tool, a means by which
humans understand and construct their worlds. Accordingly, socio-
rhetorical criticism intentionally uses the resources of sociology and
anthropology to analyse and understand the language in a text. It takes

---

4. Vernon K. Robbins, 'Beginnings and Developments in Socio-Rhetorical
Interpretation', in *Companion to the New Testament* (Malden, MA: Blackwell; forthcoming),
p. 1.

5. Vernon K. Robbins, *Exploring the Textures of Texts: A Guide to Socio-Rhetorical
Interpretation* (Valley Forge, PA: Trinity Press International, 1996); Robbins, *The Tapestry
of Early Christian Discourse*.

6. For a programmatic description, Vernon K. Robbins, 'The Present and Future of
Rhetorical Analysis', in *The Rhetorical Analysis of Scripture: Essays from the 1995 London
Conference* (ed. S. E. Porter and T. H. Olbricht; JSNTSup, 146; Sheffield: Sheffield Academic
Press, 1997), pp. 24–52; and for the most recent assessment, see Vernon K. Robbins, 'The
Rhetorical Full-Turn in Biblical Interpretation and Its Relevance for Feminist
Hermeneutics', in *Her Master's Tools? Feminist and Postcolonial Engagements of
Historical-Critical Discourse* (ed. Caroline Vander Stichele and Todd Penner; SBL Global
Perspectives on Biblical Scholarship Series, 9; Atlanta: SBL; Leiden: E. J. Brill, 2005), pp.
109–27.

7. Robbins, 'Beginnings and Developments', p. 14.

8. Robbins, 'Beginnings and Developments', pp. 2, 14.

very seriously the classical understanding of rhetoric as the art of persuasion. A rhetorical analysis concentrates fundamentally on what a text does or intends to do: it helps us understand the social, cultural and ideological nature and function of human discourse.

This essay presupposes the following: (1) the Epistle of James is a written instance of deliberative rhetoric, a text that seeks to persuade its addressees to think and act in particular ways.[9] (2) There are at least six major 'rhetorolects' that permeate early Christian discourse (wisdom, prophetic, miracle, priestly, precreation and apocalyptic); two of these (wisdom rhetorolect and prophetic rhetorolect) are crucial to the persuasive intent of James' rhetoric. (3) Two topics, 'household' and 'kingdom', are prominent in the social and cultural intertexture of the Epistle of James; and (4) these topics are fundamentally important in Christian wisdom and prophetic discourses. (5) The languages of 'household' and 'kingdom' (i.e., the languages in which these two topics play large) blend in the rhetoric of James. (6) The ways in which wisdom and prophetic rhetorolects interact with each other in the Epistle of James helps to create the configurations of speech in the text.

Our goal is to demonstrate something of the persuasive artistry of the Epistle of James by showing how it addresses communities of Christian Jews as belonging to law-abiding Israel and justifies a particular appropriation of Jesus' interpretation of the Torah as the cultural script for their thought and action.

1. *The Epistle of James as Rhetorical Discourse*[10]

The Epistle of James presents itself as a letter (1.1). As such it is, according to ancient epistolary theory, 'a substitute for oral communication and

9. This is the conclusion of Klaus Berger, *Formsgeschichte des Neuen Testaments* (Heidelberg: Quelle & Meyer, 1984), p. 147; cf. Klaus Berger, 'Der Jakobusbrief', in *Bibelkunde des Alten und Neuen Testaments*, vol. 2 *Neues Testament* (Heidelberg: Quelle & Meyer, 2nd edn, 1984), pp. 457–61 § 71; Ernst Baasland, 'Der Jakobusbrief als neutestamentliche Weisheitsschrift', *ST* 36 (1982), pp. 119–39; Ernst Baasland, 'Literarische Form, Thematik und geschichtliche Einordnung des Jakobusbriefes', *ANRW* 2.25.5, pp. 3646–84; Wilhelm H. Wuellner, 'Der Jakobusbrief im Licht der Rhetorik und Textpragmatik', *LB* 43 (1978), pp. 5–66.

10. My tentative outline of James as a rhetorical discourse is as follows: *inscriptio* (1.1); *exordium* (1.2-12); *narratio* (1.13-27); *argumentatio* (2.1–5.6); *peroratio* (5.7-20). The letter-*propositio* is Jas 1.12. See Wesley H. Wachob, '"The Rich in Faith" and "The Poor in Spirit": The Socio-Rhetorical Function of a Saying of Jesus in the Epistle of James' (unpublished doctoral dissertation; Emory University, 1993); Wesley H. Wachob, *The Voice of Jesus in the Social Rhetoric of James* (SNTSMS, 106; Cambridge and New York: Cambridge University Press, 2000), pp. 1–24, 52–58.

could function in almost as many ways as a speech'.[11] Because the Epistle of James lacks certain epistolary conventions that are typical in other NT letters (e.g., the letters of Paul), some scholars have been reluctant to accept it as a letter. Fortunately, much has been learned in the last three decades about both ancient letters and the overlap in epistolary practice and rhetorical theory. Given the incredible variety in extant letters and the obvious elasticity of the letter genre in antiquity, the scholarly majority now agree that the Epistle of James fits easily as an encyclical tailored for communities in the Diaspora.[12]

While distinctively literary approaches to texts ask what a text is, the approach in this essay is rhetorical. Distinctive to rhetorical analysis is the question of what a text does or what it intends to do. In other words, rhetorical criticism focuses on the functional aspect of texts, on language as a tool. The instrumental aspect of the Epistle of James is one of the things that most intrigue us. Rhetorical analysis looks at a text as the embodiment of an intention; it can help us discover the latent intent in James' discourse. Socio-rhetorical interpretation can illuminate the social, cultural and ideological dimensions of James' rhetoric.[13]

From a rhetorical perspective, the Epistle of James has 'a message to convey' and seeks 'to persuade an audience to believe it [the message] or to believe it more profoundly'.[14] In the terminology of Graeco-Roman rhetoric, the Epistle of James generally exhibits the characteristics of a symbouleutic or deliberative discourse.[15] Such a discourse seeks to make an effective difference in a given social history by using exhortation

---

11. David E. Aune, *The New Testament in Its Literary Environment* (LEC, 8; Philadelphia: Westminster, 1987), p. 158. Demetrius, *Eloc.* 223–24.

12. For a detailed discussion of the problems associated with classifying James' text as a letter, the overlap between epistolary and rhetorical theory in the ancient world and the analysis and interpretation of letters as rhetorical discourse, see Wachob, *The Voice of Jesus*.

13. See Wachob, *The Voice of Jesus*.

14. George A. Kennedy, *New Testament Interpretation through Rhetorical Criticism* (Chapel Hill and London: University of North Carolina Press, 1984), p. 3.

15. Συμβουλυτικόν (Aristotle, *Rhet.* 1.3.3); συμβουλή (Aristotle, *Rhet.* 1.3.3; 1.3.9); δημηγορικόν (Aristotle, *Rhet. Alex.* 1.1421b.8); δημαγορία (Aristotle, *Rhet. Alex.* 1.1421b.13); *deliberativus* ([Cicero], *Rhet. Her.* 1.2.2; Cicero, *Inv.* 1.5.7; 2.51.155–58.176; *De or.* 2.81.333–83.340; Quintilian, *Inst.* 2.4.24-25; 2.21.23; 3.3.14; 3.4.9, 14-15; [Cicero], *Rhet. Her.* 1.2.2); *deliberatio* (Cicero, *Inv.* 1.9.12; Quintilian, *Inst.* 3.8.10; [Cicero], *Rhet. Her.* 3.2-5). Also Heinrich Lausberg, *Elemente der Literarischen Rhetorik* (Munich: Max Hueber Verlag, 3rd rev. edn, 1967), vol. 1, sections 224–38; Josef Martin, *Antike Rhetorik. Technik und Methode* (Handbuch der Altertumswissenschaft, 2.3; Munich: C. H. Beck, 1974), pp. 167–76, 356–420; and George A. Kennedy, *The Art of Persuasion in Ancient Greece* (Princeton: Princeton University Press, 1963), pp. 203–206); George A. Kennedy, *The Art of Rhetoric in the Roman World* (Princeton: Princeton University Press, 1972), 18–21; George A. Kennedy, 'The Genres of Rhetoric', in *Handbook of Classical Rhetoric in the Hellenistic Period 330 B.C.–A.D. 400* (ed. S. E. Porter; Leiden: E. J. Brill, 1997), pp. 43–50.

(προτροπή) and dissuasion (ἀποτροπή) to persuade its addressees to take a particular course of action in the future (Aristotle, *Rhet.* 1.3.3-9).[16]

In what follows we shall concentrate mainly on the letter prescript (Jas 1.1), the *exordium* (1.2-13), *narratio* (1.13-27) and the first and fundamental argument in the *confirmatio* (2.1-12). The letter prescript is the fundamental element in epistolary form and, while it is not a technical feature in rhetorical arrangement, it does have an undeniable rhetorical function which is like that of the *exordium*. It joins with the *exordium* (1.2-12) to prepare the audience for the discourse that follows. Together the prescript and *exordium* introduce the author and the audience, help to establish the *ethos, pathos* and *logos* of the letter and prepare for the topics that are used in developing the discourse. The rhetorical problem of the letter ('the various trials of faith') is introduced in the *exordium* and its positive aspects and results are rehearsed. In the *narratio* the negative dimension of this problem is defined and in the first argument of the *confirmatio*, a particular trial of faith for the community, the conflict between the rich and poor, is embellished.[17] We shall be looking for the topics of 'household' and 'kingdom' and for wisdom and prophetic rhetorolects.

2. The Social and Cultural Intertexture of the Epistle of James

Intertexture concerns the ways in which a text represents, refers to and uses phenomena outside itself, things like other texts, social codes and conventions, cultural traditions and historical events.[18] We are particularly interested in James' cultural intertexture, or 'insider knowledge'. This is the sort of knowledge that one may acquire only by being involved in a particular culture or by interacting with it in some personal manner. 'Cultural intertexture appears in a text in three ways, in a reference, an allusion, or echo.'[19] In the Epistle of James cultural intertexture is conspicuous from the very beginning, in the letter prescript (1.1), in the *references* to James, God, the Lord Jesus Christ and the twelve tribes in the dispersion. The 'insider' knowledge signalled here permeates every-

---

16. James' text may be divided into eight (argumentative) sections (1.1-12; 1.13-27; 2.1-13; 2.14-26; 3.1-18; 4.1-12; 4.13–5.6; 5.7-20); each section is characterized by exhortation and dissuasion that concerns thought and action of social consequence in reference to the future or the present.

17. Wesley H. Wachob, 'The Apocalyptic Intertexture of the Epistle of James', in *The Intertexture of Apocalyptic Discourse in the New Testament* (ed. Duane F. Watson; SBLSS, 14; Atlanta: Society of Biblical Literature, 2002), pp. 165–85.

18. On 'intertexture' see Robbins, *Exploring*, pp. 40–70.

19. Robbins, *Exploring*, pp. 58–62.

thing else in the letter.[20] A brief look at these references sets the stage for our focus on topics of 'household' and 'kingdom' and their 'language worlds'.[21]

'James, a servant of God and of the Lord Jesus Christ' (Jas 1.1a). The predominant scholarly opinion holds that in early Christianity there was but one James who could have addressed a discourse in this manner and expected it to be well-received: that was James, the Lord's brother (Gal. 1.19; 2.9, 12; Mt. 13.55; Mk 6.3; Acts 12.17; 15.13; 21.18; 1 Cor. 15.7; cf. Jude 1). Whether he actually wrote our letter is not the issue before us; our question is whose identity and authority does the prescript presuppose and intend to convey? The most plausible answer is that the letter wishes to be heard as a discourse from 'the Lord's brother' and 'more than any other person in the early church', James 'was the representative figure of Jewish Christianity'.[22] Robert Grant correctly pointed out long ago that the materials in the letter may well go back to the early days of the Jerusalem church.[23] We shall try to read the letter as it intends to be read: as from the Lord's brother.

The noun δοῦλος, 'servant (or slave)', is properly an element of social intertexture.[24] Here, characterizing James in relation to God and Jesus Christ, it also broaches the Jewish-Christian cultural topic of a 'servant of the Lord'.[25] So understood, this is a status claim of great significance. The 'slave' metaphor was employed by persons who desired to present

20. The Letter of James features eight proper names: James (1.1), Jesus Christ (1.1; 2.1) Abraham (2.21, 23), Isaac (2.21), Rahab (2.25), Sabaoth (5.4), Job (5.11) and Elijah (5.17). While all of these names evoke Jewish culture, James and Jesus Christ mark it as Jewish-Christian culture.

21. For the phrase 'language world' see James Luther Mays, *The Lord Reigns: A Theological Handbook to the Psalms* (Louisville: Westminster John Knox, 1994), pp. 87–98.

22. W. Kümmel, *Introduction to the New Testament* (Nashville: Abingdon, rev. edn, 1975), p. 412; Brevard Childs, *The New Testament as Canon: An Introduction* (Philadelphia: Fortress, 1984), p. 435.

23. Robert M. Grant, *A Historical Introduction to the New Testament* (San Francisco: Harper & Row, 1963), p. 222. On the authorship of James' letter (both historical and implied), see Wachob, *The Voice of Jesus*.

24. Robbins, *Exploring*, pp. 62–63. 'Social knowledge is commonly held by all persons of a region, no matter what their particular "cultural" location may be.' Generally, it has four categories: social roles or identity, social institutions, social codes and social relationships (p. 62).

25. In the OT the servant of Lord is one who belongs to (Yahweh) and seeks to do his will; e.g., Abraham (Gen. 26.24), Moses (Exod. 14.31), Joshua (Judg. 2.8), David (2 Sam. 5.7, 8), Hezekiah (2 Chron. 32.16), Isaiah (Isa. 20.3; cf. Isa. 40–45), Zerubbabel (Hag. 2.23), Job (1.8), and the prophets, as individuals (Elijah, 2 Kgs 9.36) and as a group (Amos 3.7; Jer. 7.25). In the NT, Jesus is the servant of the Lord (Mt. 8.17; cf. Isa. 53.4); elsewhere this language is used by James (Jas 1.1); Paul, who is the servant of both Jesus Christ (Rom. 1.1; Gal. 1.10; Phil. 1.1) and God (Tit. 1.1); see also Peter (2 Pet. 1.1), Jude (1) and the author of Revelation (Rev. 1.1; 7.3).

themselves as spokespersons and representatives of their master or patron; so, in a patron–client milieu, James' use of the term 'servant' in the letter prescript claims for himself the status of a client. He speaks for his patrons, God and the Lord Jesus Christ.[26] This is a noble reference and thereby the rhetorical topic of 'honour', which is fundamental throughout the discourse, is in play (cf. Jas 2.1).[27] The only other obvious self-identifying references of our author occur in Jas 3.1, where he identifies himself as a 'teacher' (διδάσκολος) and 'brother' (ἀδελφός) of his addressees.[28] Here, too, as the unit makes clear, is a claim to honourable status (see Jas 3.1-18). Moreover, the tone of the letter exudes authority. As Demetrius puts it: the tone of the discourse is not that of a friendly letter; this is an *ex cathedra* address.[29] In other words, the sententious maxims and style of the epistle fit the image of a 'servant' of (= spokesperson for) God and the Lord Jesus Christ, who, as a wise 'teacher' and 'brother' of his addressees, is genuinely concerned for their well-being.[30]

James is a thoroughly theocentric discourse. A reference to God appears in every argumentative section of the letter. The common noun θεός occurs sixteen times (Jas 1.1, 5, 13 [2 ×], 20, 27; 2.5, 19, 23 [2 ×]; 3.9; 4.4 [2 ×], 6, 7, 8); the noun 'Lord' (κύριος) occurs fourteen times (1.1, 7; 2.1; 3.9; 4.10, 15; 5.4, 7, 8, 10, 11 [2 ×], 14, 15).[31] While 'Lord' is used of both God and Jesus Christ, it only enhances the theocentric character of our epistle. On the other hand, that it is poignantly used of Jesus Christ, who here is coordinated with God and throughout the letter is presumed to be one in will and purpose with God, tantalizingly raises the issue of James' Christology. The point: James announces for himself and presumes for his addressees the 'insider' knowledge of Jewish-Christian culture.

In referring to 'Jesus Christ' (Jas 1.1; 2.1), the issue of whether 'Christ' is used as a title or as a name is, as far as the rhetoric goes, a non-issue. The culture of the context is clear. In the mouth of the Lord's brother and

---

26. Dale B. Martin, *Slavery as Salvation: The Metaphor of Slavery in Pauline Christianity* (New Haven: Yale University Press, 1990), pp. 54–58.

27. See Wachob, *The Voice of Jesus*, pp. 64–70.

28. James uses the endearing 'my brothers' 11 times (1.2, 16, 19; 2.1, 5, 14; 3.1, 10, 12; 5.12, 19). The plural form 'brothers' occurs four times more (4.11; 5.7, 9, 10) and the singular 'brother' four times (1.9; 2.15; 4.11 [2 ×]); the term 'sister' one time (2.15). These terms evoke 'companionship, intimacy and kinship and similar relations and belong to the *topos* of "friendship"' (Aristotle, *Rhet.* 2.4.28; see 2.4.1-29).

29. Demetrius, *Eloc.* 231b-232. This style of letter certainly conforms to the status of the representative of Jewish Christianity, a 'pillar', as Paul calls him (Gal. 2.9).

30. On the rhetorical *topos* of 'friendship', see Aristotle, *Rhet.* 2.4.2.

31. 'Lord' as reference to God (1.7; 3.9; 5.4, 10, 11 [2 ×]); as reference to Jesus Christ (1.1; 2.1); as reference to God or Jesus Christ (4.10, 11; 5.7, 8, 14, 15). See Wachob, *The Voice of Jesus*, p. 68.

within communities of Jewish Christians in the diaspora a reference to 'Jesus Christ' was hardly an ambiguous reference. That Jesus is considered by the author to be the Messiah is clear enough, but Messiah is a rather slippery term. Here it is enough to note that the letter superscription (Jas 1.1a) is patently limited by the adscript, 'to the twelve tribes in the dispersion' (Jas 1.1b). One of the hallowed conceptions associated with the Messiah was the 'restoration' of Israel. This fits rather nicely with what we know of the period.[32]

The adscript (Jas 1.1b) identifies the addressees as 'the twelve tribes in the dispersion'. The 'twelve tribes' connote Israel, the Jews (Exod. 24.4; 28.21; 39.14; Josh. 4.5; Sir. 44.23; *Ass. Mos.* 2.4-5; *2 Bar.* 1.2; 62.5; 63.3; 64.5; 77.2; 78.1, 4; 84.3; *T. Abr.* 13.6; *T. Benj.* 9.2; Acts 26.7). The memory of 'the twelve tribes' continued to function even in the rabbinic period as a social and theological symbol of Israel's integrity and unity as God's chosen people.[33] Burton Mack argues that 'each of the early Jesus movements drew upon a conception of "Israel" in order to imagine its place in the scheme of things. These conceptions determined the stance each took in relation to some form of Judaism encountered directly in its particular environment.'[34] Limited by the spatial phrase 'in the dispersion', which refers to the scattering of the Jews, this seems to refer to communities outside Palestine (cf. Deut. 30.4; Neh. 1.9).

The reference to 'the twelve tribes in the dispersion' is an important conception that plays in the language world of Jewish culture and Jewish-Christian culture. With this reference the topics of the household and the kingdom begin to emerge. As part of the letter prescript, these words begin to create a discourse-picture in the minds of its readers.[35] The words evoke a particular culture, a particular story. From a socio-rhetorical perspective, the phrase 'to the twelve tribes in the dispersion' is a story-line: the story-line of the 'seed of Abraham' (Jas 2.21, 23; cf. Rom. 11.1). The story-line stands in the letter's foreground; the story of the house of Abraham itself stands in the background and permeates the entire discourse. For example, all the people who are named in James' letter are Jews who play a storied-role in the story of the twelve tribes that are now in the dispersion: James (Jas 1.1), Jesus Christ (1.1; 2.1), Abraham (2.21,

---

32. Here we have a blend of 'sacred' texture and 'historical' intertexture; see Robbins, *Exploring*, pp. 120–31 and 63–68, respectively.

33. J. H. Ropes, *A Critical and Exegetical Commentary on the Epistle of St. James* (ICC; Edinburgh: T&T Clark, 1916), pp. 120–25; and K. H. Rengstorf, 'δώδεκα, κτλ.', *TDNT* vol. 2, pp. 321–28; Christian Maurer, 'φυλή', *TDNT* vol. 9, pp. 245–50. Shaye J. D. Cohen, *From Maccabees to the Mishnah* (ed. W. A. Meeks; LEC, 7; Philadelphia: Westminster, 1987), pp. 104–23.

34. Burton L. Mack, *A Myth of Innocence: Mark and Christian Origins* (Philadelphia: Fortress, 1988), p. 127.

35. On 'rhetography', see Robbins, 'Beginnings and Developments', pp. 31–34.

23), Isaac (2.21), Rahab (2.25), the Lord Sabaoth (5.4), Job (5.11), and Elijah (5.17). The social location implied in the spatial reference 'in the dispersion' is a 'lived-experience': an 'embodied experience' in a social context. This begins to picture itself in the minds of the readers who hear James' discourse.

One facet of Abraham's story that seems to suggest itself here is that of 'movement', a 'faith journey' (Jas 2.21-23): from the house of Abraham to the house of Jacob/Israel (Gen. 17.23; 24.2; Isa. 29.22), to the twelve sons of Jacob/Israel, to the twelve tribes of Israel, to the kingdom of Israel, to the house/kingdom of David, to the twelve tribes in exile, to the promise of the restoration of the house/kingdom of Israel. The 'dispersion' itself symbolizes movement, too: out of the land of promise into 'the world' (*Pss. Sol.* 9.1).[36] The symbolic value of the dispersion and its social location of thought would not be lost on a first-century Jew, whether Christian or not.

The 'dispersion' also broaches the topic of 'shame', the opposite relation of 'honour' which is present in the 'noble' references to James, God, the Lord Jesus Christ, and in the prestigious title 'servant of God and of the Lord Jesus Christ'. Two aspects of this are important in James' text. On the one hand, Israel's dispersion is strongly associated with the topic of 'sin' (cf. *Pss. Sol.* 9.1-2, 11) and this topic plays large throughout our letter.[37] On the other hand, the dispersion carries with it the notion of a loss of status, possessions and security and connotes 'poverty'.[38] This, too, coheres ideologically with the theology of the piety of the poor, a subject that concerns more than one quarter of the entire text of the Epistle of James. James' energetic concern for the poor, on the other hand, resonates loudly with the Jesus tradition, which is powerfully exploited in our letter.[39]

Presupposing that we hear James' voice in this letter, it seems plausible that the salutation evokes as the primary audience an unspecified community or communities of Christian Jews, probably residing outside Palestine. Further, it seems probable that James of Jerusalem would have regarded as 'the twelve tribes' those Jews who embraced Jesus as the

---

36. On 'the world', as the sphere of enmity with God, see Luke Timothy Johnson, 'Friendship with the World/Friendship with God: A Study of Discipleship in James', in *Brother of Jesus, Friend of God: Studies in the Letter of James* (Grand Rapids: Eerdmans, 2004), pp. 202-20.

37. 'Sin' (ἁμαρτία) occurs seven times: Jas 1.15 (2 ×); 2.9; 4.17; 5.15, 16, 20; the cognate noun ἁμαρτωλός two times: Jas 4.8; 5.20.

38. Bruce J. Malina, *The New Testament World: Insights from Cultural Anthropology* (Atlanta: John Knox, 1981), p. 75.

39. See Wachob, *The Voice of Jesus*; cf. Wesley H. Wachob and Luke Timothy Johnson, 'The Sayings of Jesus in the Letter of James', in *Authenticating the Words of Jesus* (ed. B. Chilton and C. A. Evans; NTTS, 28; Leiden: E. J. Brill, 1999), pp. 431-50 (431).

Messiah (1.1; 2.1). The fact that among some early Christians there was a firm belief that part of the Messiah's work was the restoration of 'the twelve tribes' only strengthens this interpretation, as does the fact that celebrated conceptions of the anticipated restoration included the ideas of judgment and the re-establishment of justice as fundamental components, both of which are very prominent elements in the letter.[40] This interpretation is strongly buttressed by the thoroughly Jewish-Christian character of the document itself.[41]

The topics of 'household' and 'kingdom' are fundamental to two rhetorolects that appear in early Christian discourse. The configuration and function of these topics and other related motifs within the thoroughly deliberative discourse of the Epistle of James are what we hope to ascertain and elucidate. It is important to remember that 'topics' are networks of meanings and these meanings are shaped by their regular use in social, cultural and ideological contexts. Topics are elaborated in two ways: (1) by means of 'pictorial' speech; the language creates something of a verbal picture. When one verbal picture follows another in sequence, this produces a graphic story. This verbal-pictorial sequencing, as well as narrative description and picturesque expression, Robbins calls 'rhetography'. (2) Topics are also elaborated argumentatively, that is, enthymematically. Thus, a thesis or rule is presented, its warrant or rationale offered or implied and then by means of 'opposite, contrary, analogy, etc.' it creates an argument. Enthymematic argumentation, Robbins calls 'rhetology'. 'Each early Christian rhetorolect has its own way of blending pictorial narration and argumentation.'[42]

3. Wisdom Rhetorolect and Prophetic Rhetorolect in the Epistle of James[43]

'A rhetorolect is a form of language variety or discourse identifiable on the basis of a distinctive configuration of themes, topics, reasonings and argumentations.'[44] In each early Christian rhetorolect there is social,

---

40. *Sib. Or.* 2.171; 3.249; Acts 26.7. On Jesus and the 'restoration of Israel', see E. P. Sanders, *Jesus and Judaism* (Philadelphia: Fortress, 1985), pp. 99–119 (106).

41. See David Bartlett, 'The Epistle of James as a Jewish-Christian Document', in *Society of Biblical Literature 1979 Seminar Papers* (ed. P. Achtemeier; SBLSP, 2; Missoula, MT: Scholars Press, 1979), pp. 73–86; Luke Timothy Johnson, *The Letter of James* (AB, 37A; New York: Doubleday, 1995); Patrick J. Hartin, *James* (SP, 14; Collegeville, MN: Liturgical Press, 2003).

42. Robbins, 'Beginnings and Developments', pp. 30–31.

43. On 'rhetorolects' in the NT, see Vernon K. Robbins, 'The Dialectical Nature of Early Christian Discourse', *Scriptura* 59 (1996), pp. 353–62. Revised version online: http://www.emory.edu/COLLEGE/RELIGION/faculty/robbins/dialect/dialect353.html.

44. Robbins, 'The Dialectical Nature of Early Christian Discourse', p. 356.

cultural and ideological language that contributed to the creation of a new culture of discourse. In other words, within each rhetorolect or language environment there are social places (like the household, the empire, nature) and cultural spaces (like God's world, the Diaspora, the kingdom) in which people think, speak, feel and act to construct meaningful lives. In an effort to focus more closely on the social, cultural and ideological dimensions of these spaces, places and human activities, socio-rhetorical interpretation has begun to use critical spatiality theory with cognitive theory about 'conceptual blending' to construct typologies of spaces, places and activities in order to clarify 'the relation of social places to cultural, ideological and religious spaces in the six primary early Christian rhetorolects'.[45] These typologies, which are nothing more than heuristic tools (and always open to critical alteration and revision), enable the interpreter theoretically to sketch the ways in which the various rhetorolects appear to blend and reconfigure themselves in the invention of early Christian discourse.[46] Again, the socio-rhetorical function of language is in view.

For our purposes we shall utilize Vernon Robbins's heuristic typologies for 'wisdom rhetorolect' and 'prophetic rhetorolect'. Following Gilles Fauconnier and Mark Turner's *The Way We Think: Conceptual Blending and the Mind's Hidden Complexities*, Robbins holds that 'conceptual integration [or blending] always involves a blended space and at least two inputs and a generic space'.[47] Accordingly:

> Early Christian wisdom rhetorolect (generic space) blends human experiences of the household and the created world (firstspace: two places of social experience) with the cultural space of God's cosmos (secondspace). In the space of blending (thirdspace), God functions as heavenly Father over God's children in the world, who are to produce goodness and righteous [*sic*] through the medium of God's wisdom (light). Wisdom rhetorolect, then, features productivity and reproductivity. The goal of the conceptual blending is to create people who produce good, righteous action, thought, will and speech with the aid of God's light, which equals God's wisdom which certain people speak on earth.[48]
>
> Early Christian prophetic rhetorolect blends the speech and action of a prophet's body (firstspace) with the concept of a 'kingdom of God' that has political boundaries on the earth (secondspace). The reasoning

---

45. Vernon K. Robbins, 'Conceptual Blending and Early Christian Imagination' (unpublished paper presented at the Nordic Seminar, *Body, Mind, and Society in Early Christianity*, 31 August–3 September 2005, University of Helsinki), p. 5.

46. Robbins, 'Beginnings and Developments', p. 38.

47. Gilles Fauconnier and Mark Turner, *The Way We Think: Conceptual Blending and the Mind's Hidden Complexities* (New York: Basic Books, 2002), pp. xv, 279.

48. Robbins, 'Beginnings and Developments', p. 35.

in the rhetorolect presupposes that the prophet has received a divine message about God's will. The prophet speaks and acts in contexts that envision righteous judgments and actions by kings, who should be God's leaders who establish justice on the earth. As a result of the nature of God's message, the prophet regularly experiences significant resistance and often explicit rejection and persecution. In the space of blending, God functions as heavenly King over his righteous kingdom on earth. The nature of prophetic rhetorolect is to confront religious and political leaders who act on the basis of human greed, pride and power rather than God's justice, righteousness and mercy for all people in God's kingdom on the earth. The goal of prophetic rhetorolect is to create a governed realm on earth where God's righteousness is enacted among all of God's people in the realm with the aid of God's specially transmitted word in the form of prophetic action and speech (thirdspace).[49]

The vast majority of scholars agree that the Epistle of James is intimately connected with the wisdom tradition and it is frequently characterized as a type of sapiential discourse. According to Ernst Baasland, the Epistle of James is *the* wisdom book in the NT; he notes that 40 of its 108 verses contain parallels to wisdom literature.[50] We have already observed that the topic of 'honour' (τὸ καλόν)[51] is clearly in view in the letter prescript (Jas 1.1). Here we note that 'honour' has two divisions (*Rhet. Her.* 3.2.3; Cicero, *Inv.* 2.51.159–56.169): 'the right', which comprises topics like *wisdom*, justice, courage (a subtopic of which is endurance) and temperance; and 'the praiseworthy', which comprises those things that are praised by recognized authorities, like the gods, allies, fellow citizens and descendants. Given our epistle's sapiential leanings, what sorts of topics might we expect in its argumentative units?

'We shall be using the topics of Wisdom in our discourse if we compare advantages and disadvantages, counseling the pursuit of the one and the avoidance of the other'; and when 'we recommend some policy in a matter whose history we can recall either from direct experience or hearsay' (*Rhet. Her.* 3.3.4). In other words, the rhetoric will elaborate various topics in persuading its audience to pursue advantages and avoid disadvantages, based on experience and common knowledge.

In wisdom discourse from the Graeco-Roman world, three issues are fundamental: (1) What is God's relation to the world? (2) What is God's relation to human beings? (3) Given God's relation to the world and to

---

49. Robbins, 'Conceptual Blending and Early Christian Imagination', p. 9.

50. Baasland, 'Der Jakobusbrief als neutestamentliche Weisheitsschrift', pp. 119–39 (123–25).

51. Cf. the rhetorical topic 'glory' or 'reputation' (δόξα), an external good (Aristotle, *Rhet.* 1.5.4) and its relation to 'honour' (τιμή), another external good which is defined as 'a sign of the "reputation" for doing good' (1.5.9).

human beings, what is the relation of human beings to one another?[52] The
first chapter of our letter answers these questions. The answers given are
attributed to James, a spokesperson for God and the Lord Jesus Christ
and 'brother' to the community of faith (Jas 1.1). The *ethos* of James is
thoroughly honourable and the tone and style of his counsel is
authoritative.

There are several fundamental things that James says about God in the
exordium (1.1-12) and *narratio* (1.13-27) of the letter. (1) God gives to all
generously and without grudging (1.5). God is the creator of the world
and of human beings, and human beings are the first fruits of God's
creation (1.17-18). Because God has created the world and human beings,
human beings should face their trials of faith wisely (1.2-4) and with
complete trust in God (1.5-12, 13-18); they should act with restraint (1.19-
20) , informed by God's wisdom (1.21-25); they should care for one
another, especially the lowly (1.26-27), because all humans are the
children of God (1.18).

The exigence that prompts the Epistle of James is 'the various trials of
the community's faith' (1.2-4).[53] The proposition upon which the
discourse turns appears to be Jas 1.12, 'Blessed is the man [person] who
endures trial, for when he has stood the test he shall receive the crown of
life which [God] has promised to those who love him' (cf. 2.5). Great
benefit comes to those who endure trials of faith; the goal is to endure.
How then does one deal with trials of faith?

In the letter *exordium* (1.1-12), immediately after the author has
introduced the rhetorical topic, 'various trials' (1.2-4), the term 'wisdom'
(σοφία) makes its first appearance in the letter (1.5).[54] It occurs in the
form of a conditional statement, a piece of advice about prayer to God for
wisdom: 'If any of you lacks wisdom, let him ask God, who gives to all
generously and ungrudgingly and it will be given him.' The logic of the

---

52. Robbins, 'Argumentative Textures in Socio-Rhetorical Interpretation', in *Rhetorical
Argumentation in Biblical Texts: Essays From the Lund 2000 Conference* (ed. Anders
Ericksson, Thomas H. Olbricht and Walter Übelacker; Emory Studies in Early Christianity,
8; Harrisburg, PA: Trinity Press International, 2002), pp. 27–65 (15). See also Elisabeth
Schüssler Fiorenza, *In Memory of Her: A Feminist Theological Reconstruction of Christian
Origins* (New York: Crossroad, 1984); Leo G. Perdue, *Wisdom and Creation: The Theology of
Wisdom Literature* (Nashville: Abingdon, 1992); and John J. Collins, *Jewish Wisdom in the
Hellenistic Age* (Louisville: Westminster John Knox, 1997).

53. The term πίστις occurs 18 times: Jas 1.3, 6; 2.1, 5, 14 (2 ×), 17, 18 (3 ×), 19 (2 ×), 20,
22 (2 ×), 24, 26; 5.15. Wesley H. Wachob, 'The Epistle of James and the Book of Psalms: A
Socio-Rhetorical Perspective of Intertexture, Culture and Ideology in Religious Discourse',
in *Fabrics of Discourse* (Festschrift Vernon K. Robbins; ed. D. B. Gowler, L. Gregory
Bloomquist and D. F. Watson; Harrisburg: Trinity Press International, 2003), pp. 264–80.

54. See σοφία (Jas 1.5; 3.13, 15, 17); σόφος (3.13); ἐπιστήμων (3.13); ἐπίσταμαι (4.14);
γινώσκω (2.20; 3.13; 5.20); οἶδα (1.9; 3.1; 4.4, 17; 5.20).

rhetoric is that wisdom from God is needed to know how to deal with the various trials of faith: 'Count it all joy, my brothers [and sisters], whenever you fall into various trials, *knowing* (γινώσκοντες) that the trying of your faith produces patience. But let patience have its perfect work, in order that you might be perfect and complete, lacking in nothing' (Jas 1.2-4).

> *Rule*: Various tests of faith produce patience.
> *Case*: Your trials are tests of faith.
> *Conditional Result*: Your trials produce patience.
> *Exhortation drawn from the Case ('experience') and based on the Rule*:
> Count it all joy whenever you fall into various trials.

> *Rule*: Patience produces a perfect character.
> *Conditional Case*: Your tests of faith produce patience.
> *Conditional Result*: Your tests of faith produce a perfect character.
> *Exhortation drawn from Conditional Case ('experience') and based on the Rule*: Count it all joy whenever you fall into various trials.

Observe the attributes of God: God 'gives to all generously and ungrudgingly'. This belief in God's generosity is 'central to the wisdom rhetorolect in James'.[55]

> *Thesis*: If any of you is lacking in wisdom, ask God and it will be given you.
> *Rationale*: Because God gives to all generously and ungrudgingly.[56]

While the theme of 'various trials' structures the discourse, it should be noted that the matters addressed are very similar to those found in Ben Sira and the wisdom tradition (e.g., Sir. 2.1; Wis. 3.4-5; *Pss. Sol.* 16.14-15; Prov. 27.21). All the trials of faith belong to 'the perennial experience of life in God's service'.[57]

Fundamental to James' understanding of God is Jas 1.17: 'Every good gift and every perfect gift is from above and comes down from the Father of lights, with whom there is no variation or shadow due to change.' The pictorial-narrative dimensions in the succinct statements offered in James' first chapter are examples of 'rhetography'. For example, successive images of the instability of nature (in the waves of the sea, driven and tossed by the wind, Jas 1.6) and of the vicissitudes of life and its brevity (in the humble...being raised up; the rich...being brought low, withering like

---

55. Robbins, 'The Dialectical Nature of Early Christian Discourse', p. 357.

56. Robbins, 'The Dialectical Nature of Early Christian Discourse', p. 357.

57. Sophie Laws, *The Epistle of James* (HNTC; San Francisco: Harper & Row, 1980), pp. 51, 52; Rudolf Hoppe, *Der theologische Hintergrund* (FB, 28; Würzburg, Echter Verlag, 1977); and Richard J. Bauckham, *James: Wisdom of James, Disciple of Jesus the Sage* (New York: Routledge, 1999).

a flower in the field and passing away in the midst of a busy life, 1.9-11) are conspicuously contrasted with 'The Father of lights'. For, like the unchanging order of day and night (the 'lights' being the sun, moon, stars) but unlike the changes in nature and those due to created life's fragility and brevity (the 'variation or shadow due to change', perhaps a reference to the waxing and waning of seasons and years, 1.17), God the creator is constant and unchanging. The linear movement of the discourse, by means of pictorial-narrative elaboration (rhetography) and enthymematic–syllogistic elaboration (rhetology) gives rise to the argument that God (the creator), who 'gives to all generously and ungrudgingly', will never change (see Mt. 5.45; cf. Ps. 145.9; Wis. 15.1; Job 38.12-41). God may be trusted to give wisdom to those who pray in faith.

In the midst of various trials (Jas 1.2-4), 'the wisdom from above' (cf. 3.17) 'coming down from the Father of lights' (1.17) enables the one being tested 'to know' (1.2) that enduring the trials of faith produces a good result now: 'you may be perfect and complete, lacking nothing' (1.4) and in the future: 'having stood the test, [you] will receive the crown of life, which the Lord promises to those who love him' (1.12).

A look at Robbins's typology of wisdom rhetorolect suggests that James' letter is marked with the influence of wisdom. [*Firstspace (social experience)*]: experiences of the household are close at hand: beginning with Jas 1.1, the house of Abraham is present in 'the twelve tribes in the dispersion' (cf. 2.21, 'Abraham our father'); kinship language: brothers and sisters (20 times). [*Secondspace (social experiences of the created world/nature)*]: all of the various trials in James are those of everyday life in the world: analogies from daily life are used to interpret human life in the world: the wind and waves of the sea (1.6), the heat of the day, the flowers of the field, human transitoriness (1.11), the sun, moon, stars (1.17). [*Thirdspace*]: James clearly views God as creator and 'heavenly Father over his children in the world' (Jas 1.17, 27; 3.9). God is a generous and ungrudging giver of wisdom (1.5) and of 'every good and perfect gift' (1.17). Like the 'lights' of the heavens (1.17), God's wisdom, 'comes down from above' (1.17) and enables human beings to live productive and fruitful lives (1.25); wisdom enables one to endure trials, produce patience and become 'perfect and complete, lacking nothing' (1.4); by wisdom one guards one's words and refrains from anger and unrighteousness (1.19-20); wisdom enables one to learn self-knowledge and to discern the source of temptations to evil, sin and death (1.13-16). God's wisdom enables God's children to give to all, especially the lowly (1.27), 'generously and ungrudgingly', just as God always, freely gives to God's children who ask in faith. The reasonings within the house seem to move out into the world as God's house.[58] Wisdom rhetorolect permeates the wise words of James.

58. Robbins, 'Argumentative Textures', p. 51.

The word 'kingdom' occurs but once in the Epistle of James: 'Listen my beloved brothers [and sisters]: Has not God chosen the poor in this world to be rich in faith and heirs of the *kingdom* which he has promised to those who love him?' (Jas 2.5).

This, I think, is the principle statement in the first argument (2.1-13) of the letter *confirmatio* (2.1–5.7). It is an important allusion to a saying of Jesus.[59] It treats of the conflict between the rich and the poor, an issue that occupies more than one-quarter of the letter of James; this is also an issue of great social significance in the Jesus tradition and in much of early Christian literature. I have written extensively on Jas 2.5 and on Jas 2.1-13, so I shall only summarize and rehearse my views as needed to show the presence and nature of prophetic rhetorolect in Jas 2.1-13.[60]

First, Jas 2.5 is a crucial element in a very tightly organized and complete argument, elaborating a piece of 'apotreptic' advice set forth in Jas 2.1, 'My brothers [and sisters], do not hold the faith of our glorious Lord Jesus Christ with acts of partiality.' My outline of the argument is as follows:[61]

1.	Theme	2.1
2.	Reason	2.2-4
	(*Probatio*)	2.5-11
3.	Argument from example	2.5
	a. with opposite	2.6a
	b. with social example	2.6b-7
4.	Argument from judgment, based on the written law, in four parts:	2.8-11
	a. Proposition based on the written Torah	2.8
	b. Argument from the contrary	2.9
	c. Rationale for judgment based on Torah	2.10
	d. Confirmation of the rationale with written testimony	2.11
5.	Conclusion	2.12-13

James 2.5 is an allusion to a saying of Jesus which is found in four other performances $Q^{Mt.}$ 5.3; $Q^{Lk.}$ 6.20b; Pol. *Phil.* 2.3, and *Gos. Thom.* 54. I have argued that it is closer to $Q^{Mt.}$ 5.3 than to the others and that it stems from a sayings-source something like that hypothesized, by Hans Dieter

---

59. Wachob, *The Voice of Jesus*.

60. Wachob, ' "The Rich in Faith" ' was the programmatic socio-rhetorical study of Jas 2.1-13 containing multi-textural analysis (inner texture, intertexture, social and cultural texture and ideological implications of the rhetoric in the letter). The dissertation was published as Wachob, *The Voice of Jesus*. Cf. my article with Luke Timothy Johnson, 'The Sayings of Jesus'.

61. Wachob, *The Voice of Jesus*, 63.

Betz as the pre-Matthaean Sermon on the Mount (= SM).[62] In James' text, the saying is not attributed to Jesus; it is attributed to James, the servant of God and the Lord Jesus Christ (1.1). In its unit (2.1-13), this saying is an argument from example, the first statement in the *probatio* or confirmation of the theme in Jas 2.1.

I concluded that Jas 2.5 is, in its own rhetorical situation, a judgment from example that sets forth in a single sentence the social identity, the way of life and the goal of God's chosen poor. Evincing a social location of thought that is fundamentally theocentric in its view of social life, this artful performance of a saying of Jesus not only supports the statement in Jas 2.1, but it recalls the quality of Jesus' own faith and relates that to the way of life that it envisions for the communities in the Diaspora, the elect poor. In James' rhetoric, 'the rich in faith' and 'those who love God' are Jamesian references to 'the poor in spirit': 'the pious poor' who fulfil the Torah, as interpreted by Jesus and summarized in the love commandment.

The 'faith of our glorious Lord Jesus Christ' in Jas 2.1 is a 'global allusion' to Jesus' own faith, what he believed, said and did. For James 'faith' *is doing* God's will. It is fulfilling the Torah as Jesus interpreted it. Accordingly, the rhetoric in Jas 2.1-13 subsumes the references to the Torah (2.8-11) under 'holding Jesus' faith' (2.1). I have agreed with Helmut Koester that the Christians who are addressed in the Epistle of James are viewed as 'belong[ing] to law abiding Israel and the fulfillment of the law, though without any emphasis upon circumcision and ritual law, is the appropriate interpretation of the teachings of Jesus'.[63] Whereas the pre-Matthaean Sermon on the Mount holds that God's law is ratified in the words of Jesus and in the obedience of his followers, James argues that God's law is ratified in the faith of Jesus (and as the allusion to the saying of Jesus in Jas 2.5 shows) also in the faith of the 'servants' of the Lord Jesus Christ (cf. Jas 1.1).

A look at Robbins' typology for prophetic rhetorolect seems to suggest that this is what we have in Jas 2.1-13. In $Q^{Lk.}$ 6.20b we have a wisdom saying, but in $Q^{Mt.}$ 5.3 and Jas 2.5 we have a prophetic saying. *Firstspace*: the kingdom of God, which in the Letter of James is an eschatological kingdom. *Secondspace*: the world in which humans now live. *Blended space*: God functions as heavenly king over his righteous kingdom on earth. In James' teaching, 'holding the faith of the glorious Lord Jesus Christ' means fulfilling the 'royal' Torah, the law of the kingdom as Jesus

---

62. Hans Dieter Betz, *The Sermon on the Mount: A Commentary on the Sermon on the Mount, including the Sermon on the Plain (Matthew 5.3–7.27 and Luke 6.20–49)* (Hermeneia; Minneapolis: Fortress, 1975). Cf. John S. Kloppenborg, *Excavating Q. The History and Setting of the Sayings Gospel* (Minneapolis: Fortress; Edinburgh: T&T Clark, 2000), p. 213.

63. Helmut Koester, *Ancient Christian Gospels: Their History and Development* (London: SCM Press; Philadelphia: Trinity Press International, 1990), p. 171.

himself believed and taught. Fulfilling the Torah as Jesus taught it means fulfilling the love command (Lev. 19.18). In the *thirdspace*: God's righteousness is shown in word and deed on earth.

In the blend of wisdom and prophetic rhetorolects in the Epistle of James it seems that the wisdom and righteousness of God have come together in 'the faith of Jesus Christ' (2.1); that is, in what Jesus believed, said, and did. The cultural script for the 'beloved community' is to 'hold Jesus' faith': to love God: to do the Torah as Jesus taught it: to speak and do the love command (Lev. 19.18; cf. Jas 2.18).

4. *Conclusion*

From a socio-rhetorical perspective the Epistle of James is an intentional text, one that attempts to persuade its addressees to think and act like Jesus Christ (Jas 1.1; 2.1). Crucial to its persuasive intent are two major rhetorolects: wisdom rhetorolect and prophetic rhetorolect, which distinctively configure two topics, 'household' and 'kingdom', within the reasonings, argumentations and narrations within the letter. Socio-rhetorical criticism helps us identify and probe the social and cultural intertexture of the Epistle of James; in particular it suggests that the languages in which the topics 'household' and 'kingdom' play large in early Christian rhetoric blended in the rhetoric of James. Accordingly, it focuses on the ways in which wisdom and prophetic rhetorolects interact with each other and create the configurations of speech in the Epistle of James.

Socio-rhetorical interpretation specifically asks what the rhetoric of the Epistle of James attempts to do: it helps us identify the function of the social possession and use of language in the text. Accordingly, the Epistle of James appears to address communities of Christian Jews as members of law-abiding Israel and it justifies a particular appropriation of Jesus' interpretation of the Torah as the cultural script for their thought and action. In sum, socio-rhetorical interpretation shows us something of the persuasive artistry of the Epistle of James and suggests that the ethos, pathos and word of James, 'the Lord's brother', were important tools in the effort to persuade some Jewish Christians to hold Jesus' faith: to think and act like 'the glorious Lord Jesus Christ' (Jas 2.1).

BIBLIOGRAPHY

Adams, Edward, *Constructing the World: A Study in Paul's Cosmological Language* (SNTW; Edinburgh: T&T Clark, 2000).

Adamson, James B., *James: The Man and His Message* (Grand Rapids: Eerdmans, 1989).

—*The Epistle of James* (NICNT; Grand Rapids: Eerdmans, 1976).

Allison, Dale C., 'The Fiction of James and Its *Sitz im Leben*', *RB* 108 (2001), pp. 529–70.

Alonso Schökel, Luis, 'James 5.2 and 4.6', *Bib* 54 (1973), pp. 73–76.

Asensio, Victor Morla, 'Poverty and Wealth: Ben Sira's View of Possessions', in *Der Einzelne und seine Gemeinschaft bei Ben Sira* (ed. Renate Egger-Wenzel and Ingrid Krammer; BZAW, 270; Berlin and New York: Walter de Gruyter, 1998), pp. 151–78.

Ashcroft, Bill, Gareth Griffiths and Helen Tiffin (eds.), *Post-Colonial Studies: The Key Concepts* (London and New York: Routledge, 1998).

—*The Post-Colonial Studies Reader* (London and New York: Routledge, 1995).

Aune, David E., *The New Testament in Its Literary Environment* (LEC, 8; Philadelphia: Westminster, 1987).

—*The Westminster Dictionary of New Testament and Early Christian Literature and Rhetoric* (Louisville: Westminster John Knox, 2003).

Baasland, Ernst, 'Der Jakobusbrief als neutestamentliche Weisheitsschrift', *ST* 36 (1982), pp. 119–39.

—'Literarische Form, Thematik und geschichtliche Einordnung des Jakobusbriefes', *ANRW* 2.25.5, pp. 3646–84.

—*Jakobsbrevet* (KNT, 16; Uppsala: EFS, 1992).

Baker, William R., *Personal Speech-Ethics in the Epistle of James* (WUNT, 2.68; Tübingen: J. C. B. Mohr [Paul Siebeck], 1995).

Baldwin, C. S., *Medieval Rhetoric and Poetic (to 1400)* (Gloucester, MA: Peter Smith, 1959).

Barrett, Michèle, 'Ideology and the Cultural Construction of Gender', in *Women's Oppression Today: The Marxist/Feminist Encounter* (London: Verso, rev. edn, 1988), pp. 84–113.

Bartlett, David, 'The Epistle of James as a Jewish-Christian Document', in *Society of Biblical Literature 1979 Seminar Papers* (ed. P.

Achtemeier; SBLSP, 2; Missoula, MT: Scholars Press, 1979), pp. 73–86.

Batten, Alicia, 'God in the Letter of James: Patron or Benefactor?' *NTS* 50 (2004), pp. 257–72.

—'Unworldly Friendship: The "Epistle of Straw" Reconsidered' (unpublished doctoral dissertation, University of St. Michael's College, 2000).

Bauckham, Richard J., 'The Study of Gospel Traditions Outside the Canonical Gospels: Problems and Prospects', in *The Jesus Tradition Outside the Gospels* (ed. David Wenham; Gospel Perspectives, 5; Sheffield: JSOT Press, 1985), pp. 369–419.

—'The Tongue Set on Fire by Hell (James 3.6)', in *Fate of the Dead: Studies on the Jewish and Christian Apocalypses* (NovTSup, 93; Leiden: E .J. Brill, 1998), pp. 119–31.

—*James: Wisdom of James, Disciple of Jesus the Sage* (New Testament Readings; London and New York: Routledge, 1999).

Berger, Klaus, 'Der Jakobusbrief', in *Bibelkunde des Alten und Neuen Testaments*, vol. 2 *Neues Testament* (Heidelberg: Quelle & Meyer, 2nd edn, 1984).

—'Hellenistische Gattungen in Neuen Testament', *ANRW* 2.25.2, pp. 1031–1432, 1831–85.

—*Formsgeschichte des Neuen Testaments* (Heidelberg: Quelle & Meyer, 1984).

Berger, Peter L., *The Sacred Canopy: Elements of a Sociological Theory of Religion* (1967; repr., New York: Anchor Books, 1990).

Berger, Peter L. and Thomas Luckmann, *The Social Construction of Reality: A Treatise in the Sociology of Knowledge* (Harmondsworth: Penguin, 1967).

Bernand, Etienne, *Inscriptions métriques de l'Egypte gréco-romaine: Recherches sur la poésie épigrammatique des Grecs en Egypte* (Annales littéraires de l'Université de Besançon; Centre de recherches anciennes, 98; Paris: Société d'édition 'Les Belles-lettres', 1969).

Bernheim, Pierre Antoine, 'La mort de Jacques, l'épître de Jacques et la dénonciation des riches', in *The Catholic Epistles and the Tradition* (ed. J. Schlosser; BETL, 176; Leuven: Peeters, 2004), pp. 249–61.

Betz, Hans Dieter, *Galatians: A Commentary on Paul's Letter to the Churches in Galatia* (Hermeneia; Philadelphia: Fortress, 1979).

—*The Sermon on the Mount: A Commentary on the Sermon on the Mount, including the Sermon on the Plain (Matthew 5.3–7.27 and Luke 6.20–49)* (Hermeneia; Minneapolis: Fortress, 1975).

Bhabha, Homi K., *The Location of Culture* (London and New York: Routledge, 1994).

Brock, Sebastian, 'Ephrem's Letter to Publius', *LM* 89 (1976), pp. 261–305.

Brosend II, William F., *James and Jude* (NCBC; Cambridge: Cambridge University Press, 2004).

Bultmann, Rudolf, *Der Stil der paulinischen Predigt und die kynisch-stoische Diatribe* (FRLANT, 13; Göttingen: Vandenhoeck & Ruprecht, 1910).

Burchard, Christoph, *Der Jakobusbrief* (HNT, 15/1; Tübingen: J. C. B. Mohr [Paul Siebeck], 2000).

Calvin, John, *Commentaries on the Catholic Epistles* (trans. John Owen; Grand Rapids: Eerdmans, 1948).

Cargal, Timothy Boyd, *Restoring the Diaspora: Discursive Structure and Purpose in the Epistle of James* (SBLDS, 144; Atlanta: Scholars Press, 1993).

Carney, T. F., *The Shape of the Past: Models and Antiquity* (Lawrence, KS: Coronado Press, 1975).

Chester, Andrew and Ralph P. Martin, *The Theology of the Letters of James, Peter, and Jude* (New Testament Theology; Cambridge: Cambridge University Press, 1994).

Cheung, Luke L., *The Genre, Composition and Hermeneutics of the Epistle of James* (Paternoster Biblical and Theological Monographs; Carlisle: Paternoster, 2003).

Childs, Brevard S., *The New Testament as Canon: An Introduction* (Philadelphia: Fortress, 1984; repr., Valley Forge, PA: Trinity Press International, 1994).

Cohen, Shaye J. D., *From Maccabees to the Mishnah* (ed. W. A. Meeks; LEC, 7; Philadelphia: Westminster, 1987).

Collins, John J., *Jewish Wisdom in the Hellenistic Age* (Louisville: Westminster John Knox, 1997).

Conway, Colleen M., 'Toward a Well-formed Subject: the Function of Purity Language in the Serek ha-Yahad', *JSP* 21 (2000), pp. 103–20.

Conzelmann, Hans, *1 Corinthians: A Commentary on the First Epistle to the Corinthians* (ed. George W. MacRae; trans. James W. Leitch; Hermeneia; Philadelphia: Fortress, 1975).

—*Acts of the Apostles: A Commentary on the Acts of the Apostles* (ed. Eldon Jay Epp and Christopher R. Matthews; trans. James A. Limburg, A. Thomas Kraabel and Donald H. Juel; Hermeneia; Philadelphia: Fortress, 1987).

Cribiore, Raffaella, *Writing, Teachers, and Students in Graeco-Roman Egypt* (American Studies in Papyrology, 36; Atlanta, GA: Scholars Press, 1996).

Davids, Peter H., 'Palestinian Traditions in the Epistle of James', in *James the Just and Christian Origins* (ed. B. Chilton and C. A. Evans; NovTSup, 98; Leiden: E. J. Brill, 1999), pp. 33–57.

—'The Epistle of James in Modern Discussion', *ANRW* 2.25.5, pp. 3621–45.

—*James* (NIBC; Peabody, MA: Hendrickson, rev. edn, 1989).

—*The Epistle of James: A Commentary on the Greek Text* (NIGTC; Grand Rapids: Eerdmans, 1982).

Davis, David Brion, *The Problem of Slavery in the Age of Revolution, 1770–1823* (Ithaca: Cornell University Press, 1975).

De Ste. Croix, G. E. M., *The Class Struggle in the Ancient Greek World* (Ithaca: Cornell University Press, 1981).

Debut, Janine, 'Les documents scolaires', *ZPE* 63 (1986), pp. 251–78.

Deissmann, Adolf, *Light From the Ancient East* (trans. L. Strachan; London: Hodder & Stoughton, 1927).

Deppe, Dean B., 'The Sayings of Jesus in the Epistle of James' (D. Th. diss., Free University of Amsterdam; Ann Arbor: Bookcrafters, 1989).

Dibelius, Martin, *James: A Commentary on the Epistle of James* (ed. H. Koester; rev. Heinrich Greeven; trans. Michael A. Williams; Hermeneia; Philadelphia: Fortress, 1976).

Douglas, Mary, *In the Wilderness: The Doctrine of Defilement in the Book of Numbers* (Sheffield: JSOT Press, 1993).

—*Purity and Danger: An Analysis of the Concepts of Pollution and Taboo* (1966; repr. London: Routledge, 1991).

Dover, K. J., *Greek Popular Morality in the Time of Plato and Aristotle* (Oxford: Basil Blackwell, 1974).

Dowd, Sharon, 'Faith that Works: James 2.14-26', *RevExp* 97 (2000), pp. 195–205.

Dube, Musa, *Postcolonial Feminist Interpretation of the Bible* (St. Louis: Chalice Press, 2000).

Dunn, James D. G., *Romans 1–8* (WBC, 38A; Dallas: Word Books, 1988).

Eagleton, Terry, *Ideology* (London: Verso, 1991).

Edgar, David Hutchinson, *Has God Not Chosen the Poor? The Social Setting of the Epistle of James* (JSNTSup, 206; Sheffield: Sheffield Academic Press, 2001).

Eilberg-Schwartz, Howard, *The Savage in Judaism: An Anthropology of Israelite Religion and Ancient Judaism* (Indianapolis: Indiana University Press, 1990).

Elliott, John H., 'Disgraced Yet Graced: The Gospel According to 1 Peter in the Key of Honour and Shame', *BTB* 25 (1996), pp. 166–78.

—'The Epistle of James in Rhetorical and Social Scientific Perspective: Holiness-Wholeness and Patterns of Replication', *BTB* 23 (1993), pp. 71–81.

—*A Home for the Homeless: A Sociological Analysis of 1 Peter, Its Situation and Strategy* (Philadelphia: Fortress, 1981).

—*What is Social Scientific Criticism?* (GBS; Minneapolis: Fortress, 1993).

Fanon, Franz, *The Wretched of the Earth* (trans. Constance Farrington; New York: Grove Press, 1963).

Fauconnier, Gilles and Mark Turner, *The Way We Think: Conceptual Blending and the Mind's Hidden Complexities* (New York: Basic Books, 2002).

Fee, Gordon D., *The First Epistle to the Corinthians* (NICNT; Grand Rapids: Eerdmans, 1987).

Francis, Fred O., 'The Form and Function of the Opening and Closing Paragraphs of James and 1 John', *ZNW* 61 (1970), pp. 110–26.

Freyne, Sean, 'Vilifying the Other and Defining the Self: Matthew's and John's Anti-Jewish Polemic in Focus', in *'To See Ourselves as Others See Us': Christians, Jews and 'Others' in Late Antiquity* (ed. Jacob Neusner and Ernest S. Frerichs; Scholars Press Studies in the Humanities; Chico, CA: Scholars Press, 1985), pp. 117–43.

Gamble, Harry Y., 'The Pauline Corpus and the Early Christian Book', in *Paul and the Legacies of Paul* (ed. W. Babcock; Dallas: Southern Methodist University Press, 1990), pp. 265–80.

—*Books and Readers in the Early Church* (New Haven: Yale University Press, 1995).

Gammie, J. G. 'Paraenetic Literature: Toward the Morphology of a Secondary Genre', in *Paraenesis: Act and Form* (ed. L. G. Perdue and J. G. Gammie; Semeia, 50; Atlanta: Scholars Press, 1990), pp. 41–77.

Garnsey, Peter and Greg Woolf, 'Patronage of the Rural Poor in the Roman World', in *Patronage in Ancient Society* (ed. Andrew Wallace-Hadrill; London: Routledge, 1989), pp. 153–70.

Geertz, Clifford, *The Interpretation of Cultures* (New York: Basic Books, 1973).

Geiger, L., 'Figures of Speech in the Epistle of James: A Rhetorical and Exegetical Analysis' (unpublished doctoral dissertation; Southwestern Baptist Theological Seminary, 1981).

Geuss, Raymond, *The Idea of Critical Theory: Habermas and the Frankfurt School* (Cambridge: Cambridge University Press, 1981).

Goodacre, Mark, 'Review of Richard Bauckham, *James*', *Reviews in Religion and Theology* 7 (2000), pp. 52–54.

Goodspeed, Edgar J., *Introduction to the New Testament* (Chicago: University of Chicago Press, 1937).

Gottwald, Norman K., 'Ideology and Ideologies in Israelite Prophecy', in *Prophet and Paradigms* (Festschrift Gene M. Tucker; ed. Stephen Breck Reid; JSOTSup, 229; Sheffield: Sheffield Academic Press, 1996), pp. 136–49.

—*The Tribes of Yahweh: A Sociology of the Religion of Liberated Israel, 1250–1050 BCE* (Maryknoll, NY: Orbis, 1979).

Gowler, David B., 'The Development of Socio-Rhetorical Criticism', in Vernon K. Robbins, *New Boundaries in Old Territory: Forms and Social Rhetoric in Mark* (ed. David B. Gowler; Emory Studies in Early Christianity, 3; New York: Peter Lang Publishing, 1994).

Grant, Robert M., *A Historical Introduction to the New Testament* (San Francisco: Harper & Row, 1963).

Haenchen, Ernst, *The Acts of the Apostles: A Commentary* (Hermeneia; Philadelphia: Westminster, 1971).

Haines-Eitzen, Kim, *Guardians of Letters: Literacy, Power and the Transmitters of Early Christian Literature* (New York and Oxford: Oxford University Press, 2000).

Hanson, K. C. and Douglas E. Oakman, *Palestine in the Time of Jesus: Social Structures and Social Conflict* (Minneapolis: Fortress, 1998).

Harland, Philip A., 'Connections with Elites in the World of the Early Christians', in *Handbook of Early Christianity* (ed. Anthony J. Blasi, Jean Duhaime, and Paul-André Turcotte; Walnut Creek, Lanham, New York and Oxford: Altamira, 2002), pp. 385–408.

Harrington, Daniel J., 'The Wisdom of the Scribe According to Ben Sira', in *Ideal Figures in Ancient Judaism* (ed. George W. E. Nickelsburg and John J. Collins; Chico, CA: Scholars Press, 1980), pp. 181–88.

Hartin, Patrick J., ' "Who is Wise and Understanding Among You?" An Analysis of Wisdom, Eschatology and Apocalypticism in the Epistle of James', in *Society of Biblical Literature 1996 Seminary Papers* (SBLSP, 35; Atlanta: Scholars Press, 1996), pp. 483–503.

—'James and the Q Sermon on the Mount/Plain', in *Society of Biblical Literature 1989 Seminar Papers* (ed. David J. Lull; SBLSP, 28; Atlanta: Scholars Press, 1989), pp. 440–57.

—*A Spirituality of Perfection: Faith in Action in the Letter of James* (Collegeville, MN: Liturgical Press, 1999).

—*James* (SP, 14; Collegeville, MN: Liturgical Press, 2003).

—*James and the 'Q' Sayings of Jesus* (JSNTSup, 47; Sheffield: Sheffield Academic Press, 1991).

Hauck, Fridrich and Rudolf Meyer, 'καθαρός, κτλ.', *TDNT* vol. 3.

Heath, M., *The Poetics of Greek Tragedy* (Stanford: Stanford University Press, 1987).

Hengel, Martin, 'Jakobusbrief als antipaulinischen Polemik', in *Tradition and Interpretation in the New Testament* (ed. G. F. Hawthorne and O. Betz; Grand Rapids: Eerdmans, 1987) 248–78.

Hock, Ronald F. and Edward N. O'Neil, *The Chreia in Ancient Rhetoric*, vol. 1 *The Progymnasmata* (SBLTT, 27; Atlanta: Scholars Press, 1986).

Hock, Ronald F. and Edward N. O'Neil (eds), *The Chreia and Ancient Rhetoric: Classroom Exercises* (Writings from the Greco-Roman World, 2; Atlanta: Society of Biblical Literature; Leiden: E. J. Brill, 2002),

Hollenbach, Paul, 'Defining Rich and Poor Using Social Sciences', in *Society of Biblical Literature 1987 Seminar Papers* (ed. Kent Harold Richards; SBLSP, 26; Missoula: Scholars Press, 1987), pp. 50–63.

Holtzmann, Heinrich Julius, *Lehrbuch der neutestamentlichen Theologie* (2 vols; Freiburg im Breisgau and Leipzig: J. C. B. Mohr [Paul Siebeck], 1897).

Hoppe, Rudolf., *Der theologische Hintergrund* (FB, 28; Würzburg: Echter Verlag, 1977).

Jeremias, Joachim, 'Paul and James', *ExpTim* 66 (1955), pp. 368–71.

Johnson, Luke Timothy, 'Friendship with the World/Friendship with God: A Study of Discipleship in James', in *Brother of Jesus, Friend of God: Studies in the Letter of James* (Grand Rapids: Eerdmans, 2004), pp. 202–20.

—'James 3.13–4.10 and the *Topos* ΠΕΡΙ ΦΘΟΝΟΥ', *NovT* 25 (1983), pp. 327–47.

—*Brother of Jesus, Friend of God: Studies in the Letter of James* (Grand Rapids: Eerdmans, 2004).

—'Review of Luke Leuk Cheung, *The Genre, Composition and Hermeneutics of the Epistle of James*', *CBQ* 66 (2004), pp. 641–43.

—*The Acts of the Apostles* (SP, 5; Collegeville, MN: Liturgical Press, 1992).

—*The Letter of James* (AB, 37A; New York: Doubleday, 1995).

Jouguet, Pierre and P. Perdizet (eds.), 'Le Papyrus Bouriant n. 1. Un cahier d'écolier grec d'Egypte', in *Kolotes und Menedemos* (ed. Wilhelm Crönert; Studien zur Paläographie und Papyruskunde 6; Leipzig: E. Aveniarus, 1906; repr., Amsterdam: A. M. Hakkert, 1965), pp. 148–61.

Kennedy, George A., *The Art of Rhetoric in the Roman World* (Princeton: Princeton University Press, 1972).

—*New Testament Interpretation through Rhetorical Criticism* (Chapel Hill: University of North Carolina Press, 1984).

—*Progymnasmata: Greek Textbooks of Prose Composition and Rhetoric* (Writings from the Greco-Roman World, 10; Atlanta: Society of Biblical Literature, 2003).

—*The Art of Persuasion in Ancient Greece* (Princeton: Princeton University Press, 1963).

—The Genres of Rhetoric', in *Handbook of Classical Rhetoric in the Hellenistic Period 330 B.C.–A.D. 400* (ed. S. E. Porter; Leiden: E. J. Brill, 1997), pp. 43–50.

Klawans, Jonathan, *Impurity and Sin in Ancient Judaism* (Oxford: Oxford University Press, 2000).

Klein, Martin, *'Ein vollkommenes Werk': Vollkommenheit, Gesetz und Gericht als theologische Themen des Jakobusbriefes* (BWANT, 7/19; Stuttgart: Kohlhammer, 1995).

Kloppenborg, John S., 'Blessing and Marginality: The "Persecution Beatitude" in Q, Thomas and Early Christianity', *Forum* 2.3 (1986), pp. 36–56.

—'Patronage Avoidance in James', *HTS* 55 (1999), pp. 755–94.

—'Response to "Riches, the Rich and God's Judgment in 1 Enoch 92–105 and the Gospel According to Luke" and "Revisiting the Rich and the Poor in 1 Enoch 92–105 and the Gospel According to Luke"', in *George W. E. Nickelsburg in Perspective: An Ongoing Dialogue of Learning* (ed. Jacob Neusner and Alan J. Avery-Peck; Leiden and Boston: E. J. Brill, 2003), pp. 572–85.

—'The Reception of the Jesus Tradition in James', in *The Catholic Epistles and the Tradition* (ed. J. Schlosser; BETL, 176; Leuven: Peeters, 2004), pp. 91–139.

—'The Sayings Gospel Q: Literary and Stratigraphic Problems', in *Symbols and Strata: Essays on the Sayings Gospel Q* (ed. Risto Uro; Publications of the Finnish Exegetical Society, 65; Helsinki: Finnish Exegetical Society; Göttingen: Vandenhoeck & Ruprecht, 1996), pp. 1–66.

—*Excavating Q: The History and Setting of the Sayings Gospel* (Minneapolis: Fortress; Edinburgh: T&T Clark, 2000).

—*Q Parallels: Synopsis, Critical Notes, and Concordance* (FFNT; Sonoma, CA: Polebridge, 1988).

—*The Formation of Q: Trajectories in Ancient Wisdom Collections* (Studies in Antiquity and Christianity; Philadelphia: Fortress, 1987).

Koester, Helmut, *Ancient Christian Gospels: Their History and Development* (London: SCM Press; Philadelphia: Trinity Press International, 1990).

Konradt, Matthias, 'Review of Patrick Hartin, *A Spirituality of Perfection: Faith and Action in the Letter of James*; David Hutchinson Edgar, *Has God Not Chosen the Poor? The Social Setting of the Epistle of James*; and Matt A. Jackson-McCabe, *Logos and Law in the Letter of James: The Law of Nature, the Law of Moses and the Law of Freedom*', *JBL* 122 (2005), pp. 182–89.

—*Christliche Existenz nach dem Jakobusbrief: Eine Studie zu seiner soteriologischen und ethischen Konzeption* (SUNT, 22; Göttingen: Vandenhoeck & Ruprecht, 1998).

Konstan, David, *Friendship in the Classical World* (Cambridge: Cambridge University Press, 1997).

Kümmel, Werner G., *Introduction to the New Testament* (Nashville: Abingdon, rev. edn, 1975).

Kustas, George L., *Diatribe in Ancient Rhetorical Theory* (Center for Hermeneutical Studies in Hellenistic and Modern Culture; Protocol Series of the Colloquies of the Center, 22; Berkeley: Center for Hermeneutical Studies, 1976).

Lausberg, Heinrich, *Elemente der Literarischen Rhetorik* (Munich: Max Hueber Verlag, 3rd rev. edn, 1967).

—*Handbook of Literary Rhetoric: A Foundation for Literary Study* (trans.

David E. Orton and R. Dean Anderson; Leiden and New York: E. J. Brill, 1998).

Laws, Sophie, *The Epistle of James* (BNTC; London: A&C Black; HNTC; San Francisco: Harper & Row, 1980).

Lendon, J. E., *Empire of Honour: The Art of Government in the Roman World* (Oxford: Clarendon Press, 1997).

Lieu, Judith, *Christian Identity in the Jewish and Graeco-Roman World* (Oxford: Oxford University Press, 2004).

Lindemann, Andreas, *Paulus im älten Christentum: Das Bild des Apostels und die Rezeption der paulinischen Theologie in der frühchristlichen Literatur bis Marcion* (BHT, 58; Tübingen: J. C. B. Mohr [Paul Siebeck], 1979).

Lockett, Darian, *Pure and Worldview in the Epistle of James* (LNTS; London T&T Clark, forthcoming).

Loomba, Ania, *Colonialism/Postcolonialism* (London and New York: Routledge, 1998).

Luedemann, Gerd, *Opposition to Paul in Jewish Christianity* (trans. M. Eugene Boring; Minneapolis: Fortress, 1989).

MacDonald, Dennis R., *The Legend and the Apostle: The Battle for Paul in Story and Canon* (Philadelphia: Westminster, 1983).

Mack, Burton L., *Anecdotes and Arguments: The Chreia in Antiquity and Early Christianity* (Occasional Papers of the Institute for Antiquity and Christianity, 10; Claremont: Claremont Graduate School, 1987).

—*A Myth of Innocence: Mark and Christian Origins* (Philadelphia: Fortress, 1988).

—*Rhetoric and the New Testament* (GBS; Minneapolis: Fortress, 1990).

Mack, Burton L. and E. N. O'Neil, 'The Chreia Discussion of Hermogenes of Tarsus', in *The Chreia in Ancient Rhetoric*, vol. 1 *The Progymnasmata* (ed. Ronald F. Hock and Edward N. O'Neil; SBLTT, 27; Atlanta: Scholars Press, 1986), pp. 153–71.

Mack, Burton L. and Vernon K. Robbins, *Patterns of Persuasion in the Gospels* (Sonoma, CA: Polebridge, 1989).

Malherbe, Abraham J., 'Hellenistic Moralists and the New Testament', *ANRW* 2.26.1, pp. 267–333.

Malina, Bruce J., 'Wealth and Poverty in the New Testament and Its World', *Int* 41 (1986), pp. 354–67.

—*The New Testament World: Insights from Cultural Anthropology* (Atlanta: John Knox, 1981).

Martin, Dale B., *Slavery as Salvation: The Metaphor of Slavery in Pauline Christianity* (New Haven: Yale University Press, 1990).

Martyn, J. Louis, *Galatians: A New Translation with Introduction and Commentary* (AB, 33A; New York: Doubleday, 1997).

Martin, Josef, *Antike Rhetorik: Technik und Methode* (Handbuch der Altertumswissenschaft, 2.3; Munich: C. H. Beck, 1974).

Martin, Ralph P., *James* (WBC, 48; Waco, TX: Word Books, 1988).

Massebieau, Louis, 'L'Épître de Jacques est-elle l'oeuvre d'un chrétien?', *RHR* 31–32 (1895): 249–83.

Maurer, Christian, 'φυλή', *TDNT*, vol. 9, pp. 245–50.

Maynard-Reid, Pedrito U., *Poverty and Wealth in James* (Maryknoll, NY: Orbis Books, 1987).

Mayor, Joseph B., *The Epistle of St. James* (London: Macmillan, 1892, 3rd edn, 1913).

Mays, James L., *The Lord Reigns: A Theological Handbook to the Psalms* (Louisville: Westminster John Knox, 1994).

McKnight, Scot, 'A Parting Within the Way: Jesus and James on Israel and Purity', in *James the Just and Christian Origins* (ed. Bruce Chilton and Craig A. Evans; NovTSup, 98; Leiden: E. J. Brill, 1999), pp. 83–129.

Metzger, Bruce M., *The Canon of the New Testament: Its Origin, Development, and Significance* (Oxford: Oxford University Press, 1987).

Milgrom, Jacob, *Leviticus 1–16* (AB, 3; New York: Doubleday, 1991).

Mitchell, Margaret M., 'Rhetorical Shorthand in Pauline Argumentation: The Functions of "The Gospel" in the Corinthian Correspondence', in *Gospel in Paul: Studies on Corinthians, Galatians and Romans* (Festschrift Richard N. Longenecker; ed. L. A. Jervis and P. Richardson; Sheffield: Sheffield Academic Press, 1994), pp. 63–88.

—'The Emergence of the Written Record', in *Cambridge History of Christianity*, vol. 1 *Origins to Constantine* (ed. Margaret M. Mitchell and Frances M. Young; Cambridge: Cambridge University Press, 2006), pp. 103–24.

—*Paul and the Rhetoric of Reconciliation: An Exegetical Investigation of the Language and Composition of 1 Corinthians* (HUT, 28; Tübingen: J. C. B. Mohr [Paul Siebeck], 1991; Louisville: Westminster John Knox, 1993).

—*The Heavenly Trumpet: John Chrysostom and the Art of Pauline Interpretation* (HUT, 40; Tübingen: Mohr/Siebeck, 2000; Louisville: Westminster John Knox, 2002).

Moo, Douglas J., *The Letter of James* (PNTC; Grand Rapids: Eerdmans, 2000).

Morgan, Teresa, *Literate Education in the Hellenistic and Roman Worlds* (Cambridge Classical Studies; Cambridge and New York: Cambridge University Press, 1999).

Mount, Christopher N., *Pauline Christianity: Luke-Acts and the Legacy of Paul* (NovTSup, 104; Leiden: E. J. Brill, 2002).

Mussner, Franz, *Der Jakobusbrief* (HTKNT, 13/1; Freiburg: Herder, 1964, 3rd edn, 1975).

Niebuhr, Karl-Wilhelm, 'Der Jakobusbrief im Licht frühjüdischer Diasporabriefe', *NTS* 44 (1998), pp. 420–43.

Nienhuis, David, 'Not By Paul Alone: The Formation of the Catholic Epistle Collection and the Christian Canon' (unpublished doctoral dissertation, University of Aberdeen, 2005).

—*Not By Paul Alone: The Formation of the Catholic Epistle Collection and the Christian Canon* (Waco, TX: Baylor University Press, forthcoming).

Painter, John, 'The Power of Words: Rhetoric in James and Paul', in *The Missions of James, Peter, and Paul: Tensions in Early Christianity* (ed. B. Chilton and C. A. Evans; NovTSup, 115; Leiden: E. J. Brill, 2005), pp. 236–73.

Pardee, Dennis, *Handbook of Ancient Hebrew Letters* (SBLSBS, 15; Chico, CA: Scholars Press, 1982).

Parsons, P. J., 'A School-Book from the Sayce Collection', *ZPE* 6 (1970), pp. 133–49.

Patillon, Michel (ed.), *Aelius Théon, Progymnasmata: Texte établi et traduit par Michel Patillon avec l'assistance, pour l'Arménien, de Giancarlo Bolognesi* (Collection des universités de France; Paris: Editions 'Les belles lettres', 1997).

Pearson, Birger A., *The Pneumatikos-Psychikos Terminology in 1 Corinthians: A Study in the Theology of the Corinthian Opponents and its Relation to Gnosticism* (SBLDS, 12; Missoula, MT: Society of Biblical Literature, 1973).

Penner, Todd C., 'The Epistle of James in Current Research', *CRBS* 7 (1999), pp. 257–308.

—*The Epistle of James and Eschatology: Re-reading an Ancient Letter* (JSNTSup, 121; Sheffield: Sheffield Academic Press, 1996).

Perdue, Leo G., 'Paraenesis and the Epistle of James', *ZNW* 72 (1981), pp. 241–56.

—*Wisdom and Creation: The Theology of Wisdom Literature* (Nashville: Abingdon, 1992).

Perelman, Chaïm and Lucie Olbrechts-Tyteca, *The New Rhetoric: A Treatise on Argumentation* (trans. J. Wilkinson and P. Weaver; Notre Dame: University of Notre Dame Press, 1969).

Piper, Ronald A., 'Matthew 7,7–11 par. Lk 11,9–13: Evidence of Design and Argument in the Collection of Jesus' Sayings', in *Logia: Les Paroles de Jésus – The Sayings of Jesus* (Festschrift Joseph Coppens; ed. Joël Delobel; BETL, 59; Leuven: Peeters, 1982), pp. 411–18.

Polag, Athanasius, *Fragmenta Q: Textheft zur Logienquelle* (Neukirchen-Vluyn: Neukirchener Verlag, 1979).

Popkes, Wiard, 'James and Scripture: An Exercise in Intertexuality', *NTS* 45 (1999), pp. 213–29.

—*Der Brief des Jakobus* (THKNT, 14; Leipzig: Evangelische Verlags-Anstalt, 2001).

Porter, Stanley E. (ed.), *Handbook of Classical Rhetoric in the Hellenistic Period 330 B.C.–A.D. 400* (Leiden: E. J. Brill, 1997).

Pretorius, E. A. C., 'Drie nuwe verklaringsopsies in die Jakobusbrief (Jak 2.1; 4.5; 5.6)', *HvTSt* 44 (1988), pp. 650–64.

Pseudo-Libanius, 'Epistolary Types', in *Ancient Epistolary Theorists* (ed. A. J. Malherbe; SBLSBS, 19; Atlanta: Scholars Press, 1988), pp. 66–81.

Rabe, H. (ed.), *Hermogenis Opera* (Rhetores Graeci, 6; Leipzig: Teubner, 1913).

Reicke, Bo, *The Epistles of James, Peter, and Jude* (AB, 37; Garden City, NY: Doubleday, 1978).

Rengstorf, K. H., 'δώδεκα, κτλ.', *TDNT* vol. 2, pp. 321–28.

Robbins, Vernon K., 'Conceptual Blending and Early Christian Imagination' (unpublished paper presented at the Nordic Seminar, *Body, Mind, and Society in Early Christianity*, 31 August–3 September 2005, University of Helsinki).

—'Argumentative Textures in Socio-Rhetorical Interpretation', in *Rhetorical Argumentation in Biblical Texts: Essays From the Lund 2000 Conference* (ed. Anders Ericksson, Thomas H. Olbricht, and Walter Übelacker; Emory Studies in Early Christianity, 8; Harrisburg, PA: Trinity Press International, 2002), pp. 27–65.

—'Beginnings and Developments in Socio-Rhetorical Interpretation', in *Companion to the New Testament* (Malden, MA: Blackwell; forthcoming).

—'Introduction', in *Jesus the Teacher: A Socio-Rhetorical Interpretation of Mark* (Minneapolis: Fortress, rev. edn, 1992), pp. xiv–xliv.

—'Progymnastic Rhetorical Composition and Pre-Gospel Traditions: A New Approach', in *The Synoptic Gospels: Source Criticism and New Literary Criticism* (ed. Camille Focant; BETL, 110; Leuven: Peeters, 1993), pp. 111–47.

—'The Dialectical Nature of Early Christian Discourse', *Scriptura* 59 (1996), pp. 353–62. Revised version online: http://www.emory.edu/COLLEGE/RELIGION/faculty/robbins/dialect/dialect353.html.

—'The Present and Future of Rhetorical Analysis', in *The Rhetorical Analysis of Scripture: Essays from the 1995 London Conference* (ed. S. E. Porter and T. H. Olbricht; JSNTSup, 146; Sheffield: Sheffield Academic Press, 1997), pp. 24–52.

—'The Rhetorical Full-Turn in Biblical Interpretation and Its Relevance for Feminist Hermeneutics', in *Her Master's Tools? Feminist and Postcolonial Engagements of Historical-Critical Discourse* (ed. Caroline Vander Stichele and Todd Penner; SBL Global

Perspectives on Biblical Scholarship Series; Atlanta: SBL; Leiden: E. J. Brill, 2005), pp. 109–27.

—*Exploring the Textures of Texts: A Guide to Socio-Rhetorical Interpretation* (Valley Forge, PA: Trinity Press International, 1996).

—*New Boundaries in Old Territory: Forms and Social Rhetoric in Mark* (ed. D. B. Gowler; Emory Studies in Early Christianity, 3; New York: Peter Lang, 1994).

—*The Tapestry of Early Christian Discourse: Rhetoric, Society and Ideology* (London and New York: Routledge, 1996).

Robinson, James M., Paul Hoffmann and John S. Kloppenborg (eds), *The Critical Edition of Q: A Synopsis, including the Gospels of Matthew and Luke, Mark and Thomas, with English, German and French Translations of Q and Thomas* (Hermeneia; Leuven: Peeters; Minneapolis: Fortress, 2000).

Ropes, James H., *A Critical and Exegetical Commentary on the Epistle of St. James* (ICC; Edinburgh: T&T Clark; New York: Scribner's, 1916).

Said, Edward W., *Culture and Imperialism* (New York: Vintage Books, 1993).

—*Orientalism* (New York: Vintage Books, 1978).

Sanders, E. P., *Jesus and Judaism* (Philadelphia: Fortress, 1985).

—*Paul and Palestinian Judaism* (Philadelphia: Fortress, 1977).

Schenk, Wolfgang, *Synopse zur Redenquelle der Evangelien: Q-Synopse und Rekonstruktion in deutscher Übersetzung* (Düsseldorf: Patmos Verlag, 1981).

Schüssler Fiorenza, Elisabeth, *In Memory of Her: A Feminist Theological Reconstruction of Christian Origins* (New York: Crossroad, 1984).

Schmidt, K. L., 'θρησκεία, κτλ.', *TDNT* vol. 3, pp. 155–59.

Slemon, Stephen, 'The Scramble for Post-Colonialism', in *The Post-Colonial Studies Reader* (ed. B. Ashcroft, G. Griffiths and H. Tiffin; London and New York: Routledge, 1995), pp. 45–52.

Songer, H., 'The Literary Character of the Book of James', *RevExp* 66 (1969), pp. 379–89.

Souter, Alexander, *Pelagius' Expositions of Thirteen Epistles of St. Paul* (2 vols; Cambridge: Cambridge University Press, 1926).

Spengel, L. (ed.), *Rhetores Graeci* (Leipzig: Teubner, 1853–56).

Spitaler, Peter, '*Diakrinomai* in Mat 21.21, Mk 11.23, Acts 10.20, Rom 4.20, 14.23, Jas 1.6, and Jud 22 – The "Semantic Shift" that Went Unnoticed by Patristic Authors', *NovT* 48 (2006), forthcoming.

Spitta, Friedrich, 'Der Brief des Jakobus', in *Zur Geschichte und Litteratur des Urchristentums*, vol. 2 (Göttingen: Vandenhoeck & Ruprecht, 1896), pp. 1–239.

Spivak, Gayatri Chakravorty, 'Can the Subaltern Speak?', in *The Post-*

Colonial Studies Reader (ed. B. Ashcroft, G. Griffiths and H. Tiffin; London and New York: Routledge, 1995), pp. 24–28.

Stegemann, Ekkehard W., and Wolfgang Stegemann, *The Jesus Movement: A Social History of Its First Century* (trans. O. C. Dean; Minneapolis: Fortress, 1995).

Stendahl, Krister, 'The Apostle Paul and the Introspective Conscience of the West', in *Paul Among Jews and Gentiles and Other Essays* (Philadelphia: Fortress, 1976), pp. 78–96.

Stowers, Stanley K., 'The Diatribe', in *Greco-Roman Literature and the New Testament* (ed. David E. Aune; SBLSBS, 21; Atlanta: Scholars Press, 1988), pp. 71–83.

—*Letter Writing in Greek Antiquity* (LEC, 5; Philadelphia: Westminster, 1986).

—*The Diatribe and Paul's Letter to the Romans* (SBLDS, 57; Chico, CA: Scholars Press, 1981).

Streeter, B. H., *The Primitive Church: Studied with Special Reference to the Origins of Christian Ministry* (London: Macmillan, 1929).

Sugirtharajah, Rasiah S., *Postcolonial Criticism and Biblical Interpretation* (Oxford: Oxford University Press, 2002).

Syreeni, Kari, 'James and the Pauline Legacy: Power Play in Corinth?', in *Fair Play: Diversity and Conflicts in Early Christianity* (Festschrift Heikki Räisänen; ed. Ismo Du Dunderberg, Christopher Tuckett and Kari Syreeni; NovTSup, 103; Leiden: E. J. Brill, 2002), pp. 397–437.

Taatz, Irene, *Frühjüdische Briefe: die paulinischen Briefe im Rahmen der offiziellen religiösen Briefe des Frühjudentums* (NTOA, 16; Göttingen: Vandenhoeck & Ruprecht, 1991).

Tamez, Elsa, *The Scandalous Message of James: Faith Without Works Is Dead* (trans. Mortimer Arias; New York: Crossroad, 1990).

Thompson, John B., *Ideology and Modern Culture* (Stanford: Stanford University Press, 1990).

Thurén, Lauri, 'Risky Rhetoric in James?', *NovT* 37 (1995), pp. 262–84.

Thyen, H., *Der Stil der jüdisch-hellenistischen Homilie* (Göttingen: Vandenhoeck & Ruprecht, 1955).

Tiller, Patrick A., 'The Rich and Poor in James: An Apocalyptic Proclamation', in *Society of Biblical Literature 1998 Seminar Papers* (SBLSP, 37; Missoula: Scholars Press, 1998), pp. 909–20.

Trobisch, David, *Die Entstehung der Paulusbriefsammlung: Studien zu den Anfängen christlicher Publizistik* (NTOA, 10; Göttingen: Vandenhoeck & Ruprecht, 1989).

—*Paul's Letter Collection: Tracing the Origins* (Minneapolis: Fortress, 1994).

Tuckett, Christopher M., 'The Beatitudes: A Source Critical Study', *NovT* 25 (1983), pp. 193–207.

Vananhoozer, Kevin, *The Drama of Doctrine: A Canonical-Linguistic*

Approach to Christian Theology (Louisville: Westminster John Knox, 2005).

Van der Westhuizen, J. D. N., 'Stylistic Techniques and Their Functions in James 2.14-26', *Neot* 25 (1991), pp. 89–107.

Verseput, Donald, 'Wisdom, 4Q185, and the Epistle of James', *JBL* 117 (1998), pp. 691–707.

Volten, Aksel, 'Die moralischen Lehren des demotischen Pap. Louvre 2414', in *Studi in memoria di Ippolito Rosellini nel primo centenario della morte (4 guigno 1843)* (Pisa: V. Lischi, 1955), vol. 2, pp. 271–80.

Wachob, Wesley H., ' "The Rich in Faith" and "The Poor in Spirit": The Socio-Rhetorical Function of a Saying of Jesus in the Epistle of James' (unpublished doctoral dissertation; Emory University, 1993).

—'The Apocalyptic Intertexture of the Epistle of James', in *The Intertexture of Apocalyptic Discourse in the New Testament* (ed. Duane F. Watson; SBLSS, 14; Atlanta: Society of Biblical Literature, 2002), pp. 165–85.

—'The Epistle of James and the Book of Psalms: A Socio-Rhetorical Perspective of Intertexture, Culture, and Ideology in Religious Discourse', in *Fabrics of Discourse* (Festschrift Vernon K. Robbins; ed. D. B. Gowler, L. Gregory Bloomquist, and D. F. Watson; Harrisburg: Trinity Press International, 2003), pp. 264–80.

—*The Voice of Jesus in the Social Rhetoric of James* (SNTSMS, 106; Cambridge and New York: Cambridge University Press, 2000).

Wachob, Wesley H. and Luke Timothy Johnson, 'The Sayings of Jesus in the Letter of James', in *Authenticating the Words of Jesus* (ed. B. Chilton and C. A. Evans; NTTS, 28; Leiden: E. J. Brill, 1999), pp. 431–50.

Wall, Robert W., 'A Unifying Theology of the Catholic Epistles: A Canonical Approach', in *The Catholic Epistles and the Tradition* (ed. J. Schlosser; BETL, 176; Leuven: Peeters, 2004), pp. 43–71.

—*Community of the Wise: The Letter of James* (Valley Forge, PA: Trinity Press International, 1997).

Watson, Duane F., 'James 2 in Light of Greco-Roman Schemes of Argumentation', *NTS* 39 (1993), pp. 94–121.

—'Rhetorical Criticism of Hebrews and the Catholic Epistles Since 1978', *CRBS* 5 (1997), pp. 175–207.

—'Rhetorical Criticism of the Pauline Epistles Since 1975', *CRBS* 3 (1995), pp. 219–48.

—'The Rhetoric of James 3.1-12 and a Classical Pattern of Argumentation', *NovT* 35 (1993), pp. 48–64.

Watson, Duane F. (ed.), *The Intertexture of Apocalyptic Discourse in the New Testament* (SBLSS, 14; Atlanta: Society of Biblical Literature, 2002).

Watson, Duane F. and A. J. Hauser, *Rhetorical Criticism of the Bible: A*

Comprehensive Bibliography with Notes on History and Method (BIS, 4; Leiden: E. J. Brill, 1994).

Wendland, Paul, *Die hellenistische–römische Kultur in ihren Beziehungen zu Judentum und Christentum* (HNT, 1: Tübingen: J. C. B. Mohr [Paul Siebeck], 2nd edn, 1912).

Wifstrand, A., 'Stylistic Problems in the Epistles of James and Paul', *ST* 1 (1947), pp. 170–82.

Wilcken, Ulrich, 'Zur ägyptisch-hellenistischen Litteratur', in *Aegyptiaca* (Festschrift Georg Ebers; Leipzig: Wilhelm Engelmann, 1897), pp. 142–52.

Windisch, Hans, *Die katholischen Briefe* (HNT, 4.2; Tübingen: J. C. B. Mohr [Paul Siebeck], 1911).

Witherington, Ben, *Conflict and Community in Corinth: A Socio-Rhetorical Commentary on 1 and 2 Corinthians* (Grand Rapids: Eerdmans; Carlisle: Paternoster; 1995).

—*Jesus the Sage: The Pilgrimage of Wisdom* (Minneapolis: Fortress, 1994).

—*The Acts of the Apostles: A Socio-Rhetorical Commentary* (Grand Rapids: Eerdmans; Carlisle: Paternoster, 1998).

Wuellner, Wilhelm H., 'Der Jakobusbrief im Licht der Rhetorik und Textpragmatik', *LB* 43 (1978), pp. 5–66.

Yee, Gale A., 'Ideological Criticism', in *Dictionary of Biblical Interpretation* (ed. John H. Hayes; Nashville: Abingdon, 1999), pp. 534–37.

—*Poor Banished Children of Eve: Woman as Evil in the Hebrew Bible* (Minneapolis: Fortress, 2003).

Young, Robert, *White Mythologies: Writing History and the West* (London and New York: Routledge, 1990).

Zahn, Theodor, *Introduction to the New Testament* (Edinburgh: T&T Clark, 1909).

Ziebarth, Erich Gustav Ludwig, *Aus der antiken Schule: Sammlung griechischer Texte auf Papyrus, Holztafeln, Ostraka* (Kleine Texte für Vorlesungen und Ubungen, 65; Bonn: A. Marcus & E. Weber, 1910).

Zmijewski, Josef, 'Christliche "Vollkommenheit": Erwägungen zur Theologie des Jakobusbriefes', *SNTU* 5 (1980), pp. 50–78.

INDEX OF ANCIENT TEXTS

INDEX OF AUTHORS